Making the most of *Vegetables*

ROBERT CARRIER'S KITCHEN

Making the most of
Vegetables

Marshall Cavendish   London Sydney & New York

Editor	Grizelda Wiles
Editorial Staff	Carey Denton
	Roz Fishel
Designer	Ross George
Series Editor	Pepita Aris
Production Executive	Robert Paulley
Production Controller	Steve Roberts

Photography
Bryce Attwell: 56, 103
Paul Bussell: 13, 18, 59, 66, 82, 84, 88, 94
Alan Duns: 90
Laurie Evans: 9, 78, 102
Edmund Goldspink: 96, 104
Melvin Grey: 83
James Jackson: 17, 33, 48, 67, 71, 76, 77, 99, 101, 108
Chris Knaggs: 10, 12, 26, 27, 39, 42, 44, 45, 58, 65, 85, 95, 98
Peter Myers: 11, 19, 23, 24, 30, 50, 52, 58, 61
Paul Webster: 32, 57, 89
Paul Williams: 37, 38, 60, 72
Cover picture: **Theo Bergstrom**

Weights and measures
Both metric and imperial measurements are given. As these are not exact equivalents, please work from one set of figures or the other. Use graded measuring spoons levelled across.

Time symbols
The time needed to prepare the dish is given on each recipe. The symbols are as follows:

 simple to prepare and cook

 straightforward but requires more skill or attention

 time-consuming to prepare or requires extra skill

 must be started 1 day or more ahead

On the cover: Vegetable terrine, page 70

This edition published 1986
© Marshall Cavendish Limited 1984/85

Printed in Italy by
L.E.G.O. S.p.a Vicenza

Typeset by Performance Typesetting, Milton Keynes

Published by Marshall Cavendish House
58 Old Compton Street
London W1V 5PA
ISBN 0 86307 264 X (series)
ISBN 0 86307 332 8 (this volume)

Contents

Boiling & steaming vegetables   8
The simplest way to preserve all the goodness

Sautéed vegetables   16
From quick-fried savoury dishes to creamy omelettes

Deep frying vegetables   22
The secrets of perfect fritters and French fries

Puréed vegetables   30
Clever contrasts with colour and texture

Stuffed vegetables   36
A variety of stuffings for every occasion

Braising vegetables   42
A simple method produces maximum flavour

Oriental-style vegetables   48
The welcome influence of the East

Baking & roasting vegetables   56
Delicious potatoes, wholesome pies and crispy gratins

Vegetable casseroles   64
Unusual and satisfying – vegetables from the pot

Terrines & moulded vegetables   70
Try hot or cold mousses and artistic terrines

Cold vegetable dishes   76
Interesting combinations that put salads to shame

Vegetable soups   82
Hearty or delicate – a soup for all seasons

Cooking pulses   88
All you need to know, from choosing to serving

Vegetables à la grecque   92
An aromatic way to start your meal

Vegetable sauces   96
Perfect partners for pasta, fish, meat and poultry

Chutneys, pickles & preserves   100
Home-made relishes revive traditional flavours

Freezing vegetables   104
Long-term storage made easy

Vegetable garnishes   108
Clever ideas for those finishing touches

Index   111

Making the most of vegetables is a volume crammed full of recipes to make all sorts of vegetable dishes: to accompany your Sunday roast, substantial main courses for family and friends and unusual, delicate dishes from the Orient.

Really mastering those supposedly simple techniques of boiling and steaming, baking and roasting or sautéing vegetables as accompaniments can be more tricky than you may imagine. For maximum flavour, texture and goodness it is imperative to prepare and cook your vegetables correctly. Follow my detailed instructions for the perfect end results.

There are certain types of vegetables and methods of preparation which make dishes that are filling enough to serve as the central dish of a meal. Pulses – peas, beans and lentils – have long been known as the central part of a vegetarian diet. They are also important in many Oriental, Eastern and Middle-Eastern cuisines, making unusual dishes. For example, Falafel, popular in Israel and Egypt, is a mixture of ground chick-peas and spices, deep-fried and served in pitta bread.

Vegetables such as green peppers, marrow, onions or aubergines used as containers can be the basis of some interesting meals. The variety of fillings that can be used may also surprise you – try herby peanuts and cashews for marrow, or tomato and garlic with olive oil for an aubergine dish called Imam bayeldi. The literal translation of this Turkish dish is 'the imam (priest) faints' – but whether he fainted with delight or from horror on hearing how much the oil in the dish cost, we shall never know!

We are all used to using vegetables as a padding for meat casseroles, but in fact there are many types of vegetable that combine together well, and with herbs and spices make delicious casseroles in their own right. Ratatouille is equally good served hot or cold, and my Vegetable hotpot will keep the worst winter weather at bay.

Vegetables have also found their own special place in nouvelle cuisine. As with the cooking and presentation of many other ingredients, the Oriental-style of cooking vegetables has contributed a lot to this new cuisine. The emphasis on the quality of the ingredients, the importance of texture and the exquisite look of the finished dish are all part and parcel of this unique style of cooking. The renewed interest in puréeing vegetables is reflected by this cuisine, focusing on the colour of the vegetables, versatility of appearance and, of course, the flavour.

This is a volume for the adventurous cook. Experimenting with different methods of cooking may give new life to vegetables you had all but forgotten, as well as adding sparkle to those old family favourites.

Happy cooking and bon appétit!

Robert Carrier

Vegetables

BOILING & STEAMING VEGETABLES

Properly cooked boiled or steamed vegetables are nutritious as well as delicious – the vitamins and minerals are preserved by these simple, rapid methods of cooking.

Vegetables do taste good if they are washed, prepared, cooked and served in quick succession and this is how boiled or steamed vegetables are prepared and presented.

Choosing vegetables
Most vegetables can be boiled or steamed, except those with a high water content such as tomatoes, aubergines and mushrooms, which are better suited to other methods. Also, red cabbage and peppers lose their firmness if boiled or steamed.
Boiling: in general, boiling is most suitable for hard root vegetables such as celeriac, parsnips and carrots, though even these can be steamed if they are cut into even-sized, small pieces and steamed for a longer time.
Steaming: this method is especially suited to delicate vegetables that lose their shape or become waterlogged easily, such as leeks, asparagus, broccoli, spinach and marrow.

Preparing vegetables
Wash all vegetables quickly but thoroughly in clean water – don't soak them as this will remove their vitamins. Scrub grit from root vegetables.
Artichoke (globe): trim the stems, cut the top, spiky leaves level and trim off the tops of any leaves that are discoloured.
Artichoke (Jerusalem): wash and scrub, but do not peel.
Asparagus: trim off ends and scrape lower section of stems to remove woody parts, then tie into bundles.
Broad beans: pod, or cook whole if very small and tender.
Broccoli: cut off tough stalks, divide large heads into two or three.
Brussels sprouts: remove discoloured leaves and trim the base, marking the bottom of larger sprouts with a cross.
Cabbage: trim, cut into halves or quarters, remove stalk and shred.
Carrots: scrub young carrots and cook whole. Peel and slice old ones.
Cauliflower: trim and remove leaves, divide into florets.
Celery: remove grit, separate stalks and cut into small lengths.
Courgettes: trim, cook whole if small, slice across or into lengths if large.
Leeks: remove all grit. Trim root and remove tough, green leaves.
Parsnips and turnips: trim and scrub if young, peel and cut old ones into pieces.
Peas: pod, or top and tail mange tout.
Potatoes: peel and cut into quarters if old, scrub and cook whole if new.
Spinach: remove grit, trim and cut off tough stalks.
Swede: peel and cut into pieces.

Boiling
This is an excellent way to cook vegetables, it is so quick that few nutrients are lost, and this means that colour and flavour are also retained. To call this process boiling, though, is slightly misleading, as vegetables should in fact be cooked at a slow simmer for best results.
The saucepan: a pan with a well-fitting lid is essential. Stainless steel, non-stick or hard enamel pans are all suitable, but not copper, as this destroys vitamin C on contact. The size of the pan depends on the quantity of vegetables you are cooking. Choose the smallest pan possible – this means there will be less water to dissolve the valuable vitamins. Use only enough water to barely cover the vegetables. Add just a pinch of salt – too much will encourage the vegetable juices to leak out. If the vegetables are to be added to boiling water, make sure that it really is boiling when you add them – this retains colour and vitamin C. Keep the heat high, cover the pan and bring back to the boil as quickly as possible, then reduce the heat and simmer gently. Keep the pan covered throughout. Simmering will cook vegetables just as fast as boiling.

Length of cooking
The vegetables are cooked as soon as they are tender, or *al dente* (firm to the bite). It is a good idea to keep a sharp eye on them so that you catch them at the exact moment when they are done. Test with a skewer or fork, and lift a piece from the pan to taste. Never leave vegetables to cook until they are soft – not only will they lose their flavour and vitamins but the resulting texture will be unpleasant.

Draining
Drain boiled vegetables thoroughly as soon as they are cooked (save the liquid for gravies, health drinks or stock). Tip them into a colander or a sieve (metal is best) and drain away the liquid. Leafy vegetables such as spinach and shredded cabbage, which absorb water easily, should be lightly squeezed with the back of a wooden spoon to release surplus liquid.

Return the drained vegetables to the rinsed-out pan and place over a very low heat for a few seconds to drive off any excess moisture, then add butter, season to taste with salt and freshly ground black pepper, turn into a warm vegetable dish and serve as soon as possible.

Steaming vegetables
Steaming is a method of cooking vegetables over, rather than in, water. It is a technique gaining in popularity as people learn how good the flavour and texture of vegetables are when cooked this way. Because they are not immersed in water, they are never soggy. Steaming takes slightly longer than boiling, and some special equipment is needed. This does not have to be expensive or elaborate, and, if you wish, you can improvise with what you have already.

There are two ways to steam vegetables:
Open steaming: this means that the vegetables are placed in a perforated container over a pan of simmering water and are cooked in the steam that penetrates the holes.
Closed steaming: with this method of steaming the vegetables are placed in a solid container over a pan of simmering water; they cook in the steam formed inside the container.

Vegetables cook more quickly when they are open steamed but the closed method preserves more flavour.

Types of steamers
Flower steamer: this is the cheapest type of steamer to buy and is first-rate provided you use a saucepan with a well-fitting lid. The sides are perforated 'petals' hinged to a

perforated base which stands on three or four legs to raise it clear of the water so that only steam penetrates the holes and cooks the vegetables. You can open the petals wide or close them tight, depending on how many vegetables and what size pan you are using.

Lidded steamer: this has solid sides, a perforated bottom and its own lid. It is designed to sit on top of a saucepan which is half full of water. The steamer has graduated ridges underneath so it can fit snugly on saucepans of varying sizes. Some models are divided into compartments so that you can cook two or three vegetables simultaneously.

Chinese steamers: these are little basketwork containers with solid sides, open-weave bases and their own lids. They are designed to fit on top of a small saucepan. You can build a 'tower block' of several containers with a lid on the top one, which is ideal for steaming small portions of several different vegetables. Chinese steamers can be bought from most Chinese supermarkets.

Double boiler or porringer: this is a set of two saucepans (one fitting on top or just inside the other) with one lid. You put water in the larger, bottom saucepan, putting your vegetables in the upper pan, so that the vegetables are cooked by the closed method of steaming.

Improvised steamer: if you don't possess a steamer of any kind and are eager to start steaming straight away, you can improvise. A stainless steel or enamel colander which fits snugly inside a saucepan can be used for open or closed steaming. For open steaming, place the vegetables directly in the colander; for closed steaming, wrap them loosely but firmly in a foil parcel. In both cases, cover the top of the colander carefully with a double layer of kitchen foil to prevent steam from escaping.

How much water?

The amount of water placed in the pan depends on which steaming method you are using. If you are using the open method, use very little water – it must never be able to bubble up through the holes and touch the

Curried new potatoes

vegetables. If you are using the closed method, the water should come no more than halfway up the vegetable container. Always wait until the water is boiling and the steam is rising before you put the vegetables in the steamer. Once the vegetables are in the steamer, cover it immediately or steam will escape into the air and your vegetables will take unnecessarily long to cook.

A fast boil is not necessary, just keep the water bubbling gently – the same amount of steam will rise.

Serving

Plainly boiled or steamed vegetables served with melted butter are a feast in themselves, but they can also be served with a variety of sauces, such as cheese, hollandaise and bechamel. Alternatively, add herbs to the vegetables when closed steaming, also a knob of butter and some wine, to make a wonderful 'instant' sauce. And, for a different serving idea, try garnishing green vegetables with crumbled, crispy bacon.

Curried new potatoes

For a delicious, unusual and simple variation on new potatoes, serve them tossed in curry butter.

🔪 30–40 minutes

Serves 6
900 g /2 lb new potatoes
coarse salt
75 g /3 oz butter
5 ml /1 tsp curry powder
5 ml /1 tsp dry mustard
60 ml /4 tbls finely chopped spring onion
30 ml /2 tbls finely chopped fresh parsley

1 Wash and scrape the potatoes, or simply rub off the skins, if they peel easily.
2 If steaming, cook for 25–30 minutes for the open method. Add a few more minutes for closed steaming.
3 If boiling, put the potatoes in a saucepan. Cover with cold water and add a generous amount of coarse salt. Bring to the boil.
4 Simmer the potatoes for 15–20 minutes, or until they feel soft when pierced with a fork.
5 Meanwhile, heat 25 g /1 oz butter in a large saucepan. Stir in the curry powder, dry mustard and finely chopped spring onion. Cook over a medium heat for 5–7 minutes, or until the onion is tender but not browned, stirring occasionally with a wooden spoon.
6 Stir in the remaining butter and then add the finely chopped parsley and keep warm.
7 Drain the cooked potatoes well and toss them in the curry butter for 1–2 minutes, or until well coated. Season with coarse salt to taste and then transfer the curried new potatoes to a heated serving dish. Serve them immediately.

Boiled asparagus

🔪 12–20 minutes

Serves 4
900 g /2 lb fresh green asparagus
salt

1 If the asparagus is young, the spears will just need to be trimmed at the cut end. For tougher stalks, check where they begin to thicken and shave off the skin downwards, using a sharp knife. Rinse well.
2 Arrange in bundles of 8–12 spears, and stand them in tall, straight-sided jars. Fill to just below the tips with boiling, salted water.
3 Cover the tips with a 'dome' of foil, secured on the jar sides.
4 Set the jars in a pan of simmering water, and cook until tender.
5 Drain well and serve.

Sauces for hot asparagus
● **Quick hollandaise:** see the recipe on page 13.
● **Cream sauce:** thin a bechamel sauce (for recipe see page 87) by beating in thin, fresh cream. Sharpen lightly with lemon juice, adding finely chopped herbs.
● **Melted butter:** bring 30 ml/2 tbls water to the boil in a small saucepan. Remove

from the heat, add 100 g /4 oz fresh butter cut into dice and swirl it around until it melts but remains creamy. Avoid overheating. Season lightly with lemon juice and white pepper.

Sauces for cold asparagus
● **Vinaigrette:** make with 4 or 5 parts olive oil to 1 part lemon juice and tarragon

Use a tall jar for boiling asparagus.

Boiled asparagus

vinegar mixed. Add chopped, fresh herbs.
● **Mayonnaise chantilly:** fold whipped cream into mayonnaise. Add lemon juice to taste.
● **Asparagus Milanese:** arrange cooked asparagus in a buttered ovenproof dish, sprinkling the layers and top with Parmesan cheese. Pour over 25 g /1 tbls lightly browned butter. Grill for 2 minutes and serve.

Peas with water chestnuts

🔪 20–25 minutes

Serves 4
500–600 g /1–1¼ lb frozen peas
5 mm /¼ in thick slice bacon, rind removed
15 ml /1 tbls olive oil
225 g /8 oz can water chestnuts, drained
50 g /2 oz butter
60 ml /4 tbls chicken stock, home-made or
*   from a cube*
15 ml /1 tbls caster sugar
salt
freshly ground black pepper
lettuce leaves

1 Put the peas in a small pan and cover with cold water. Cover and bring to the boil. When boiling, drain the peas, refresh under cold water and drain again.
2 Cut the bacon into 5 mm /¼ in strips, and sauté in the olive oil until golden. Remove the bacon from the pan and keep to one side.
3 Slice the drained water chestnuts thinly. Put them in a saucepan with the peas and bacon and add the butter, stock, sugar, salt and pepper to taste. Cook gently for about 10 minutes, or until most of the liquid is absorbed.
4 Serve on a bed of lettuce leaves.

Spring vegetable medley

🍴🍴 1 hour

Serves 4
250 g /8 oz new carrots
250 g /8 oz new potatoes
salt and freshly ground black pepper
250 g /8 oz asparagus tips
250 g /8 oz small courgettes
50–75 g /2–3 oz butter

1 Peel the carrots and potatoes and cut into equal-sized pieces. Trim them neatly into olive shapes. Add to 2 separate saucepans of salted water and bring to the boil. Simmer for 10–15 minutes, or until tender and still firm. Remove from the water with a slotted spoon and keep warm.
2 Blanch the asparagus tips in salted, boiling water for 10–12 minutes, depending on quality and thickness. Remove with a slotted spoon and keep warm.
3 Meanwhile, wipe the courgettes with a damp cloth, slice them thinly and blanch them in boiling, salted water for 2 minutes. Remove the courgettes with a slotted spoon and keep them warm.
4 In a large, heavy-based frying-pan melt the butter. Add the blanched vegetables, season with freshly ground black pepper to taste and toss over a moderate heat for 2–3 minutes. Transfer to a shallow, heated serving dish and serve immediately.

Skirlie mirlie

This is a traditional Scottish dish made from mashed turnips and potatoes. The Welsh version is called Punch-nep.

🔪 45 minutes

Serves 5–6
450 g /1 lb turnips, peeled and thickly sliced
450 g /1 lb floury potatoes, peeled and thickly sliced
salt and freshly ground black pepper
45–60 ml /3–4 tbls creamy milk
25 g /1 oz butter
For the garnish
freshly chopped parsley or chives
small triangles of crisply fried bread

1 Put the turnips into a pan of boiling, salted water, cover and simmer for 15 minutes.
2 Add the potatoes, cover and continue cooking gently for another 15 minutes, or until both the turnips and potatoes are tender. Drain well, then mash them very thoroughly with a potato masher.
3 Add the milk and butter, heat for 1–2 minutes, then whisk with an electric or wire whisk until light and fluffy. Season well with pepper.
4 Pile into a hot dish, sprinkle with the herbs and garnish with the fried bread.

Creamed chopped spinach

Although this recipe uses boiled spinach, you can steam it – 12 minutes for the closed method, 15 for the open.

🔪 30 minutes

Serves 4–6
1 kg /2 lb fresh spinach
15 g /½ oz butter
15 ml /1 tbls cornflour
150 ml /5 fl oz milk
45–60 ml /3–4 tbls thin cream
a pinch of nutmeg
salt and freshly ground black pepper
1 hard-boiled egg, sliced

1 Wash the spinach to remove any dirt and discard any yellowed, pale or blemished leaves, then pull away the stems. If they are tender, they will snap off at the base of the leaf, if tough, the stem will probably rip away along the whole length of the leaf.
2 Shake the leaves – not too energetically – to get rid of excess moisture, and pack them into a saucepan. Cover tightly, place over high heat and allow to cook in the water left clinging to the leaves; no salt is added at this stage.
3 From the moment you hear sizzling noises coming from the pan, cook for 1–2 minutes longer, uncovering the pan to turn the leaves over with a fork, so that the uncooked layer on top replaces the cooked leaves underneath. Remove from the heat.
4 Drain the cooked spinach in a colander, pressing firmly to extract any remaining moisture. Chop up the drained spinach using two sharp knives, one in each hand alternately cutting across each other.
5 Melt the butter in a pan. Add the cornflour and stir into the butter to make a roux. Gradually add the milk, stirring constantly. Leave the sauce to simmer for 1–2 minutes over very low heat.
6 Put the spinach in a pan, add the sauce, cream, nutmeg and salt and freshly ground black pepper to taste. Place over low heat for 1 minute to reheat. Transfer the spinach mixture to a serving dish and garnish with slices of hard-boiled egg.

Spring vegetable medley

Julienne of potatoes, celery and carrots

🔪🔪 clarifying butter,
then 30 minutes

Serves 4
6 large celery sticks
3 medium-sized potatoes, peeled
4 medium-sized carrots, scraped
salt and freshly ground black pepper
45 ml /3 tbls clarified butter
sprigs of fresh mint and celery leaves, to
garnish

1　Wipe the celery with a damp cloth, then cut into 4 cm /$1\frac{1}{2}$ in lengths. Slice each length into 3 mm /$\frac{1}{4}$ in wide batons.
2　Square off the potatoes and carrots, then cut them into batons as for the celery.
3　Bring a large saucepan of salted water to the boil. Add the potato and carrot batons and boil for 2 minutes.
4　Add the celery batons, then simmer for a further 6 minutes, or until the vegetables are tender but still firm. Drain well.
5　In a large frying-pan, heat the clarified butter. Add the drained vegetable batons and toss with a spatula over a moderate heat for 2 minutes, or until well coated in butter.
6　Season to taste with salt and freshly ground black pepper and transfer to a heated serving dish. Garnish with sprigs of fresh mint and celery leaves and serve.

Julienne of potatoes, celery and carrots

Broad beans with herb butter

Potato gnocchi

🔪🔪 50 minutes,
plus 1 hour chilling

Serves 4
450 g /1 lb floury potatoes
salt and freshly ground black pepper
65 g /$2\frac{1}{2}$ oz butter
100 g /4 oz flour, or more if necessary, plus
extra for flouring hands
1 small egg, beaten
50 g /2 oz freshly grated Parmesan cheese

1　Drop the potatoes into slightly salted, boiling water and simmer for about 20 minutes, or until tender. Drain, peel, mash and sieve them.
2　Mix the potatoes with 15 g /$\frac{1}{2}$ oz of the butter and the flour, egg, salt, pepper and nutmeg to taste. Work the mixture to a firm dough, adding a little extra flour if the dough is wet. Chill for 1 hour.
3　Form into small cylindrical shapes with floured hands.
4　Bring a very large pan of lightly salted water to the boil. Gently lower the gnocchi into the water and simmer for about 5 minutes, or until they rise to the surface.
5　Meanwhile, melt the remaining butter. Lift the gnocchi out carefully using a slotted spoon and place on a heated serving dish. Pour the melted butter over the top, sprinkle with Parmesan cheese and serve.

Broad beans with herb butter

🔪 15–25 minutes

Serves 4
500 g /1 lb shelled, young broad beans, fresh
or frozen
salt
25 g /1 oz butter
5 ml /1 tsp finely chopped fresh chervil
10 ml /2 tbls finely chopped fresh parsley
freshly ground black pepper
a sprig of chervil or parsley, to garnish

1　If using large, fresh beans, remove the tough, outer skins. Slit the skin of each bean along the indented edge with your thumbnail and then squeeze out the green kernel.
2　In a saucepan, bring enough salted water to the boil to cover the prepared beans. Add the beans and simmer for 12–15 minutes if fresh, and 5 minutes if frozen, until just tender.
3　Meanwhile, in a bowl, mix the butter with the finely chopped chervil and parsley, working with a fork until blended.
4　Drain the cooked beans thoroughly and put them into a heated serving dish.
5　Season to taste with salt and freshly ground black pepper. Add the herb butter and toss to coat the beans thoroughly. Serve immediately, garnished with a sprig of chervil or parsley.

Green beans with button onions

🍴🍴 35 minutes

Serves 8
900 g /2 lb green beans
salt
450 g /1 lb button onions, peeled
50 g /2 oz butter
freshly ground black pepper

1 Top and tail the beans, stringing them if necessary.
2 Bring a large saucepan of salted water to the boil. Add the peeled button onions and cook for 8 minutes, or until tender. Drain well and keep warm.
3 Bring a large saucepan of salted water to the boil. Add the beans and cook for 6 minutes, or until tender but still crisp. Drain well and keep warm.
4 In a clean saucepan, heat the butter. Add the drained beans and onions and toss over a moderate heat for 1–2 minutes, or until well coated in butter.
5 Season to taste with salt and freshly ground black pepper and transfer to a heated serving dish. Serve immediately.

Caramelized turnips

🍴 35 minutes

Serves 4
600 g /1¼ lb small, young turnips, pared and
  quartered
salt
25 g /1 oz butter
25 g /1 oz soft, brown sugar
30 ml /2 tbls stock, home-made or from a
  cube

1 Put the turnips into a saucepan, almost cover with boiling water and add 5 ml /1 tsp salt. When the water boils again, cover the pan and simmer until the turnips are just tender (15–20 minutes). Drain off the water leaving the turnips in the pan.
2 Add the butter, sugar and stock and heat briskly for a few minutes, turning the turnips gently now and then, just until they are coated with a shiny, syrupy glaze. Remove from the heat and serve hot.

Broccoli with quick hollandaise sauce

🍴 25 minutes

Serves 6
700 g /1½ lb broccoli
salt
225 g /8 oz butter
6 egg yolks
45–60 ml /3–4 tbls lemon juice
pinch of cayenne pepper

Green beans with button onions

1 Put the cleaned broccoli in a pan of cold, salted water, cover and bring to the boil. Simmer for 10 minutes, or until tender but still firm. Drain and arrange the broccoli neatly in a heated serving dish.
2 Meanwhile, slowly melt the butter in a heavy pan, removing it from the heat as soon as it begins to bubble.
3 Rinse the goblet of an electric blender with very hot water and shake dry.
4 Put the egg yolks, lemon juice and a pinch of salt into the goblet and start blending at the lowest speed. When the egg yolks are well mixed, trickle in hot, melted butter as you would for mayonnaise, leaving behind the white sediment which will have settled at the bottom of the pan. Stop blending as soon as the sauce is thick and velvety.
5 Prepare a double boiler or a bowl fitted on top of, but not touching, a pan of simmering water.
6 Pour in the egg mixture, stirring as you do, and continue to stir until the sauce is hot. If it becomes too thick, you can thin it down again by beating in a little boiling water.
7 Season to taste with more salt, if necessary, and a pinch of cayenne pepper. Spoon over the broccoli and serve.

● You can also steam the broccoli – 15 minutes open method, 20 minutes closed. If you are using frozen broccoli, cook it according to the instructions on the packet.

Brussels sprouts with almonds

Serves 4
500 g /1 lb small Brussels sprouts
salt
25 g /1 oz butter
15 ml /1 tbls olive oil
25 g /1 oz flaked almonds
freshly ground black pepper

1   Cut off the stem ends and remove any wilted or damaged outer leaves from the Brussels sprouts. (If the Brussels sprouts are older, remove the tough outer leaves entirely.) Nick a small cross in their stems to help them cook evenly.
2   Drop the sprouts into a large saucepan of boiling, salted water and simmer, uncovered, for 5 minutes. Cover the pan and continue to cook for 5 (if very young) – 15 minutes longer, or until the sprouts are just tender.
3   Meanwhile, heat the butter and the olive oil in a small, heavy-based saucepan, add the flaked almonds and sauté until golden.
4   Drain the sprouts thoroughly and put them in a serving dish. Pour the buttery almond sauce over the sprouts, season with salt and freshly ground black pepper to taste, and toss lightly. Serve immediately.

30 minutes

Runner beans with yoghurt sauce

Serves 4
500 g /1 lb fresh runner beans
salt
For the yoghurt sauce
150 ml /5 fl oz natural yoghurt
2 egg yolks
50 g /2 oz butter, diced
½ Spanish onion, finely grated
45 ml /3 tbls finely chopped fresh parsley
10 ml /2 tsp Dijon mustard
salt and freshly ground black pepper
30 ml /2 tbls snipped fresh chives

1   String the runner beans and slice them diagonally into 5 cm /2 in segments. Sprinkle the beans generously with salt.
2   To make the sauce, beat the yoghurt and egg yolks together in a heatproof mixing bowl. Place the bowl over a pan of gently simmering water. Cook the sauce for about 15 minutes, whisking frequently, until the sauce has thickened. Whisk in the diced butter. Add the grated onion, finely chopped parsley and mustard, and season with salt and freshly ground black pepper to taste. Keep the sauce warm over warm water.
3   Cook the beans in boiling, salted water, uncovered, for 5–10 minutes. Strain the beans and place in a heated serving dish.
4   To serve, spoon the sauce over the beans, leaving part of the beans exposed to give a good colour contrast. Sprinkle with the snipped chives and serve.

45 minutes

Lemon dill potatoes

Serves 4

700 g /1½ lb new potatoes, scraped
salt
15 g /½ oz butter
22.5 ml /1½ tbls flour
300 ml /10 fl oz milk
5 ml / 1 tsp dill seeds
30 ml /2 tbls lemon juice
15 ml /1 tbls finely chopped fresh parsley
freshly ground black pepper

1   Put the potatoes in a saucepan of cold, salted water. Bring to the boil and simmer for 15–20 minutes, or until the potatoes are tender.
2   Meanwhile, melt the butter in a saucepan. Blend in the flour with a wooden spoon. Add the milk, dill seeds and lemon juice, whisking vigorously with a wire whisk to prevent lumps forming. Simmer for 2–3 minutes, or until the sauce has thickened, stirring constantly. Add the finely chopped parsley and season to taste with salt and freshly ground black pepper.
3   Drain the potatoes and slice them thickly. Transfer to a heated gratin dish. Season with salt and freshly ground black pepper to taste. Pour over the lemon dill sauce and serve immediately.

● Dill is often used in Scandinavian and Eastern European cooking, especially with fish and potatoes. The flavour of dill seeds is similar to that of caraway. This herb is also used in another form – dill weed, with its dried, feathery leaves.

Creamed peas with lettuce

Serves 4–6

700 g /1½ lb small frozen peas
30 ml /2 tbls finely chopped onion
15 ml /1 tbls finely chopped fresh parsley
150 ml /5 fl oz boiling water
a pinch of sugar
salt and freshly ground black pepper
½ lettuce
90 ml /6 tbls thin cream

1   Put the peas, finely chopped onion and parsley into a saucepan. Add the boiling water and season to taste with sugar, salt and freshly ground black pepper. Cover the saucepan and simmer for 3–4 minutes, until the peas are tender.
2   Split up the lettuce leaves, wash and drain them well, then shred them finely.
3   Strain the peas, then return them to the pan. Add the cream. Heat through, being careful not to allow the cream to boil, and season to taste. Toss in the finely shredded lettuce leaves and serve immediately.

● This is a summery vegetable dish, much loved by the French. It is a convenient way of using up the outer leaves of a lettuce which may not be in a good enough condition for a salad. Frozen peas are used for this dish, which means it is easy and quick to make on almost any occasion.

40 minutes

15 minutes

SAUTEED VEGETABLES

Like many easy methods of cooking, sautéing is wonderfully versatile. Fry fresh, plump vegetables in a little oil and butter to make a whole range of dishes, including unusual omelettes.

Sautéing is a traditional method of frying food using a shallow pan and just enough hot fat to prevent the food being cooked from sticking. It is a quick and simple method but one which depends for success on using top-quality ingredients.

All kinds of vegetables are suited to this method of cooking, although different kinds need different treatment. The tender vegetables such as aubergines, tomatoes, courgettes and spinach, for instance, can be put straight into the hot fat in the pan (as can onion slices), but other vegetables, such as peppers and green beans, benefit from being blanched first (*see page 36*). Other vegetables, such as potatoes and sweet potatoes, need to be parboiled and then thoroughly drained before they are sautéed. (Both blanching and parboiling tenderize vegetables and cut down the time that they will need for sautéing.)

Fats: when sautéing, many cooks mix equal quantities of oil and butter for maximum flavour, and to prevent the butter from burning. I like to use butter as the main fat, with just a little oil added to keep the butter clear and free from any bitter taste. Use only the finest quality butter – unsalted butters are the best as they do not brown as quickly as the salted ones. Of the oils, olive oil is my particular favourite, although you may prefer to use one of the lighter ones, such as sunflower oil.

The pan: use a heavy-based pan, large enough to take all the food in a single layer. This is important with this particular cooking method because if the food overlaps rather than lying flat to the surface of the pan the direct heat will be dissipated and the food will stew or steam rather than fry. Likewise, to prevent stewing or steaming – and consequently soggy food – it is usually best to sauté in an uncovered pan so any moisture formed during the cooking process can evaporate.

Preparing vegetables: thoroughly wipe, wash or scrub the vegetables, depending on their type, preferably leaving them un-peeled. If you do need to peel them, do so very thinly. Alternatively, simply scrape young vegetables. Usually the vegetables are then cut into small, uniform size so that they will cook easily and evenly but some, such as small potatoes, can be left whole. Do your preparation just before cooking so the vegetables are fresh and don't dry out, and *never* leave them to soak or soluble mineral and vitamin goodness will be lost.

Cooking: heat the oil and butter first and when the foaming subsides, add the vegetables. Shake the pan gently and turn the food with a spatula when the first side is fried to a crisp, golden brown. Fry the second side in the same way. For some vegetables, such as the tender ones, this may be all the cooking required. Other ones, such

as cabbage, may need longer, gentle cooking to ensure tenderness, but take care never to overcook the vegetables.

Omelettes

Sautéed vegetables make an excellent filling for French and flat omelettes. French omelettes are the kind which are cooked on one side only while the top is left very moist. To fill this kind of omelette, spoon or spread a little precooked vegetable mixture down the centre and then fold the omelette over.

There are two ways of making flat omelettes. For a Spanish *tortilla* or an Italian *frittata* the filling is sautéed in an iron frying-pan. The lightly beaten eggs are then poured over (or the mixture added to the eggs) and the omelette cooked.

In France the filling is sautéed in one pan and the omelette is then cooked in another. The filling is added just as the eggs begin to set on the bottom. The French omelette is perhaps a little easier to cook, as sometimes the acids in the vegetable fillings of the *frittata* and *tortilla* tend to make them stick to the pan, but both are delicious.

Flat omelettes are mostly served hot, but they can be served cold as *tortilla* wedges, or roll up flat omelettes and slip them into hollowed-out French bread. (Tiny, flat omelettes, hardly bigger than a biscuit, are inspired by the cuisines of the Orient – see Little courgette omelettes.)

Fennel with tomatoes

🍴 35 minutes

Serves 4
350 g /12 oz fennel
60 ml /4 tbls olive oil
1 large onion, thinly sliced
1 garlic clove, finely chopped
1.5 ml /¼ tsp cayenne pepper
350 g /12 oz tomatoes, blanched, skinned, seeded and chopped
50 g /2 oz freshly grated Parmesan cheese
flat-leaved parsley, to garnish

1 Trim the fennel, cut it into quarters lengthways and thinly slice it.
2 Heat the oil in a large frying-pan over a low heat. Add the onion and garlic and cook for 2 minutes, stirring. Add the fennel and cayenne, stir, cover the pan and cook gently for 10 minutes.
3 Mix in the tomatoes and cook them, uncovered, for a further 10 minutes, or until they are very soft.
4 Turn the vegetables into a warmed serving dish, scatter the cheese over the top, garnish with parsley and serve at once.

Herbed mustard carrots

🍴🍴 45 minutes

Serves 4
450 g /1 lb carrots
25 g /1 oz butter
90 ml /6 tbls dry white wine
150 ml /5 fl oz chicken stock, home-made or from a cube
15 ml /1 tbls finely chopped fresh thyme
5 ml /1 tsp Dijon mustard
salt and freshly ground black pepper
a pinch of cayenne pepper
10 ml /2 tsp lemon juice
15 ml /1 tbls finely chopped fresh parsley

1 Scrape and trim the carrots. Cut each carrot into 5 mm /¼ in thick slices.
2 In a heavy-based saucepan, melt the butter over a moderate heat. Add the sliced carrots and stir to coat in the hot butter.
3 Add the white wine and the chicken stock. Bring to the boil, then reduce the heat to a simmer and stir in the finely chopped thyme and the Dijon mustard. Season, cover

and simmer gently for 20 minutes, shaking the pan occasionally.

4 Uncover and simmer for 5 more minutes, or until the liquid has evaporated and reduced to a glaze and the carrots are tender.

5 Adjust the seasoning and add a pinch of cayenne pepper and the lemon juice.

6 Transfer to a heated serving dish, sprinkle with parsley and serve.

Pommes parisiennes

25–30 minutes

Serves 4–6
1 kg /2 lb large, floury potatoes
40 g /1½ oz butter
15 ml /1 tbls olive oil
salt and freshly ground black pepper
15 ml /1 tbls finely chopped fresh parsley

1 Peel, wash and dry the potatoes. Holding a potato firmly in one hand, press the bowl of a 25 mm /1 in parisienne cutter (or melon baller) into the flesh, open side down. Gently scoop out a neat ball of potato. Scoop as many balls as you can out of each potato.

(Save the potato trimmings under cold water for other use.)

2 Dry the potato balls thoroughly on absorbent paper.

3 Select a heavy-based frying-pan large enough to hold all the potato balls in a single layer and heat the butter and olive oil. When the foaming subsides, add the potato balls and sauté over a moderate heat for about 15 minutes, shaking the pan frequently so that the potato balls brown evenly. The potatoes are cooked when they are crisp and golden on the outside and feel soft inside when pierced with the point of a knife.

4 Season the cooked potato balls with salt and freshly ground black pepper to taste, then drain thoroughly on absorbent paper. Serve them immediately, sprinkled with the finely chopped fresh parsley.

Pipérade

This is equally delicious hot or cold. Use it to fill a hollowed-out French loaf spread with garlic butter and crisped in the oven.

40–50 minutes

Fennel with tomatoes

Serves 4
50 g /2 oz butter or bacon fat
1 large Spanish onion, peeled and chopped
2 garlic cloves, peeled and chopped
2 medium-sized peppers, seeded, blanched and chopped
3 large tomatoes, skinned and chopped
salt and freshly ground black pepper
8 eggs, lightly beaten

1 Heat the fat in a large, heavy-based saucepan. Add the onion and garlic and cook them for 5–7 minutes, or until the onion is soft in texture.

2 Stir in the peppers and cook gently for 10 minutes. Increase the heat, add the tomatoes and season lightly. Cook briskly, stirring frequently, for 5–10 minutes, or until the mixture is soft but not watery.

3 Reduce the heat to low and pour in the eggs. Cook gently, stirring constantly, until the eggs are just set and the mixture is thick and creamy.

● For a spicy Latin American version, add 5 ml /1 tsp each of chilli powder, dried oregano and powdered cumin at the stage when the tomatoes are added.

1 Put the potatoes and greens in a bowl and stir with a fork to break them up. Mix together thoroughly and season well with salt and pepper.
2 Heat the dripping or butter in a frying-pan and add the vegetables. Press the mixture down with a wooden spoon. Fry over a moderate heat for 6–7 minutes, turning occasionally, until the mixture is lightly browned, crisp and dry.
3 Sprinkle the bubble and squeak with the vinegar, turn it onto a heated serving dish and serve immediately.

● This goes well with cold roast meat or poultry or with boiled beef.

Sautéed new potatoes with herbs

35 minutes

Serves 4
1 kg /2 lb small new potatoes, scraped
salt and freshly ground black pepper
4 shallots, finely chopped
1 garlic clove, finely chopped
60–90 ml /4–6 tbls olive oil
15 ml /1 tbls finely chopped fresh parsley
15 ml /1 tbls finely chopped fresh chives
15 ml /1 tbls chopped fresh chervil
lemon juice

1 Parboil the whole potatoes for 10 minutes in salted boiling water. Drain and reserve.
2 Sauté the finely chopped shallots and garlic in 30 ml /2 tbls of the olive oil for 10 minutes, until soft and golden. Remove with a slotted spoon and reserve.
3 Add the parboiled potatoes to the pan and sauté over a high heat for about 10 minutes adding more olive oil if necessary, and turning the potatoes occasionally until they are crisp and golden all over.
4 Return the shallots and garlic to the pan, add the finely chopped herbs, and season to taste with salt, pepper and lemon juice. Stir well to coat the potatoes thoroughly with herbs. Sauté until well heated through. Serve as soon as possible.

Creole green beans

40 minutes

Serves 6
450 g /1 lb green beans, topped and tailed
salt and freshly ground black pepper
50 g /2 oz butter
30 ml /2 tbls finely chopped onion
½ green pepper, finely chopped
60 ml /4 tbls tomato ketchup
60 ml /4 tbls wine vinegar
15 ml /1 tbls Dijon mustard
30 ml /2 tbls chicken stock, home-made or from a cube
5 ml /1 tsp curry paste
a pinch of cayenne pepper
a sprig of flat-leaved parsley, to garnish

Aubergine and tomato omelette

1¼ hours, including draining

Serves 2
2 large aubergines
salt and freshly ground black pepper
60 ml /4 tbls olive oil
900 g /2 lb tomatoes, blanched, skinned, seeded and diced
1 garlic clove, finely chopped
6 eggs
25 g /1 oz butter
2 sprigs of parsley, to garnish

1 Peel the aubergines, then cut into 15 mm /½ in dice. Place in a colander. Sprinkle generously with salt and leave to drain for 30 minutes.
2 Rinse the aubergines well under cold, running water, then pat dry firmly, using absorbent paper, to remove any excess moisture.
3 In a large frying-pan, heat the olive oil and sauté the diced aubergines for 3 minutes, tossing with a spatula. Add the prepared tomatoes, then season to taste with the salt and pepper. Simmer for 20 minutes, uncovered, to reduce the tomatoes to a thick pulp, stirring occasionally with a wooden spoon.
4 About 5 minutes before the end of cooking, stir in the garlic and adjust the

Aubergine and tomato omelette

seasoning. Keep the vegetable mixture hot.
5 Meanwhile, in a bowl, stir the eggs with a fork or whisk until thoroughly blended, and season with salt and pepper.
6 In a 15 cm /6 in omelette pan, melt half the butter. When it is hot but not coloured, pour in half the egg mixture. Stir the egg lightly with the back of a fork until the mixture is just starting to set. Lift the edges of the omelette so that the soft uncooked egg comes into contact with the pan.
7 When the omelette is set and golden underneath but still very moist on top, spread the centre with ¼ of the cooked aubergine and tomato mixture. Fold the omelette in 3 and turn it out onto a heated serving dish. Keep hot while you make and fill the second omelette. Spoon the remaining aubergine and tomato mixture down the centre of each omelette and serve, garnished with a sprig of parsley.

Bubble and sqeak

10 minutes

Serves 4
450 g /1 lb cold cooked potatoes, mashed
450 g /1 lb cold cooked cabbage or Brussels sprouts, or a mixture of both
salt and freshly ground black pepper
50 g /2 oz beef dripping or butter
5 ml /1 tsp vinegar

1 Bring a saucepan of salted water to the boil. Add the beans, bring back to the boil and cook for 5–7 minutes, or until tender. Drain and refresh the beans under cold, running water; drain again.
2 In a large frying-pan, heat the butter. Add the finely chopped onion and green pepper and cook over a moderate heat for 7–10 minutes, or until tender, stirring occasionally with a wooden spoon.
3 Stir in the ketchup, wine vinegar, mustard, chicken stock and curry paste and simmer for 5 minutes. Add the drained beans, then season with salt and freshly ground black pepper and cayenne pepper to taste. Simmer until the beans are heated through, turning them with a spatula. Transfer the beans to a heated serving dish, garnish with a sprig of flat-leaved parsley and serve immediately.

Sweet potatoes with orange

❙❙ 45 minutes

Serves 4
450 g /1 lb sweet potatoes
salt and freshly ground black pepper
50 g /2 oz butter
grated zest of ½ orange
juice of 1 orange

1 Peel the sweet potatoes, cut them into chunks and add them to a saucepan of boiling, salted water. Cook for 15–20 minutes. The sweet potatoes should be soft when tested with the point of a knife. Drain the potatoes thoroughly and then cut them into 5 mm /¼ in dice.
2 Melt the butter in a frying-pan, add the sweet potatoes and sauté gently for 5 minutes, turning them to colour them evenly all over.
3 Add half the orange zest and continue to sauté until crisp and golden.
4 Remove the pan from the heat. Sprinkle with the orange juice, toss lightly and season to taste with salt and pepper. Turn into a heated serving dish, sprinkle with the remaining orange zest and serve at once.

Little courgette omelettes

❙ 20 minutes

Serves 2 or 3
6 small courgettes, trimmed
4 medium-sized eggs, lightly beaten
1 garlic clove, finely chopped
50 g /2 oz freshly grated Parmesan cheese
5 ml /1 tsp salt
freshly ground black pepper
45 ml /3 tbls flour
50 g /2 oz butter
60 ml /4 tbls olive oil
2 spring onions, cut into 5 mm /¼ in slices and tossed in a little olive oil

1 Coarsely grate the courgettes onto a thick wad of absorbent paper. Wrap the paper around the grated courgettes and squeeze out the excess moisture.
2 Transfer the courgettes to a mixing bowl. Stir in the eggs, garlic, Parmesan cheese, and salt and freshly ground black pepper to taste. Sift in the flour and mix well. The batter should be of a slightly thick dropping consistency – add a little more flour if necessary.
3 Heat a large, heavy-based frying-pan over a moderate heat and add 15 g /½ oz of the butter and 15 ml /1 tbls of the olive oil. When the fat has foamed and the foam has subsided, drop tablespoonfuls of the batter into the pan, well spaced out. (Each omelette should be about 7 cm /3 in in diameter.) Fry the omelettes for about 1 minute, then turn them over with a palette knife or spatula and fry on the other side for about 1 minute, or until golden.
4 Transfer the little omelettes to a warmed serving dish. Keep them warm while you fry the remaining omelettes in the same way, adding a little more butter and olive oil to the pan between each session.
5 When all the omelettes are cooked sprinkle them with the sliced spring onions and serve immediately.

Juniper cabbage

❙ 20 minutes

Serves 4
100 g /4 oz thick slices of streaky bacon, diced
1 Spanish onion, sliced
45 ml /3 tbls olive oil
10 ml /2 tsp juniper berries, crushed
450 g /1 lb shredded white cabbage
salt
freshly ground black pepper

1 Sauté the diced bacon and sliced onion in the olive oil in a flameproof casserole for 5 minutes, or until the onion is slightly softened.
2 Add the crushed juniper berries and cook for 1–2 minutes more. Add the shredded cabbage and toss in the oil. Season with salt and freshly ground black pepper to taste. Cook, stirring occasionally, for 10 minutes; the cabbage will be cooked but still crunchy in texture. (At this time, if you prefer your cabbage to be softer, cover the pan while it is cooking and the steamy vapour will cook it faster.)

● Aromatic and pungent, with a hint of pine, juniper berries are always sold whole and need to be crushed to release their flavour. They are best known for their use in gin – they give it both its oiliness and its 'scented' flavour. They are also used in the kitchen, to season pâtés, game and pork. Partnering them with cabbage makes an unusual and delicious combination.

Juniper cabbage

Carrots italienne

Serves 4
50 g /2 oz butter
30 ml /2 tbls olive oil
1 Spanish onion, finely chopped
100 g /4 oz long-grain rice
300 ml /10 fl oz chicken stock, home-made or from a cube
a pinch of dried, powdered thyme
salt and freshly ground black pepper
350 g /12 oz carrots, grated
250 g /8 oz cooked ham, diced
150 g /5 oz strong Cheddar cheese, grated
flat-leaved parsley, to garnish

1   In a large, heavy-based saucepan, heat 15 g /½ oz butter and 15 ml /1 tbls olive oil. When the foaming subsides, add half the finely chopped onion and the rice and cook for 5 minutes over a moderate heat, stirring constantly with a wooden spoon. The rice should not colour.
2   Add the chicken stock and powdered thyme. Season with salt and freshly ground black pepper to taste. Simmer gently for 15 minutes, or until the rice has cooked and the liquid has been absorbed, stirring occasionally. Heat the grill to high.
3   Meanwhile, in a large frying-pan, heat the remaining butter and olive oil. Add the grated carrots and remaining finely chopped onion. Cook for 10 minutes over a moderate heat, stirring constantly. Season with salt and freshly ground black pepper to taste.
4   Stir the carrots into the rice mixture with the diced ham and half of the grated cheese. Adjust the seasoning and transfer it to a flameproof gratin dish. Sprinkle with the remaining cheese and brown under the heated grill for 5 minutes. Garnish with the flat-leaved parsley and serve immediately.

 45 minutes

Spinach with pimento and hard-boiled eggs

Serves 4
1 kg /2 lb fresh spinach
25 g /1 oz butter
30 ml /2 tbls olive oil
salt and freshly ground black pepper
1 small garlic clove, finely chopped
2 hard-boiled eggs, sliced
2 canned pimentos, cut into fine strips

1   Wash the spinach in several changes of cold water, nipping off any tough stems and discarding any yellowed leaves. Drain thoroughly.
2   Heat the butter and the olive oil in a large, heavy-based saucepan. Add the spinach and season to taste with salt and freshly ground black pepper and the finely chopped garlic. Cook over a high heat, stirring carefully and turning the top to the bottom with a large spoon or fish slice, for 30–40 seconds, until the spinach is soft.
3   Transfer the spinach to a heated serving dish. Garnish with slices of hard-boiled egg. Make a lattice over the top with the pimento strips. Serve immediately.

● This colourful dish of green, red and yellow, *espinaca con huevos*, is typically Spanish. It is important that the spinach is drained well, or the resulting dish will be soggy.

hard boiling eggs, then 20 minutes

Potato cake with celery

Serves 4

75 g /3 oz butter
3 celery sticks, diced
700 g /1½ lb potatoes, mashed (see below)
salt and freshly ground black pepper
freshly grated nutmeg

1   Melt 25 g /1 oz of the butter in a frying-pan and sauté the diced celery for 1–2 minutes.
2   Mix the celery with the mashed potatoes, season with salt and freshly ground black pepper and freshly grated nutmeg to taste.
3   Melt another 25 g /1 oz butter in the frying-pan and, when it is sizzling, pile in the potato and celery mixture. Spread into a flat cake with a palette knife and cook gently until golden brown underneath – about 15 minutes. Turn the potato cake out onto a flat dish and then slip it back into the frying-pan on the uncooked side. Add the remaining butter to the pan and cook for 10 minutes, or until golden brown. Turn out onto a heated plate and serve immediately, cut into wedges.

●   When you are making mashed potato for this recipe do not put milk or butter in it. You need a purée of a firm consistency to make effective cakes.
●   This delicious potato cake can be served with a number of other flavourings besides celery. Try onions or mushrooms or crisply fried bacon.

making mashed potato,
then 35 minutes

Sautéed fresh tomatoes

Serves 4

450 g /1 lb fresh tomatoes
15 g /½ oz butter
7.5 ml /½ tbls olive oil
2 spring onions, finely chopped
15 ml /1 tbls tomato purée
1 garlic clove, finely chopped
5 ml /1 tsp sugar
salt and freshly ground black pepper

1   Prepare the tomatoes. Place them in a bowl and cover with boiling water. Leave for 1 minute, then drain and peel off the skins. Cut the skinned tomatoes into quarters and remove the little core from each quarter.
2   In a large frying-pan, heat the butter and olive oil. When the foaming subsides, add the finely chopped spring onions and sauté over a moderate heat for 1 minute, stirring occasionally with a wooden spoon.
3   Add the tomato purée and stir to blend with the wooden spoon.
4   Stir in the finely chopped garlic, then add the tomato quarters. Sprinkle with sugar and season to taste with salt and freshly ground black pepper. Simmer over a moderate heat for 2 minutes only, tossing gently with a spatula. The juices will make a sauce, but the tomatoes should keep their shape.
5   Pour the tomatoes and their juices into a heated serving dish, and serve as soon as possible.

15–20 minutes

DEEP FRYING VEGETABLES

Deep-fried vegetables are full of flavour and taste really delicious. From perfect, crisply-fried chips to mouth-watering croquettes they illustrate the delights of this method of cooking.

Deep frying is the perfect method of cooking for many vegetables because the high heat of the oil forms a crisp shell on the outside of the food and seals all the natural juices inside. As a result the centre is juicy, tender and full of flavour.

Deep frying is a simple method of cooking; all the equipment you really need for successful results is a large, heavy saucepan with a tightly fitting lid, and a wire draining spoon. Life will be easier, however, if you have a frying basket to fit the saucepan and a thermometer to measure the temperature of the fat. Easiest of all is an electrically-controlled deep-fat frier with a built-in thermostat.

Vegetables suitable for frying
In the Western world the most popular deep-fried vegetable is the potato. It is the ideal candidate for this method of cooking because, fried just as it is, it will be crisp on the outside, fluffy and melting on the inside. But many other vegetables are suitable, though the less robust have to be coated in some way before they are deep-fried or the heat of the oil will dry them out. Egg and breadcrumbs or batter are the most common coatings, but vegetables can also be wrapped in a light pastry such as filo or Chinese spring roll wrappers.

My favourite deep-fried vegetables are mushrooms, aubergines, courgettes and onions. The only vegetables that are not suitable are very watery ones such as tomatoes. These release too much of their own liquid into the oil and won't become crisp.

Preparing the vegetables
Potatoes are the most straighforward vegetables to deep-fry but they still need a certain amount of careful preparation.

First of all, choose the right type of potato for the recipe: for chips a good all-round potato, not too waxy, not too floury, is ideal; for Potato baskets (see recipe) a more floury potato is required.

Peel the potatoes and cut them carefully into the shape and size recommended in the recipe. For chips and other dishes where you do not want the potatoes to stick together, rinse them under cold, running water to remove some of their starch and then pat them dry with absorbent paper. Make sure that they are well dried before you start frying; any water coming into contact with the hot fat causes spitting and splashing.

Vegetables that are to be dipped in batter or coated before frying should be cut into uniform slices, sticks or rings, or left whole if they are small enough. Cauliflower can be divided into florets.

If the vegetable is very firm and will not cook through in the time it takes for the coating to become golden, it should be partly cooked before coating. Cook the prepared pieces in boiling, salted water until just tender, then drain and refresh them under cold, running water. Dry the vegetables well before coating them.

For croquettes made from vegetables combined with other ingredients there are no hard and fast rules for preparation; each individual recipe is different. Sweetcorn croquettes (see recipe) are made from a panade – a thick sauce made with the creamed sweetcorn.

Coating
A coating of egg and breadcrumbs (or sometimes flour, egg and breadcrumbs) or batter protects the surface of the vegetables and prevents them from hardening.

Egg and breadcrumbing: first prepare the coating ingredients in separate shallow containers: one for seasoned flour (if using), the second for the beaten egg and the third for breadcrumbs. The flour is not always necessary, but it helps to give a good clean surface for the other coatings. I use fresh breadcrumbs made from a day-old loaf of white bread. Cut off the crusts and crumb the bread in a blender or on the coarse side of a grater, then sieve the crumbs.

Place a piece of vegetable or a shaped croquette in the flour, roll it lightly until coated all over, then shake off any excess. Place it in the beaten egg, turn it lightly with 2 palette knives or spoons, lift it out and let the excess liquid drain off, then place it in the breadcrumbs. Turn it until well coated, lightly pressing on the crumbs with a palette knife. Lay the coated vegetables on a flat dish and place them in the refrigerator for 15 minutes for the coating to set. For an extra firm coating, the egg and breadcrumbing can then be repeated.

Batter: a batter is a delicious way to coat vegetables; if properly prepared, it is always crisp and light and there are many interesting variations on the basic recipe.

My favourite batters all have whisked egg whites folded in to lighten them, and I like to ring the changes with seasonings.

Always prepare the batter well in advance; it should rest for at least 30 minutes at room temperature. This allows the gluten in the flour to develop, making its coating properties more even. The addition of more liquid to the batter makes it thinner and crisper, but it will tend to spread out when it comes in contact with the hot oil. Less liquid will give the batter a thicker, more spongy texture. If the batter contains egg whites, fold them in at the last moment.

When the batter is ready, coat the vegetables, a few pieces at a time, evenly in the batter. Fry them immediately.

Wrapping: the best example of this method of protection are Spring rolls (see recipe). Buy ready-made wrappers from Chinese suppliers or use filo pastry from Greek grocers. Vegetables are lightly softened in oil before being placed on the wrapper. They are then rolled up, with the ends folded in, brushed with beaten egg and fried.

Fat for deep frying
My choice of fat for deep frying is always olive oil. I like the deep, nutty flavour but, if for reasons of taste or economy, you do not agree, then choose a less strongly flavoured vegetable oil. Lard is also a good choice, but it burns more quickly than oil.

Oil used for deep frying can be re-used several times. After use, leave it to cool, then strain it carefully through a muslin-lined sieve to make sure all traces of food are removed. Wash the pan; the cool oil can then be stored in the pan, if you wish. Discard it as soon as it begins to smell stale. It helps to keep the oil sweet if you add a little fresh oil to it each time you use it.

Frying
To deep-fry, never fill the pan more than half-full with oil. When cold food is added to hot oil it foams considerably and there is a danger that it will overflow. Always keep the lid of the pan to hand in case of fire.

Temperature: the temperature is the most crucial part of deep-frying so put the oil on to heat in plenty of time. If the oil is too hot, the food will burn on the outside before it has time to cook on the inside; if it is not hot enough, the food will absorb the oil and become soggy. There is no question that a thermometer is the correct way to check the temperature (the same thermometer can be used for jams and sugar syrups, so it is quite versatile). But if you do not have a thermometer, you can make an approximate check with a cube of bread.

Take a loaf of day-old bread and cut from it a 15 mm /$\frac{1}{2}$ in cube without any crust. Heat the oil until you think it is somewhere near the right temperature, then add the bread and time how long it takes to go a crisp, golden brown. At 180C /350F it will take 60 seconds; at 190C /375F it will take 50 seconds; at 200C /400F it will take 40 seconds.

When the oil reaches the correct temperature, lower the source of the heat and try to keep the temperature constant. Without a thermostatically-controlled pan this can be difficult, but you may be able to do it by moving the pan off the heat occasionally. If the oil is really getting too hot, add some more cold oil to the pan to reduce the temperature quickly.

Leave the frying basket in place while you heat the oil so that it, too, is hot. Lift the basket out of the oil and place the food in the basket a small portion at a time. There must be room for each piece of food to fry and turn in the fat without crowding the others. Lower the basket into the oil and fry for the stated time, or until the outside is just golden and crisp.

Draining: as soon as the food is cooked remove the basket from the fat, shaking any excess oil back into the pan, and turn the food out onto absorbent paper.

Spring rolls

Spring rolls

1 hour 10 minutes

Serves 4
4 courgettes
30–45 ml /2–3 tbls olive oil
125 g /4 oz bean sprouts
2.5 ml /½ tsp soy sauce
30 ml /2 tbls dry sherry
2.5–5 ml /½–1 tsp ground ginger
salt and freshly ground black pepper
8 spring roll wrappers or 4 sheets of filo
*   pastry*
1 egg, beaten
oil for deep frying
spring onion 'flower', to garnish

1   Wipe the courgettes, trim the ends and cut into quarters, lengthways, then cut into small batons.
2   In a large frying-pan, heat the olive oil and add the courgettes and the bean sprouts. Cook them for 1–2 minutes, or until the courgettes have softened slightly. Add the soy sauce, sherry and ground ginger and season to taste with salt and pepper.
3   Place 30 ml /2 tbls of the mixture at the top end of a spring roll wrapper and roll up, folding in the ends and brushing the surface with beaten egg as you roll. Repeat with the remaining wrappers and vegetable mixture to make 8 spring rolls. (If using the filo pastry, cut the sheets in half and brush off any excess flour.)
4   Heat the oil in a deep-fat frier to 180C / 350F and when the oil is hot, fry the rolls for 1–2 minutes or until golden brown. Drain, garnish and serve immediately.

Deep-fried stuffed mushrooms

20 minutes

Makes about 24
225 g /8 oz button mushrooms
50 g /2 oz Stilton
1 garlic clove, finely chopped
1 large egg yolk
freshly ground black pepper
a pinch of cayenne pepper
1 egg, beaten
50 g /2 oz fresh, white breadcrumbs
oil for deep frying
parsley, to garnish

1   Pull the stalks out of each mushroom carefully and save for another recipe. Wipe the caps with a damp cloth.
2   In a small bowl, mash the Stilton with a fork, to a smooth paste. Combine with the finely chopped garlic and egg yolk and season with the black and cayenne peppers.
3   Fill the centre of each mushroom with enough mixture to form a mound to equal the size of the mushroom. Dip it in beaten egg and coat with breadcrumbs.
4   Heat the oil in a deep-fat frier to 180C / 350F. When hot, deep-fry the mushrooms

for 1 minute, or until they are golden brown. Drain on absorbent paper and serve garnished with a sprig of parsley.

Deep-fried artichoke hearts

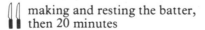
making and resting the batter, then 20 minutes

Makes 6
400 g /14 oz canned artichoke hearts
oil for deep frying
For the batter
125 g /4 oz flour
a pinch of salt
30 ml /2 tbls olive oil
150 ml /5 fl oz tepid water
2 egg whites
45 ml /3 tbls finely chopped fresh parsley
parsley, to garnish

1   To make the batter: sift the flour and salt in a bowl. Make a well in the centre.
2   Pour in the olive oil and tepid water and stir with a wooden spoon, gradually incorporating the flour from the sides of the well, until blended to a smooth batter. (It should be the consistency of thick cream.) If necessary, add extra water, otherwise the batter becomes glutinous and it is very difficult to fold in the egg whites. Leave to rest for 30 minutes.
3   When ready to use the batter, whisk the egg whites until stiff but not dry and fold in gently but thoroughly. Then fold in the finely chopped parsley.
4   Preheat the oil in the deep-fat frier to 190C /375F.
5   Drain the artichoke hearts and dry them on absorbent paper. Coat the artichoke hearts in the batter and deep-fry them for 1½–2 minutes until they are golden brown. Drain, garnish with a sprig of parsley and serve immediately.

Potato baskets

 35 minutes

Serves 4
450 g /1 lb floury potatoes
oil for deep frying
salt and freshly ground black pepper
butter and freshly chopped parsley

1 Heat the oil in a deep-fat frier to 200C / 400F.
2 Peel the potatoes and cut them into paper-thin slices – use a food processor or mandolin cutter – then into julienne strips.
3 Line a wire ladle with a thin layer of potatoes and place another wire ladle on top, so that the potatoes are held between the two. Deep-fry the potatoes for 1–2 minutes until crisp and golden. Remove from the ladles and drain on absorbent paper. Keep them warm while you fry the rest.
4 To serve, season with salt and freshly ground black pepper. Fill the baskets with butter balls coated with parsley as an accompaniment to a grilled dish.

Aubergine fritters with piquant sauce

 40 minutes

Serves 4
2 medium-sized eggs, beaten
75 g /3 oz cornmeal
2 medium-sized aubergines, cut across into
*   6 slices each*
30 ml /2 tbls seasoned flour
oil for deep frying
fennel sprigs and lemon slices, to garnish
For the sauce
15 ml /1 tbls oil
1 medium-sized onion, chopped
450 g /1 lb tomatoes, blanched, skinned,
*   seeded and chopped*
15 ml /1 tbls tomato purée
15 ml /1 tbls wine vinegar
5 ml /1 tsp Worcestershire sauce
few drops of Tabasco sauce

1 First make the sauce. Heat the oil in a small saucepan. Fry the onion for 2–3 minutes, add the remaining ingredients and bring to the boil. Reduce the heat and simmer for 20 minutes, then sieve or purée.
2 Heat the oil in a deep-fat frier to 200C / 400F. At this temperature a cube of day-old bread will brown in 40 seconds.
3 Meanwhile, place the beaten eggs and the cornmeal in two separate soup bowls. Sprinkle the aubergine slices with the seasoned flour. Dip each slice in the egg and then lightly coat with cornmeal. Deep-fry the aubergine slices for about 2 minutes, or until golden brown on both sides.
4 Remove from the oil with a slotted spoon, drain on absorbent paper, place on a heated serving dish and keep warm.
5 Reheat the sauce, garnish the fritters and serve with the sauce in a sauce-boat.

Deep-fried artichoke hearts and Deep-fried stuffed mushrooms

Sweetcorn croquettes

 15 minutes, 1¼ hours chilling, then 1 hour

Serves 6
40 g /1½ oz butter
75 ml / 5 tbls flour
400 g /14 oz canned creamed sweetcorn
1 egg yolk
salt and freshly ground black pepper
pinch of cayenne pepper
200 g /7 oz canned sweetcorn kernels,
*   drained*
1 egg, beaten
75 g /3 oz fresh white breadcrumbs
oil for deep frying

1 In a saucepan, melt the butter and add 45 ml /3 tbls of the flour. Cook for 1–2 minutes, stirring, to make a pale roux. Add the creamed sweetcorn; bring to the boil, then simmer for 5 minutes.
2 Remove from the heat, stir in the egg yolk and season well with salt, black pepper and cayenne. Add the sweetcorn kernels.
3 Line an 18 cm /7 in square tin with cling-film. Pour the mixture into the tin and refrigerate until chilled – about 1½ hours.
4 Place the remaining flour, beaten egg and fresh breadcrumbs in 3 flat containers. Divide the sweetcorn mixture into 12 portions. Shape each croquette with 2 dessert-spoons. Roll the croquette in flour and coat with the beaten egg and finally the breadcrumbs. Refrigerate for 30 minutes.
5 Heat the oil in a deep-fat frier to 180C / 350F, then deep-fry the croquettes for 1 minute, or until golden brown. Remove from the oil and drain on absorbent paper.

Potato chips

🔪 45 minutes

Serves 4
450–700 g /1–1½ lb potatoes
oil for deep frying
salt and freshly ground black pepper

1 Heat the oil in a deep-fat frier to 190C / 375F.
2 Peel the potatoes and cut them into sticks about 3 mm /⅛ in square and 7.5 cm / 3 in long. Rinse in cold water to remove any excess starch and drain thoroughly; dry on absorbent paper.
3 Fill the frying basket half to two-thirds full of potatoes and immerse it gently in the hot oil. Shake the basket from time to time while frying to keep the potatoes from sticking together. Continue to fry until the potatoes are nearly tender but only slightly coloured. Drain them well and spread on a baking tray lined with absorbent paper to absorb the excess oil while you fry the remaining potatoes in the same way.
4 Reheat the oil to 190C /375F and fry the potatoes again in small quantities until golden brown. Drain on absorbent paper.
5 Sprinkle with salt and freshly ground black pepper and serve immediately.

Potato chips

Parsnip fritters

🔪 15 minutes, 1 hour chilling, then 30 minutes

Serves 4
550 g /1¼ lb parsnips, peeled and sliced
salt
1 medium-sized egg
25 g /1 oz butter, softened
15 ml /1 tbls flour
50 g /2 oz walnuts, roughly chopped
oil for deep frying
maple syrup or golden syrup heated with a
*   few drops of lemon juice, to serve*

1 Put the parsnips in a pan, cover with boiling water, add 5 ml /1 tsp salt and when the water boils again, cover the pan and simmer for 10–15 minutes, until the parsnips are tender when pierced.
2 Drain well, shake over heat for a minute and then mash thoroughly.
3 Beat in the egg, butter, flour and salt to taste. Stir in the walnuts. Leave in the refrigerator for an hour to firm up.
4 Heat the oil in a deep-fat frier to 190C / 375F or until a cube of bread browns in 50 seconds. Slip in dessertspoonfuls of the parsnip mixture and fry until golden, 2-3 minutes.
5 Lift out with a slotted spoon, drain on crumpled kitchen paper and keep hot until all are fried. Serve very hot, with syrup.

Japanese mushroom fritters

These fritters, made with a light-as-air tempura batter, are delicious as appetizers or as a side dish to grilled meat. In Japan sweet cooking wine, *mirin*, and *daishi*, which is a golden, delicate fish-based stock, are used for the sauce. Japanese radish, *daikon*, sold as mooli in Europe, is used for the garnish; this is milder than the red radish, with a less peppery taste, so you will find that turnip is the best and most easily available substitute for it.

🔪 15 minutes, plus 30 minutes soaking time if using dried mushrooms

Serves 8
450 g /1 lb mushrooms, ceps, or 150 g /5 oz
*   dried shiitake mushrooms, soaked in*
*   boiling water and patted dry*
250 g /8 oz mooli or turnip, coarsely grated
oil for deep frying
For the tempura batter
1 small egg
50 g /2 oz flour
50 g /2 oz cornflour
1.5 ml /¼ tsp salt
1.5 ml /¼ tsp monosodium glutamate
2.5 ml /½ tsp baking powder
1 small ice cube

For the tempura sauce
250 ml /8 fl oz good chicken consommé or Japanese daishi
30 ml /2 tbls sweet sherry
30 ml /2 tbls soy sauce

1 First make the tempura sauce: heat the ingredients together in a small saucepan until the liquid boils. Remove the pan from the heat and leave the sauce to cool while you make the tempura batter.
2 To make the tempura batter: beat the egg and 75 ml /3 fl oz water lightly together. Using a fork or chopsticks, mix the dry ingredients together. Lightly beat the egg mixture into them and add the ice cube. The ingredients should just be blended and the batter should be thin and lumpy. Do not beat out the lumps.
3 In a *wok* or deep-fat frier, heat the oil until it smokes. Use chopsticks to dip one mushroom at a time in the batter, shaking off any excess, then drop them into the oil. Cook the mushrooms for 1–2 minutes, or until the batter sets and turns pale golden. Remove them with a slotted spoon and drain them on absorbent paper.
4 Serve the fritters accompanied by the sauce in a bowl or sauce-boat and the mooli or turnip in a separate dish.

Jerusalem artichoke fritters

Serve these delicious nutty-flavoured fritters with roast lamb as a change.

45 minutes

Serves 4
125 g /4 oz flour
5 ml /1 tsp paprika
2.5 ml /½ tsp cayenne pepper
a pinch of salt
1 medium-sized egg, separated
300 ml /11 fl oz milk
700 g /1½ lb Jerusalem artichokes
oil for deep frying
parsley, to garnish
Creamy tomato sauce (see page 96)

1 Place the flour, paprika, cayenne pepper and salt in a bowl, make a well in the centre and gradually beat in the egg yolk and milk. Leave in a cool place for 30 minutes.
2 Meanwhile, peel the artichokes and cut them into 5 mm /¼ in slices. Leave them until needed in a bowl of water to which has been added a dash of lemon juice or vinegar.
3 Whisk the egg white until stiff, then fold it into the batter.
4 Heat the oil in a deep-fat frier to 190C / 375F, or until a cube of bread browns in 50 seconds. Dry the artichoke slices on absorbent paper. A few at a time, dip the slices in the batter and deep fry them in the hot oil until they are golden brown, about 1½ minutes. Lift them out with a slotted spoon, drain on absorbent paper, and keep them hot while you cook the rest in the same way. Garnish with parsley and serve with the tomato sauce.

Fried onion rings

A traditional garnish for hamburgers.

making and resting the batter, then 15 minutes

Serves 4
1 small Spanish onion, sliced into 5 mm /¼ in rings
oil for deep frying
For the batter
125 g /4 oz flour
a pinch of salt
30 ml /2 tbls olive oil
150 ml /5 fl oz tepid water
2 egg whites

1 To make the batter: sift the flour and salt into a bowl and make a well in the centre.
2 Pour in the olive oil and tepid water and stir with a wooden spoon, gradually incorporating the flour from the sides of the well, until blended to a smooth batter. The batter should be the consistency of thick cream. If necessary, add extra water, otherwise the batter becomes glutinous and it is very difficult to fold in the egg whites. Leave the batter for 30 minutes at room temperature.
3 When ready to use the batter, whisk the egg whites until stiff but not dry, and fold in gently but thoroughly.
4 Heat oil in a deep-fat frier to 190C / 375F (a cube of bread will brown in 50 seconds).
5 Coat the onion rings, several at a time, and fry for 1 minute, until golden brown. Drain on absorbent paper. Repeat until all the onion rings are cooked. Reheat the onion rings, if necessary, by frying them again very quickly just before serving.

Fried onion rings

Deep-fried or buttered courgettes

Serves 4–6
For deep-fried courgettes
700 g /1½ lb small courgettes
½ Spanish onion, coarsely chopped
1 bay leaf
1.5 ml /¼ tsp ground nutmeg
freshly ground black pepper
275 ml /10 fl oz milk
seasoned flour
oil for deep frying
For buttered courgettes
700 g /1½ lb small courgettes, trimmed
salt
60 ml /4 tbls butter
60 ml /4 tbls chicken stock, home-made or from a cube
5 ml /1 tsp sugar
freshly ground black pepper

For deep-fried courgettes, trim and thinly peel the courgettes; cut into strips about 5 cm /2 in long and place in a bowl with the chopped onion, bay leaf, ground nutmeg and freshly ground black pepper to taste. Pour over the milk and leave to soak for 30 minutes.
2   Drain the strips, dry well on absorbent paper and roll in seasoned flour.
3   Heat the oil in a deep-fat frier to 180C /350F. A bread cube will turn brown in 60 seconds at this temperature. Deep-fry the courgettes in the hot oil for 2 minutes until golden. Drain on absorbent paper and serve immediately.
For the buttered courgettes, cut the unpeeled courgettes into quarters lengthways. Slice each quarter into 5 cm /2 in segments and blanch in salted, boiling water for 3 minutes; drain well and reserve.
2   Melt the butter in a heavy-based, shallow saucepan over a low heat. Add the drained courgettes, chicken stock, sugar and freshly ground black pepper to taste. Bring the liquid to simmering point, cover the pan, reduce the heat and simmer gently for 10 minutes, or until the liquid has almost disappeared and the courgettes are tender. Serve immediately.

40–50 minutes including soaking, deep-fried   25 minutes, buttered

Deep-fried cauliflower

Serves 4
1 large cauliflower
oil for deep frying
fresh tomato sauce, to serve (see below)
For the batter
100 g /4 oz flour
a pinch of salt
1 medium-sized egg
150 ml /5 fl oz milk
30 ml /2 tbls dry white wine

1   First make the batter: sift the flour and salt into a mixing bowl and make a well in the centre. Beat together the egg, milk and white wine, add to the well and stir with a wooden spoon, gradually incorporating the flour and beating until smoothly blended. Set the batter aside to rest until needed.
2   Trim away the green outer leaves, then rinse the cauliflower under cold running water. Drain and separate into florets. Poach the florets in boiling water for 5 minutes, then drain and pat dry on absorbent paper.
3   Pour enough oil into a deep-fat frier to come one-third of the way up the sides. Set the pan over a low heat and heat the oil to 190C /375F. (At this temperature a small cube of bread will brown in 50 seconds.)
4   Dip the poached florets in the batter, then deep-fry them until golden brown. Use skewers to lower them into the oil and cook in batches, if necessary, to avoid overcrowding the pan.
5   Remove the cooked florets from the pan with a slotted spoon and drain on absorbent paper. Serve hot, accompanied by a tomato sauce.

● Either the smooth texture of the Creamy tomato sauce (page 96) or the chunky Matriciana sauce (page 98) will go well with these deep-fried cauliflower florets.
● This dish makes a delicious appetizer, but can also be served as a side dish.

1 hour

Deep-fried celery

Serves 6
1 head of celery
90 ml /6 tbls olive oil
30 ml /2 tbls lemon juice
salt and freshly ground black pepper
oil for deep frying
1 small bunch of parsley, cut into sprigs
For the beer batter
150 g /5 oz flour
salt
30 ml /2 tbls olive oil
200 ml /7 fl oz lager
1 egg white

1   To prepare the batter, sift the flour and the salt into a mixing bowl and make a well in the centre. Pour in the olive oil and gradually add the lager, stirring with a wooden spoon to incorporate the flour from the sides. The batter should be completely smooth. Leave to rest for 2 hours.
2   Wash the celery and, with a sharp knife, remove any stringy parts. Cut the stalks into 25 mm /1 in pieces. In a large bowl, combine the olive oil and the lemon juice and season with salt and freshly ground black pepper to taste. Beat with a fork until the mixture emulsifies. Toss the celery pieces in this mixture and leave to marinate for 1 hour, stirring occasionally.
3   Heat the oil in a deep-fat frier to 190C /375F (a 15 mm /½ in cube of day-old bread takes 50 seconds to turn crisp and golden brown at this temperature).
4   Remove the celery pieces from the marinade with a slotted spoon. Pat each piece dry with absorbent paper. Coat each piece in the batter and deep-fry a small batch at a time for 5 minutes, or until golden. Drain on absorbent paper, transfer to a heated serving dish and keep warm.
5   Deep-fry the parsley sprigs in the same oil for a couple of seconds – it will sizzle and spit. Drain on absorbent paper quickly. Garnish the dish of deep-fried celery with a cluster of deep-fried parsley at either end and serve immediately.

 making and resting the batter,
then marinating, plus 20 minutes

Fried aubergines slices

Serves 4
2 large, ripe aubergines
salt
olive oil for deep frying
seasoned flour
1 tomato, to garnish

1   Wipe the aubergines clean with a damp cloth and trim off the stem ends.
2   Cut the aubergines into thin slices, crossways or lengthways, depending on their shape. Sprinkle with salt and leave to drain in a colander for at least 30 minutes, to allow the salt to draw out the bitter juices.
3   Heat the oil in a deep-fat frier to 190C /375F. At this temperature a 15 mm /½ in cube of day-old bread will take 50 seconds to turn crisp and golden brown.
4   Rinse the aubergine slices thoroughly. Pat them dry with absorbent paper, pressing firmly to get rid of as much moisture as possible. Dust lightly with seasoned flour.
5   Deep-fry the slices in 4 batches, for 4–5 minutes, or until crisp and golden brown. Drain thoroughly on absorbent paper and keep warm. Repeat with the remaining batches.
6   Arrange on a heated serving dish. To garnish, cut the tomato into 6 wedges, leaving them joined at the stalk end. Remove the seeds. Arrange in a flower shape at one end of the dish, then serve.

●   The fried aubergine slices will go limp very quickly, so serve them immediately.

1 hour, including draining

PUREED VEGETABLES

The nouvelle cuisine method of puréeing boiled or steamed vegetables produces purées that can be used as sauces, piped as a border or stuffed into vegetable cases to give new eye appeal to your dishes.

It is only too easy to run out of ideas when it comes to cooking vegetables and I find that puréeing vegetables adds a new dimension to my cooking. I serve the thinner purées as sauces and spoon the thicker ones into baked pastry barquettes or hollowed-out vegetables of a different colour.

It is the lovely contrast of colours and textures that make puréed vegetables such a creative alternative to those which have been prepared conventionally.

What vegetables to use

You can purée almost any vegetable, although the consistency of the purée will alter from vegetable to vegetable. For example, broccoli, leeks and watercress will all give thin purées, swedes, turnips and peas make much thicker ones.

The quality of the vegetables is very important – just because they are puréed does not mean you can begin with produce that is past its best; you may be able to disguise the appearance, but the flavour will let you down. Always choose fresh, unblemished vegetables.

Preparing and cooking

Prepare the vegetables as you would normally for boiling or steaming; trim and wash them, peel those with tough skins and remove any strings from beans. Cut the prepared vegetables into similar-sized pieces so that they cook through evenly. They can then be boiled or steamed.

Cooking times: if you are normally a fan of the 'crunchy' vegetable school, you will have to cook your vegetables longer than usual for puréeing. They should be completely tender before you purée them, but take care – avoid overcooking or the resulting purée will be thin and watery.

Draining: once the vegetables are cooked, drain them carefully to remove all excess water. If you are preparing several vegetables to purée together, try cooking them in the same water. Start with the vegetable with the strongest flavour and cook that first, then reserve the cooking water for the other vegetables. This way the flavour of the finished purée will be stronger.

Green vegetables like broccoli and watercress should be drained, refreshed under cold, running water and then drained again, to preserve the colour of the purée.

Leave cooked vegetables to cool slightly before puréeing them; they will be easier to handle and will splash less.

How to purée

There are several different ways to purée cooked and drained vegetables and the method you choose will depend on the equipment you have and the texture you want.

Mashing: any vegetable that does not have tough fibres can be puréed with a potato masher. Concentrating on a little of the vegetable at a time, pound it with the masher until it is quite smooth and then add more unpuréed vegetable and continue mashing until it is completely smooth.

Sieving: you can sieve the vegetables through a fine-meshed wire sieve, using a pestle or wooden spoon to push it through. This method, used on its own, will give a fairly fine textured purée. Or you can sieve vegetables you have already mashed to give them an even smoother consistency.

Food mill: a food mill or *mouli legume* copes very well with firmer textured vegetables. A plate at an incline is turned by a handle and this gradually forces the food through perforated plates in the base of the mill. Different plates, with smaller or larger holes, can be fitted to the mill to give a smoother or coarser purée. The coarsest plate when used to grind potatoes or boiled chestnuts will give small morsels like rice so this is sometimes known as a 'ricer'.

Electric blender or food processor: both of these will purée vegetables in seconds but some of the drier types of vegetable can be too thick for a blender and will clog up the blades. Chestnut purée is an example of this, and these purées are better done in a food mill should you not have a processor.

Vegetables that have tough fibres or strings will benefit from sieving after they have been puréed in a blender or mill. This will ensure that the finished purée is smooth.

Checking the consistency: now is the time to check the consistency of your basic purée and to take any corrective measures necessary. If you have overcooked the vegetables, they will have absorbed too much water and the purée will be watery. To remove excess moisture, return the purée to a saucepan. Beat the purée vigorously with a wooden spoon over a low heat. The liquid will evaporate and the purée will become stiffer. If it still seems too slack and watery, beat in some hot mashed potato or thicken it with instant potato.

Finishing the purée

Seasoning: season the purée generously with salt and freshly ground black pepper; a pinch of sugar will also bring out the natural sweetness of many vegetables. Try adding a pinch of crumbled stock cube to a simple dish of puréed peas, carrots or sweetcorn – it really does enhance it. Finely chopped herbs can be sprinkled in at this point, too: savory with broad beans or chervil with carrots.

Cream and butter: finish off the purée with either a dash of cream to enrich it, or stir in some diced, cold butter.

Serving

Puréed vegetables can be served in a number of ways: nouvelle cuisine-style as a 'bed' for meat, fish or poultry; piped decoratively around the serving dish; or piled into an accompanying dish.

Reheating: a great advantage of puréed vegetables is that most can be made in advance and reheated later. Do not reheat purées containing potato, which turns waxy, or watercress, which may turn yellow.

Leek purée with scallops

🍴 1 hour

Serves 4
900 g /2 lb leeks
salt
4 large scallops, opened
1 shallot
50 g /2 oz cold butter, diced
freshly ground black pepper
freshly grated nutmeg
sprigs of fresh herbs, to garnish

1 Cut the leeks into slices and cook in boiling, salted water for 15–20 minutes.

Leek purée with scallops

2 Meanwhile, remove the scallops from their shells by sliding a knife between the flesh and the flat side. Remove the thin, black membrane from behind the corals.

3 When the leeks are soft, drain them well, allow to cool a little and purée them in a blender or food processor. Press the purée through a fine sieve into a saucepan.

4 Place the saucepan over a low heat. Grate the shallot finely into the purée and gradually whisk in the butter. Season with salt, freshly ground black pepper and nutmeg. Keep it hot.

5 Place the scallops in a steamer and steam over simmering water for 2 minutes. Remove the scallops from the steamer and cut off the corals. Cut each coral in half horizontally and slice the scallops in 3 horizontally. Return all the pieces to the steamer, cut sides down, for 1 minute.

6 Spoon leek purée into individual dishes and arrange the scallop slices and corals on top. Garnish each one with a sprig of fresh herbs.

Hot avocado purée

20 minutes

Serves 4
2 large avocados
lemon juice
salt and freshly ground black pepper
15 g /½ oz unsalted butter
To garnish
4 small tomatoes
4 spring onions

1 Make 4 tomato roses and 4 spring onion curls for the garnish. To make the tomato roses, thinly cut a long, narrow strip of tomato peel and wind it round several times to make a 'rose' shape. To make the spring onion curls, slit the green ends of the spring onions into narrow strips and soak in iced water to open. Refrigerate both garnishes until needed.

2 Peel the avocados, halve them and remove the stones. Put the flesh in a bowl and mash with a fork until nearly smooth. Add the lemon juice to taste and season with salt and freshly ground black pepper.

3 Melt the butter in a small, heavy-based saucepan, add the mashed avocado and stir with a wooden spoon over a low heat for 3–4 minutes, or until heated through. Adjust the seasoning and transfer to a shallow, heated serving dish or individual dishes. Garnish and serve immediately.

Broccoli purée

35 minutes

Serves 4
350 g /12 oz fresh broccoli
salt and freshly ground black pepper
15 ml /3 fl oz thick cream
15 ml /1 tbls lemon juice

1 Cut away just the end of the broccoli stalks and any large leaves. Wash and drain.

2 In a large saucepan, bring 300 ml /10 fl oz salted water to the boil. Place the broccoli in the water and cook, uncovered, for 10 minutes, or until the broccoli is very soft. Drain and refresh under cold, running water; drain again.

3 Leave to cool a little, then purée in an electric blender or food processor and pass the purée through a fine sieve into a small saucepan. Add the thick cream and lemon juice, season to taste with salt and freshly ground black pepper and reheat.

4 Spoon a bed of broccoli purée onto each of 4 individual, heated serving plates and then top it with your chosen main course or, serve separately.

Purée of Brussels sprouts

 1 hour

Serves 4
450 g /1 lb Brussels sprouts
salt
150 ml /5 fl oz thin cream
freshly ground black pepper
about 225 g /8 oz potato, puréed
a pinch of grated nutmeg
flat-leaved parsley, to garnish

1   Cut off the stem ends and remove any wilted or damaged outer leaves from the Brussels sprouts. (If the sprouts are older, remove the tough outer leaves entirely.) Nick a small cross in their stems to help them cook evenly.
2   Drop the sprouts into a large pan of boiling, salted water and simmer, uncovered, for 5 minutes. Cover the pan and continue to cook for 15–20 minutes longer, or until tender. Drain well.
3   Allow to cool a little, then purée the sprouts in an electric blender, together with the thin cream, and then rub the purée through a sieve. Season with salt and freshly ground pepper. Gradually add the potato purée to the puréed sprouts, beating vigorously. Add enough potato so that the purée holds its shape when lifted with a spoon. (The amount of potato needed depends entirely on the moisture content of the sprout purée.) Add more salt and freshly

Purée of Brussels sprouts

ground black pepper, if necessary, and season with a pinch of nutmeg.
4   Keep the purée hot over a pan of simmering water until ready to serve. Garnish with flat-leaved parsley.

Celeriac purée

45 minutes

Serves 4
700 g /1½ lb celeriac
300–425 ml /11–15 fl oz milk
4 medium-sized tomatoes
salt and freshly ground black pepper
25–40 g /1–1½ oz butter

1   Heat the oven to 180C /350F /gas 4.
2   Peel the celeriac and cut it into chunks. Put the chunks in a saucepan, cover them with the milk and simmer for 10–15 minutes, or until very soft.
3   Meanwhile, cut a small slice from the top of each tomato and scoop out the seeds with a teaspoon. Season inside the tomato shells with salt and freshly ground black pepper and put them on a baking sheet. Place them in the oven to heat through – about 5 minutes.
4   When the celeriac is soft, remove it from the heat and leave to cool a little, then purée it with the milk used for cooking in an electric blender or food processor. Then pass the purée through a fine sieve.
5   Return the purée to a saucepan, season it

with salt and freshly ground black pepper and add a little extra milk, if necessary, to make a soft purée. Reheat gently and stir in the butter.
6   Spoon or pipe the purée into the warm tomato shells and serve immediately as a vegetable accompaniment.

Aligot

 45 minutes

Serves 6
700 g /1½ lb potatoes, peeled weight
salt
50 g /2 oz butter
275 ml /10 fl oz thick cream
350 g /12 oz strong Cheddar cheese, grated
freshly ground white pepper

1   Cut the peeled potatoes into even-sized pieces. Bring a large saucepan of salted water to the boil and cook the potatoes for 20–25 minutes, or until tender. Do not overcook, or the potates, and the resultant purée, will be watery.
2   Drain the cooked potatoes, then push them through a sieve into a clean saucepan, using the back of a wooden spoon.
3   Over a low heat, beat the butter into the sieved potatoes until well mixed, using the wooden spoon. Gradually beat in the cream until smooth. Stir in the grated Cheddar cheese and continue beating until the mixture becomes stringy.
4   Remove the pan from the heat and season to taste with salt and pepper.
5   Turn the potato and cheese mixture into a heated serving dish and serve very hot.

●   This is one of the few potato dishes that can be made well ahead. The fat content of the cheese prevents the potatoes from turning waxy.

Pumpkin purée with dill

 40 minutes

Serves 4
700 g /1½ lb fresh pumpkin
50 g /2 oz butter
salt and freshly ground black pepper
15–30 ml /1–2 tbls lemon juice
15–30 ml /1–2 tbls finely chopped fresh dill

1   Remove the peel and seeds from the pumpkin and cut the flesh into large cubes.
2   Place the cubed pumpkin in a large, wide saucepan and add the butter. Cover and cook over a gentle heat for 10–15 minutes, until the pumpkin is very soft.
3   Leave to cool a little, then purée the pumpkin in an electric blender or food processor.
4   Return the purée to the saucepan and reheat gently. Season to taste with salt, freshly ground black pepper, lemon juice and finely chopped dill. Serve immediately.

Purée of green beans

🔪 45 minutes

Serves 4
500 g /1 lb whole green beans, fresh or
*   frozen*
salt and freshly ground black pepper
60 ml /4 tbls thick cream
freshly grated nutmeg

1   If using fresh beans, trim them.
2   Bring a pan of water to the boil. When it begins to bubble, add a generous pinch of salt and the beans. Boil briskly for 30 minutes – less for frozen beans – or until the beans are very tender. Drain thoroughly.
3   Purée in an electric blender or food processor, or work through a vegetable mill. Then, using a wooden spoon, press the purée through a fine sieve and return to the pan. Reheat over a moderate heat, beating with a wooden spoon to evaporate excess moisture. Add the cream, mix well and season to taste with salt, freshly ground black pepper and a pinch of freshly grated nutmeg.
4   Spoon the bean purée into a heated serving dish and serve immediately.

● This dish is excellent served cold, mixed with a little well-flavoured mayonnaise.

Garlic purée

🔪 1 hour

Serves 4
700 g /1½ lb potatoes
salt
8 very large garlic cloves, unpeeled
coarse salt
125 ml /4 fl oz milk
125 g /4 oz butter
freshly ground black pepper

1   Heat the oven to 190C /375F /gas 5.
2   Peel the potatoes, cut them into even-sized pieces and place in a saucepan of cold, salted water. Bring to the boil and cook for 20–30 minutes, until soft.
3   Meanwhile, make a cut in each garlic clove. Place them in a small ovenproof dish and cover with coarse salt. Place in the oven and cook for 20 minutes, or until soft.
4   When the potatoes are cooked, drain them and pass them through a sieve into a saucepan.
5   Remove the cooked garlic cloves from the salt (the salt can be used again). Peel the garlic and place in an electric blender or food processor with the milk. Blend to a smooth purée and add to the potato purée.
6   Place the saucepan over a low heat, add the butter and heat through gently, season-ing to taste with salt and freshly ground black pepper. Serve immediately, with lamb, pigeon, quail or wild duck.

Garlic purée

Jerusalem artichoke purée

🔪🔪 1 hour

Serves 4
900 g /2 lb Jerusalem artichokes
salt and freshly ground black pepper
30 ml /2 tbls thick cream, whipped
25 g /1 oz butter, diced
2 egg yolks
2 chilli flowers, to garnish (see below)

1   Scrub the artichokes clean. Bring a saucepan of salted water to the boil. Add the unpeeled artichokes, bring back to the boil, then lower the heat and simmer for 25–30 minutes, or until tender, according to size.
2   Drain the artichokes in a colander. Hold them in a cloth and peel them.
3   Purée the artichokes in a blender or food processor, then press the purée through a sieve into a clean saucepan, using the back of a wooden spoon.
4   Over a moderate heat, simmer the purée for 3–4 minutes, to evaporate any excess moisture, stirring with the wooden spoon. The purée will thicken considerably and the flavour will intensify.
5   Beat in the whipped cream, then add the diced butter gradually, stirring after each addition until incorporated into the purée.
6   When all the butter has melted, remove the pan from the heat, beat in the egg yolks one at a time and season to taste with salt and freshly ground black pepper.
7   Transfer the purée to a heated serving dish. Garnish and serve.

● To make chilli 'flowers', cut the tops off fresh chillies, then cut down in strips towards the stalk ends; remove the seeds. Fold back the strips to make the flowers.

Whipped swedes with nutmeg

Serves 4
900 g / 2 lb swedes
salt
150 ml / 5 fl oz milk
125 g / 4 oz butter, softened
45 ml / 3 tbls thick cream
freshly ground black pepper
freshly grated nutmeg
a sprig of parsley, to garnish

1 Roughly cut the swedes into even-sized pieces.
2 Boil the swedes in salted water until they feel soft when pierced with a fork but are not disintegrating – approximately 20 minutes. Overcooked swedes will produce a water-sodden purée, not a fluffy one as you might expect.
3 As soon as the swedes are cooked, drain them thoroughly and toss in a dry pan over a moderate heat until any remaining moisture has completely evaporated.
4 Mash the swedes to a smooth purée, or rub them through a fine wire sieve. Return the purée to the pan. Warm the milk and gradually beat it into the purée with a wooden spoon. (If the swedes are particularly dry, you may need to use more milk.) Add the softened butter and thick cream and continue to beat vigorously until the purée is light and fluffy.
5 Season the purée to taste with salt, freshly ground black pepper and freshly grated nutmeg, and beat over a moderate heat until the purée is thoroughly hot again. Take great care not to let the purée boil or it may discolour. Serve immediately, garnished with a sprig of parsley.

🕯 45 minutes

Purée of carrots

Serves 4
700 g / 1½ lb carrots
salt
15 g / ½ oz butter
5 ml / 1 tsp sugar
75 ml / 3 fl oz thick cream
freshly grated nutmeg
freshly ground black pepper
To garnish
1 shiny green leaf
carrot flowers (see below)

1 Cut the carrots into thin slices.
2 Bring a large saucepan of salted water to the boil and cook the carrots for 20 minutes, or until very tender. Drain well. Reserve a little cooking liquid if you are using an electric blender.
3 Place the drained carrots in a blender with a little liquid and blend until smooth, or work them until smooth in a food processor. Transfer to a clean saucepan. Alternatively, purée the carrots in a vegetable mill, or press them through a fine sieve into a clean saucepan, using the back of a wooden spoon.
4 Beat the butter and sugar into the puréed carrots. Stir in the thick cream and heat through gently over a low heat. Season to taste with nutmeg, salt and freshly ground black pepper.
5 Spoon the purée into a heated serving dish. Garnish with the green leaf and arrange the carrot flowers around the leaf. Serve immediately.

● To make carrot flowers, cut a carrot into thin slices. Using a small, very sharp knife, neatly and regularly cut notches around each slice to make a flower shape.

🕯 45 minutes

Purée Saint-Germain

Serves 4–6
700 g /1½ lb frozen peas
60 ml /4 tbls chicken stock, home-made or from a cube
50 g /2 oz butter
15–30 ml /1–2 tbls instant potato powder
15–30 ml /1–2 tbls thick cream
5–15 ml /1–3 tsp lemon juice
salt and freshly ground black pepper

1 Place the frozen peas, chicken stock and butter in a heavy-based saucepan. Set the pan over a high heat and bring the liquid to the boil. Push a sheet of greaseproof paper down into the pan on top of the peas, then reduce the heat to moderate and simmer for about 5 minutes, or until the peas are very tender. Remove the pan from the heat and allow to cool slightly.
2 Reserve 15–30 ml /1–2 tbls of the cooked peas for a garnish, if you wish. Purée the remainder of the peas and the instant potato powder in a blender or food processor. Alternatively, reduce the peas to a purée in a vegetable mill or by rubbing them through a fine nylon sieve.
3 Return the purée to a clean pan. Beat vigorously with a wooden spoon over a moderate heat until heated through, adding the cream, lemon juice and salt and freshly ground black pepper to taste. Serve immediately, garnished with the reserved peas, if you like.

● This purée of peas is often used for garnishing: the name Saint-Germain tells you that peas are included in the dish.

Puréed potatoes

Serves 4–6
1 kg /2 lb floury potatoes
salt
150 ml /5 fl oz hot milk
50 g /2 oz butter, softened
2 egg yolks
1.5 ml /¼ tsp dry mustard
freshly ground black pepper
a sprig of parsley, to garnish

1 Roughly cut the potatoes into even-sized pieces.
2 Boil them in salted water for approximately 20 minutes, or until they feel soft when pierced with a fork, but are not disintegrating. (Overcooked potatoes will produce a water-sodden purée, not a fluffy one.)
3 As soon as the potatoes are cooked, drain them thoroughly and toss them in the dry pan over a moderate heat until the remaining moisture has completely evaporated.
4 Mash the potatoes to a smooth purée in a bowl, or rub them through a fine wire sieve, and return them to the pan.
5 Gradually beat in the hot milk with a wooden spoon. (If the potatoes are particularly dry, you may need to use more milk.) Then add the softened butter and egg yolks and continue to beat vigorously until the purée is light and fluffy.
6 Add the dry mustard and season the purée to taste with salt and freshly ground black pepper. Beat over a moderate heat until the purée is thoroughly hot again. Take great care not to let the purée boil, or it may discolour. Serve immediately in a heated serving bowl, garnished with parsley.

15 minutes

40 minutes

STUFFED VEGETABLES

The fillings you choose for your vegetables can range from the simple to the exotic; either way, stuffed vegetables are a superb way to enjoy them in their own right, not just as accompaniments.

In this section I aim to bring back some of the surprise and delight into cooking vegetables. Stuffed, they should be served as a separate course, either before or after the main course. This way, they receive the attention they really deserve.

In addition, this method of cooking allows you to make the most of the cooked vegetable, to introduce subtle seasonings and flavours that might otherwise go unappreciated if it were to be served simply as an accompaniment to meats, poultry, fish or game. Serve stuffed vegetables, too, on their own as tempting main courses for lunch or supper.

Varying the stuffings
The fillings you choose for your vegetables can range from the simple to the exotic. Blanched vegetable cases can be filled with minced meat and aromatic vegetables mixed with breadcrumbs or rice and bound with egg yolks; or, more simply, filled with diced, cooked vegetables tossed in butter or soured cream, or even a delicious bechamel sauce. If you use this type of stuffing, add a topping of herbs and breadcrumbs or of grated cheese. If you are looking for new variations on the stuffed vegetable theme, try filling the vegetable case with a contrasting purée of cooked vegetable. One of the most effective colour contrasts is tomato cases filled with spinach purée. For contrasting tastes, try puréed green beans in green pepper cases, puréed mushrooms in artichoke cases, or puréed onions in beetroot cases.

Buying and preparing vegetables
Choose vegetables that are crisp and fresh looking. No amount of attention will restore flavour, texture and goodness to a limp, wilted vegetable that is past its prime.

Trim and clean the vegetables in the usual way. Do not peel them unless absolutely necessary. Scrub root vegetables (except beetroot) with a stiff brush. In the case of delicate vegetables – tomatoes or mushrooms, for instance – simply wipe them with a damp cloth.

Blanching: you will find that many vegetables benefit from being softened by blanching before they are actually stuffed or

baked. This preliminary stage tenderizes the vegetables, shortens the cooking time and makes them more receptive to the subtle flavourings of herbs, spices and aromatics.

Blanching is not truly a cooking process, merely a preparatory one, so watch your blanching times carefully to avoid loss of texture and colour. Bring a large saucepan of water to the boil, immerse the vegetables in boiling water, allow the water to come to the boil again, then time your blanching according to the chart below.

Drain blanched vegetables immediately and refresh them under cold, running water to 'fix' their fresh colour, then drain again.

Preparing leaves
Cabbage: strip off and discard any leaves that are tough or discoloured. Separate the remainder and trim off the hard stalk at the base of each leaf. Wash them thoroughly in cold water, drain well and then blanch them in boiling, salted water for one minute before draining and refreshing them in cold water. This softens the leaves and makes them pliable for use.

Vine leaves: fresh vine leaves, which are available from specialist shops, should be trimmed and blanched as for cabbage. Tinned leaves which have been preserved in brine or ones which have been vacuum-sealed simply need to be rinsed.

Cheese-stuffed peppers

 1 hour

Serves 4-5
4-5 plump peppers
25 g /1 oz butter, plus extra for greasing
30 ml /2 tbls olive oil
175-225 g /6-8 oz onions, chopped
1 garlic clove, chopped
175-225 g /6-8 oz easy-cook Italian rice
300 ml /11 fl oz chicken stock, home-made or from a cube
2 hard-boiled eggs
100 g /4 oz Cheddar cheese, chopped
100 g /4 oz walnuts, chopped
45 ml /3 tbls grated Parmesan cheese
30 ml /2 tbls freshly chopped parsley
5 ml /1 tsp oregano
salt and freshly ground black pepper
100 g /4 oz Mozzarella cheese, sliced in 4
Ratatouille, to serve (page 66)

1 Heat the oven to 180C /350F /gas 4. Heat the butter and oil in a large pan and fry the onions and garlic until soft. Add the rice and cook, stirring, for about 2 minutes.
2 Meanwhile, slice the tops from the peppers and seed them. Parboil the peppers

for 2-4 minutes, then drain them, turn them upside down and reserve until needed.
3 Meanwhile, chop the uncooked trimmings from the tops and add these to the rice. Add the stock to the rice, stir once, cover and cook for 12 minutes, adding more stock as necessary for the larger quantity of rice.
4 Peel and chop the eggs and add these, plus the chopped cheese, walnuts, Parmesan, parsley and oregano to the rice and season to taste with salt and pepper.
5 Arrange the peppers in a greased baking dish in which they fit snugly. Fill them with the stuffing and top this with the slices of Mozzarella. Bake for 30 minutes and serve with ratatouille, if wished.

Provençal-style vegetables

🔪🔪 1 hour

Serves 4
4 small aubergines, trimmed
4 medium-sized onions, peeled
4 courgettes, trimmed
salt and freshly ground black pepper
4 tomatoes
105 ml /7 tbls olive oil
175 g /6 oz veal, minced
50 g /2 oz lean bacon, diced
1 Spanish onion, finely chopped
1-2 garlic cloves, crushed
30 ml /2 tbls finely chopped fresh tarragon or chives
30 ml /2 tbls finely chopped fresh parsley
1 medium-sized egg, beaten
90-120 ml /6-8 tbls cooked rice
50 g /2 oz freshly grated Parmesan cheese
butter

1 Poach the whole aubergines and onions for 3-5 minutes and the whole courgettes for 3 minutes in boiling, salted water. Drain and leave until cool enough to handle.
2 Slice off and discard the tops of the tomatoes, courgettes, aubergines and onions. Using a small spoon, scoop out the pulpy flesh of the vegetables, taking care not to break the skins and leaving the shells about 3 mm /⅛ in thick. Reserve the pulp of the aubergines, courgettes and tomatoes (but not the onion) for use in the stuffing. Heat the oven to 190C /375F /gas 5.
3 Prepare the stuffing. Heat 60 ml /4 tbls olive oil in a large, heavy-based pan. Add the minced veal, diced bacon and chopped onion and sauté until lightly browned. Mix together the garlic, herbs, egg, rice and reserved vegetable pulp, then add to the pan. Season generously and sauté for a few minutes, stirring continuously. Remove the pan from the heat and stir in the grated Parmesan cheese.
4 Use the mixture to stuff the scooped-out vegetables. Pour 45 ml /3 tbls olive oil into a large, shallow ovenproof dish. Arrange the stuffed vegetables in the dish and place a knob of butter on top of each one. Bake for about 30 minutes or until tender.

Cheese-stuffed peppers

Blanching times

Artichokes	6-8 minutes
Beetroot	cook until almost tender
Brussels sprouts	4-6 minutes
Cabbage	5-10 minutes
Courgettes	3-5 minutes
Onions	cook until almost tender
Parsnips	2-4 minutes
Peppers	2-4 minutes
Potatoes	cook until almost tender
Turnips	cook until almost tender

Stuffed vine leaves

 1 hour

Serves 8
25 g /1 oz butter
1 Spanish onion, finely chopped
225 g /8 oz cooked rice
500 g /1 lb lean minced lamb
2.5 ml /½ tsp paprika
2.5 ml /½ tsp ground coriander
1.5 ml /¼ tsp cumin powder
1.5 ml /¼ tsp ground ginger
a pinch of cayenne
5 ml /1 tsp crushed dried rosemary
salt and freshly ground black pepper
425 g /15 oz canned vine leaves, drained
about 850 ml /1½ pt chicken stock
150 ml /5 fl oz soured cream, to serve

Stuffed vine leaves

1   Melt the butter in a frying-pan and sauté
the onion until lightly coloured.
2   Mix the sautéed onion with the rice and
lamb. Add the ground spices and crushed
rosemary and season with salt and freshly
ground black pepper to taste, mixing well.
3   Lay out the vine leaves on a flat surface
and divide the stuffing among them. Fold
round the stuffing to make a neat parcel.
4   Put the stuffed leaves in a large saucepan in a single layer and add enough stock
to cover. Put a plate directly on top of the
vine leaves to stop them floating. Bring the
stock to the boil, then lower the heat, cover
the pan and simmer for 30 minutes.
5   Remove each parcel carefully from the
pan with a slotted spoon and arrange in a
warm serving dish. Garnish with soured
cream, serving the remainder separately.

Savoury marrow with peanuts and cashews

 1½ hours

Serves 4
1.2 kg /2¾ lb whole marrow
salt and freshly ground black pepper
75 g /3 oz peanuts, shelled and skinned
75 g /3 oz cashew nuts
60 ml /4 tbls oil
1 large onion, finely chopped
1 garlic clove, finely chopped
125 g /4 oz fresh wholemeal breadcrumbs
30 ml /2 tbls freshly chopped parsley
15 ml /1 tbls freshly chopped marjoram
15 ml /1 tbls tomato purée
90 ml /6 tbls dry white wine
oil for greasing

1   Heat the oven to 200C /400F /gas 6. Cut
off both ends of the marrow and reserve.
Scoop out and discard the seeds.
2   Put the marrow and both the reserved
ends into a large saucepan containing lightly
salted boiling water, return to the boil and
simmer for 5 minutes. Drain well.
3   Grind the nuts in a blender or coffee
grinder. Heat the oil in a frying-pan over a
low heat. Add the onion and garlic and cook
until they are soft but not coloured.
4   Remove the pan from the heat and mix
in the breadcrumbs, nuts, herbs, tomato
purée, wine and seasonings.
5   Fill the marrow with the stuffing and
anchor the ends back on with cocktail sticks.
Place the marrow in a large, lightly greased
casserole, cover and cook for 1 hour.
6   To serve, discard the ends and cut the
marrow into 4 thick slices.

Stuffed cabbage

 2 hours

Serves 4
1 small white or green smooth-leaved
   cabbage
salt and freshly ground black pepper
50 g /2 oz butter
1 medium-sized onion, sliced
1 clove garlic, crushed
350 g /12 oz sausage-meat
5 ml /1 tsp dried mixed herbs
100 g /4 oz 1-day-old white breadcrumbs
50 g /2 oz walnuts, chopped
1 hard-boiled egg, finely chopped

1   Remove any discoloured or loose outer
leaves from the cabbage until it is a neat,
round shape. Blanch it whole in a saucepan
of boiling, salted water for about 5 minutes,
then drain it thoroughly.
2   Transfer the cabbage to a board and,
using 2 spoons, gently pull the leaves out-
wards to make a hollow in the centre. With a
curved grapefruit knife, carefully cut out the
centre of the cabbage, without cutting

Fold each leaf around the stuffing.

Roll it up to make a neat parcel.

through to the base. Chop the removed cabbage centre finely and reserve.

3   Melt half of the butter in a large frying-pan and fry the onion over a moderate heat for 3 minutes. Add the garlic and fry for 1 minute, stirring. Add the sausage-meat and stir until it is evenly browned. Stir in the herbs and half the breadcrumbs and season with salt and pepper. Add the chopped cabbage and mix well.

4   Spoon the filling into the cabbage shell and wrap the whole cabbage tightly in foil. Put a trivet in the bottom of a large sauce-pan, half fill it with boiling water, add the cabbage parcel and cover the pan. Boil, topping up with boiling water when necessary, for 1½ hours, or until the cabbage is tender when pierced with a fine skewer.

5   To make the topping, melt the remaining butter in a small frying-pan, add the walnuts and remaining breadcrumbs and fry over a moderate heat until the mixture is dry. Stir in the chopped egg.

6   Unwrap the cabbage, transfer it to a heated serving dish and top it with the golden crumb mixture. Serve very hot.

Herby mushrooms

⏲ 45 minutes,
including cooling

Serves 6
700 g /1½ lb open button mushrooms
175 g /6 oz pork sausage-meat
½ onion, finely chopped
½ large garlic clove, finely chopped
15 g /½ oz finely chopped fresh parsley
2.5 ml /½ tsp dried thyme
1 bay leaf, finely crumbled
a pinch of dried tarragon, or sprig of fresh
*   tarragon, finely chopped*
salt and freshly ground black pepper
60 ml /4 tbls olive oil
For the topping
25 g /1 oz fine dry breadcrumbs
15 g /½ oz finely chopped fresh parsley

1   Heat the oven to 190C /375F /gas 5. Wipe the mushrooms clean and trim away the discoloured stem ends. Pull out the stems carefully to avoid damaging the caps.

2   Chop the stems finely and combine them with the sausage-meat, finely chopped onion, garlic and herbs. Mix well and season to taste with salt and black pepper.

3   Heat 15 ml /1 tbls of the olive oil in a heavy pan over moderate heat. Add the sausage meat mixture and cook for about 5 minutes, crumbling and blending it with a fork until it is lightly browned. Remove the pan from the heat and cool.

4   Divide the stuffing equally among the mushroom caps. Mix together the bread-crumbs and parsley for the topping and sprinkle over the stuffed mushrooms.

5   Heat the remaining oil in a wide, flameproof baking dish. Arrange the stuffed mushrooms in a single layer and cook over a moderate heat for about 2 minutes, or until the bottoms are lightly coloured, shaking the dish gently from time to time.

6   Cook in the oven for 15 minutes, or until the mushrooms are tender.

Roast stuffed onions

⏲ 1 hour

Serves 4
4 large Spanish onions
salt
50 g /2 oz butter, plus extra for greasing
1 medium-sized onion, finely chopped
1 garlic clove, crushed
225 g /8 oz sausage-meat
60 ml /4 tbls fresh white breadcrumbs
10 ml /2 tsp chopped fresh oregano or
*   5 ml /1 tsp dried oregano*
freshly ground black pepper
30 ml /2 tbls thick cream
25 g /1 oz Cheddar cheese, grated
flat-leaved parsley, to garnish

1   Peel the Spanish onions and trim away the root ends and brown part at the top. Parboil the onions in boiling, salted water for 10 minutes; drain well and leave until completely cold.

2   Melt half the butter in a heavy-based frying-pan. Add the finely chopped onion and fry over a moderate heat for 3 minutes. Stir in the crushed garlic, the sausage-meat, 45 ml /3 tbls of the breadcrumbs and the oregano and season to taste with salt and black pepper. Cook, stirring occasionally, for 10 minutes. Stir in the cream and remove the pan from the heat.

3   Heat the oven to 190C /375F /gas 5.

4   Gently open out the cooked onions; using a small spoon, scrape out and reserve the centre of the bulbs. Chop half the reserved onion flesh and stir it into the filling. Divide the filling among the onions and arrange them in a buttered, shallow ovenproof dish.

5   Melt the remaining butter in a small, heavy-based saucepan. Remove from the heat and stir in the remaining breadcrumbs and the grated cheese. Sprinkle the bread-crumb mixture over the stuffed onions in the ovenproof dish.

6   Bake the onions for about 30 minutes, until they are tender and the filling is crispy-brown on top. Serve them on 4 warmed plates and garnish each one with a sprig of flat-leaved parsley.

Roast stuffed onion

Aubergines
Imam bayeldi

Serves 6
3 aubergines, weighing about
   225 g /8 oz each
salt
1 large Spanish onion, thinly
   sliced
225 g /8 oz canned tomatoes,
   drained and chopped

45 ml /3 tbls finely chopped
   fresh parsley
1.5 ml /¼ tsp sugar
freshly ground black pepper
120–150 ml /8–10 tbls olive oil
6 large garlic cloves
juice of 1 lemon
flat-leaved parsley, to garnish

1   Wipe the aubergines with a damp cloth. Leave about 10 mm /¼
in of the stalk intact, but peel away the leaves.
2   Peel the aubergines lengthways in 15 mm /¼ in wide strips,
leaving alternate strips of peel intact. Cut the aubergines in half
lengthways and make deep slashes in the cut surface with a knife,
about 25 mm /1 in apart, taking great care not to pierce through to
the other side. Rub the cut surfaces, and the bare strips on the
outside, with salt. Put the aubergines in a colander, place a dish on
top and weight them down. Leave them for 1 hour to allow the
bitter juices to drain away.
3   Meanwhile, sprinkle the sliced onion with salt and allow to
mellow for 30 minutes. Rinse thoroughly in warm water and
squeeze dry in a cloth. Combine the rings in a bowl with the drained
tomatoes, 30 ml /2 tbls parsley, sugar, salt and pepper to taste.
4   Rinse the drained aubergine halves in cold, running water,
squeezing them gently to rid them of as much excess liquid as
possible. Dry thoroughly. Pour 30–60 ml /2–4 tbls olive oil into a
shallow flameproof casserole.
5   Arrange the aubergines in the casserole, cut sides up. Cover each
half with the tomato and onion mixture, stuffing it down into the
slashes and piling the rest on top. Lay a garlic clove on each and
pour 15 ml /1 tbls of the olive oil over each; sprinkle with lemon
juice.
6   Pour in enough water to come half-way up the sides of the
aubergines. Bring to the boil, cover the casserole and simmer gently
for 30 minutes. Remove the casserole from the heat and cool.
7   To serve, carefully transfer the aubergines to a deep serving
dish, remove the garlic cloves, sprinkle with the remaining parsley,
pour some of the cooking juices around them and garnish with
parsley. Serve lukewarm, with plenty of bread to soak up the sauce.

2 hours, plus cooling

Stuffed baked
potatoes

Serves 4
4 large potatoes
1 medium-sized onion, finely chopped
25 g /1 oz butter
175 g /6 oz lean minced beef
75 g /3 oz Cheddar cheese, grated
5 ml /1 tsp Worcestershire sauce
2.5 ml /½ tsp dried oregano or marjoram
salt and freshly ground black pepper

1   Heat the oven to 190C /375F /gas 5. Scrub the potatoes until
absolutely clean. Pat them dry and prick them all over with a fork.
Bake the potatoes for 1–1¼ hours, or until they are cooked through.
2   Towards the end of this cooking time, sauté the onion in the
butter for 4–5 minutes, or until soft and golden brown. Add the
beef and sauté over low heat for 5 minutes, crumbling it with a fork.
Stir in 50 g /2 oz of the cheese, the Worcestershire sauce and
oregano or marjoram, and season generously with salt and freshly
ground black pepper. Mix well and keep hot.
3   Heat the grill to hot. Cut a thin slice from the top of each potato
and discard. Scoop out the flesh from the potato with a sharp spoon,
taking great care not to break the skin. Leave a shell about 5 mm /¼
in thick.
4   Sieve or mash the potato flesh to a purée and blend thoroughly
with the hot meat mixture. Taste for seasoning and pile back into
the potato shells.
5   Sprinkle the top of each potato with a little of the remaining
cheese. Place under the grill and cook until the cheese is golden
brown and bubbling, and the potatoes are heated through.

● These make a simple and economical supper dish; they are also a
popular alternative to plain baked potatoes at a children's party.

1¼ hours

Baked avocado in tomato shells

Serves 6–8
6–8 medium-sized tomatoes
salt
225 g /8 oz button mushrooms
50 g /2 oz butter
1 large avocado pear
120 ml /8 tbls fresh breadcrumbs
freshly ground black pepper
15 ml /1 tbls onion juice
15–20 ml /3–4 tsp lemon juice

1   Heat the oven to 180C /350F /gas 4. Cut a 5 mm /¼ in thick
slice from the top of each tomato. Using a teaspoon, scoop out the
pulp and seeds and reserve for another use. Sprinkle the inside of
the tomato shells lightly with salt and turn them upside down on
absorbent paper to drain while you prepare the stuffing
2   To make the stuffing, wipe the mushrooms and trim off the
discoloured stem ends. Slice the mushrooms thinly, reserving 8
whole stems. Melt the butter in a frying-pan and sauté the
mushroom slices for about 3–5 minutes until softened.
3   Peel the avocado and remove the stone. Mash the flesh to a pulp
with a fork, gradually adding the fresh breadcrumbs. Remove the
sautéed mushrooms from the pan with a slotted spoon and stir into
the avocado mixture. Season to taste with salt and freshly ground
black pepper, and flavour with onion juice.
4   Season inside the tomato cases with freshly ground black
pepper. Fill the cases generously with the avocado stuffing. Push a
reserved mushroom stem into the centre of each tomato and then
sprinkle with lemon juice.
5   Arrange the tomato cases side by side in a baking dish and bake
for 15–20 minutes, or until they are very hot and tender but not
disintegrating. Serve immediately.

● Use firm fresh tomatoes for this dish. They make an excellent
appetizer with their rich, buttery avocado filling.

 45 minutes

Len Evans' stuffed mushrooms

Serves 4
8 large open mushroom caps
50 g /2 oz butter
salt and freshly ground black pepper
8 lambs' kidneys
4 small leeks, white part only
15 ml /1 tbls beef stock, home-made or from a cube
15 ml /1 tbls finely chopped fresh parsley
parsley sprigs, to garnish

1   Heat the oven to 190C /375F /gas 5. With a sharp knife trim the
stalks of the mushrooms level with the caps.
2   In a small saucepan melt 25 g /1 oz of the butter. Grease a large,
flat baking tray with a little of the melted butter. Brush the
mushrooms all over with the remaining melted butter and lay them,
cap side down, on the prepared baking tray. Season with salt and
freshly ground black pepper to taste, and bake in the oven for 10
minutes. Keep warm.
3   Remove the skin from the kidneys, halve them and cut out the
core with scissors. Chop the kidneys roughly. Slice the leeks into fine
rings, wash and drain well.
4   In a large frying-pan, melt the remaining butter and cook the
leeks for 4 minutes, stirring with a wooden spoon. Remove the leeks
with a slotted spoon and keep warm. Add the chopped kidney to the
pan and sauté for 3 minutes, or until they are cooked but still
slightly pink inside, turning with a spatula. Return the leeks to the
pan and add the beef stock. Season the sauce with salt and freshly
ground black pepper to taste, and bring to a simmer.
5   Place 2 mushroom caps per warmed serving plate and spoon the
leek and kidney sauce over the mushrooms. Sprinkle with finely
chopped parsley, garnish and serve immediately.

● This recipe came originally from Len Evans' Melbourne
restaurant and wine bar.

25 minutes

BRAISING VEGETABLES

If you feel, as I do, that vegetables deserve better treatment than they often get, then try braising them. To slowly, gently cook vegetables in a little butter or olive oil is simplicity itself, and brings out the best in them.

Braising vegetables means cooking them gently in a little butter or olive oil with just enough liquid to keep them moist. You can braise vegetables on top of the stove or in the oven – either way the vegetables emerge meltingly tender and buttery with none of their flavour or goodness boiled away in cooking water which is then thrown away.

A dish of braised vegetables is so delicious that I often prefer to follow French tradition and serve it as a separate course before the main one. Not only does this allow the meat, fish or game to be fully savoured, it also means that you can make the most of your vegetables and introduce flavours which might otherwise go unappreciated.

Many braised vegetables do, of course, perfectly complement a main dish. If you are looking for a particularly interesting vegetable accompaniment to meat, try Braised peas with bacon, or Braised cabbage with tomatoes.

Choosing vegetables for braising

Braising suits a wide variety of vegetables as a cooking method, including roots such as parsnips and swedes, and leafy green vegetables such as spinach and endive. Even the most delicate of vegetables – asparagus – can be braised, and braising is perhaps the best way to cook lettuce, peas and chicory.

Braising is a suitable method of cooking both mild and strongly flavoured vegetables: vary the strength of accompanying herbs, spices and cooking liquids accordingly.

Preparing vegetables for braising

Having picked the best fresh vegetables available, only the minimum of preparation should be necessary. Simply trim away outer leaves of vegetables such as cabbage, and use a damp cloth to wipe over mushrooms and tomatoes. Try not to peel away goodness from root vegetables, scrubbing them clean is usually an adequate alternative.

Baby carrots, mushrooms and other small vegetables can be left whole; larger ones are usually cut in half or into small pieces – try following the Chinese technique of slicing them across the grain into uniformly small pieces so that they will cook evenly.

Some vegetables will need to be blanched (see page 36) as a preparation to braising. This applies to firm vegetables which would take too long to cook through otherwise, and to vegetables which are to absorb the flavours of other ingredients being cooked with the dish.

Delicate vegetables such as mushrooms, courgettes and broccoli can be precooked for braising by first lightly frying them in butter or oil, rather than by parboiling them, if precooked at all.

Braising vegetables

Braising is simplicity itself, but you do need a suitable cooking pan. I like to use a shallow, heavy-based saucepan or flameproof casserole with a tight-fitting lid. For some braised vegetable dishes, such as Braised chicory and Oven-braised mushrooms it is necessary to cook the vegetables in a single layer – use a large, gratin-type ovenproof or flameproof dish.

Braised peas with bacon

How to braise vegetables

Trim and clean the vegetables. Leave them whole, or cut them in half or into dice depending on size. Parboil the vegetables, if necessary, drain, refresh and drain again.

Heat the butter or olive oil in a shallow saucepan or flameproof casserole. Add the prepared vegetables, flavourings and a little liquid if required. Season.

Cover the pan tightly and simmer the vegetables very gently until tender. Turn out the cooked vegetables and any cooking juices into a heated dish.

Add your prepared vegetables to some heated butter or olive oil in the saucepan or casserole, then add a little flavouring. Most vegetables benefit from the fragrance of fresh herbs, or the scent of garlic. A few strips of cooked bacon marry well with celery and other very strongly flavoured vegetables. Add a pinch of sugar to accentuate the sweetness of young carrots and peas. You can also use crushed or ground spices, but be very sparing. Do not forget the salt and a grinding of pepper.

Next, add a small amount of liquid – just enough to keep the vegetables moist. Vegetables with a naturally high water content, such as mushrooms, spinach and courgettes, need very little liquid, or none at all, as they will produce their own cooking juices. You can use water, stock, wine or even citrus juice, whichever best suits the vegetable's character. Leeks, for instance, take kindly to a splash of red wine, while the pronounced flavour of celery can withstand a robust beef or veal stock. A spoonful or two of cream gives a luxurious touch, but add it at the end of the cooking time.

When you have added the liquid, cover the pan or dish tightly so that no steam can escape. If there is a large gap between the surface of the vegetables and the lid of the pan, I like to lay a sheet of buttered greaseproof paper snugly over the vegetables to ensure that they stay really moist.

Let the vegetables simmer very gently so that all the flavours develop and mingle. Check the vegetables now and again and turn them over, if necessary, so that they braise evenly. When the vegetables are tender and have absorbed most of the liquid, they are cooked. Bite a piece to make sure they are done; if not, braise them for a couple of minutes more.

Serve braised vegetables with their own cooking juices. If there is a lot of liquid left at the end of cooking, drain it off and reduce it by rapid boiling, or thicken it with a *beurre manié*.

Braised peas with bacon

🔪 25 minutes

Serves 4–6
1.8–2 kg /4–4½ lb young peas in the pod, shelled
12 button onions
5 mm /¼ in thick slice of bacon, rind removed
15 ml /1 tbls olive oil
lettuce leaves
50 g /2 oz butter
60 ml /4 tbls chicken stock
about 15 ml /1 tbls sugar
salt

1   Place the button onions in a pan and cover them with cold water. Cover the pan, place it over a high heat and bring to the boil, then reduce the heat and simmer the onions for about 5 minutes, or until they are just tender. Drain well and reserve.
2   Cut the bacon into 5 mm /¼ in wide strips. Heat the olive oil in a frying-pan and sauté the bacon strips until they are golden. Remove the strips from the pan with a slotted spoon, drain and reserve.
3   Wash the lettuce leaves, gently pat them dry with absorbent paper and reserve.
4   Place the peas, button onions and bacon strips in a clean pan and add the butter and chicken stock, and sugar and salt to taste. Bring to the boil, then simmer gently for about 10 minutes, shaking the pan occasionally, until the peas are tender and the liquid has been absorbed. Serve on a bed of lettuce leaves.

● When peas in the pod are out of season, for simplicity and speed you can replace the fresh peas with 450–550 g /1–1¼ lb thawed frozen peas.

Leeks in red wine

🔪 30 minutes preparation,
30 minutes cooking

Serves 4
12–16 small leeks
4 slices back bacon, finely diced
60–90 ml /4–6 tbls finely chopped onion
50 g /2 oz butter
60 ml /4 tbls olive oil
275 ml /10 fl oz well-flavoured chicken stock, home-made or from a cube
150 ml /5 fl oz red wine
freshly ground black pepper

1   Heat the oven to 190C /375F /gas 5.
2   Wash the leeks, trim off the roots and cut off the green tops to within 25 mm /1 in of the white. Split the leeks from the top almost to the root end and wash them thoroughly under cold, running water.
3   Sauté the bacon in a small, dry frying-pan until it is crisp. Remove from the pan with a slotted spoon and reserve for the garnish. Add the finely chopped onion to the pan and sauté in the bacon fat until soft. Remove from the pan with a slotted spoon and reserve.
4   Use some of the butter to generously grease a flameproof, ovenproof dish. Lay the prepared leeks in the dish and dot with the remaining butter. Pour over the olive oil, chicken stock and red wine and sprinkle with the sautéed onion. Season to taste with freshly ground black pepper.
5   Place the dish over a medium heat and bring the liquid to a simmer. Cover the dish with foil and braise the leeks in the oven for 25–30 minutes.
6   Transfer the leeks to a heated serving dish and keep warm. Place the dish over direct heat and boil to reduce the liquid to a glaze – about 75 ml /3 fl oz. Spoon the glaze over the leeks and garnish with the reserved bacon. Serve immediately.

and season to taste with salt and freshly ground black pepper.

3 Lay a piece of buttered greaseproof paper over the chicory, buttered side down, and cover the casserole with a tight-fitting lid. Simmer over a very low heat for 20 minutes, turning the chicory from time to time.

4 Sprinkle the chicory with the lemon or orange juice, replace the paper and lid and simmer gently for a further 5–10 minutes, or until the chicory is tender.

● If it is more convenient, you can braise this dish in an oven heated to 180C /350F / gas 4. Allow 35–45 minutes cooking time.

Oven-braised mushrooms

⫯ 20–25 minutes

Serves 4
12–16 flat mushrooms, wiped and trimmed
3 shallots, finely chopped
1 garlic clove, finely chopped
175 g /6 oz sausage-meat
15 ml /1 tbls finely chopped fresh chervil
15 ml /1 tbls finely chopped fresh tarragon
1.5 ml /¼ tsp dried thyme
2 bay leaves, crumbled
salt
freshly ground black pepper
30–60 ml /2–4 tbls olive oil
30–45 ml /2–3 tbls toasted breadcrumbs
15–30 ml /1–2 tbls finely chopped fresh
   parsley

1 Heat the oven to 190C /375F /gas 5. Carefully remove the stems from the mushrooms caps. Chop the stems finely and place in a bowl. Add the finely chopped shallots, garlic, sausage-meat and herbs to the bowl. Season to taste with salt and freshly ground black pepper and then thoroughly mix the ingredients together.

2 Heat 15–30 ml /1–2 tbls of the olive oil in a heavy-based frying-pan. Add the sausage-meat mixture and sauté until golden. Remove the pan from the heat.

3 Season the insides of the mushroom caps with salt and brush them with a little olive oil. Divide the sautéed sausage-meat mixture among the mushroom caps, heaping it in the centre. Sprinkle lightly with the breadcrumbs and parsley.

4 Select a shallow, ovenproof gratin dish large enough to hold the mushrooms in a single layer. Pour the remainder of the olive oil into the dish, then place it in the oven to heat the oil.

5 When the oil is hot, remove the dish from the oven and arrange the stuffed mushrooms in the dish. Return the dish to the oven and cook for about 10 minutes, or until the mushrooms are tender.

Braised chicory

⫯ 40 minutes

Serves 4
8 heads chicory
50 g /2 oz butter
salt and freshly ground black pepper
juice of ½ lemon or orange

Oven-braised mushrooms

1 Trim the root end of each head of chicory, removing the bitter core at the base. Discard any withered leaves. Wash the chicory well in cold water and drain thoroughly.

2 Select a shallow, flameproof casserole dish large enough to hold the chicory in a single layer. Melt the butter in the dish over a low heat. Arrange the chicory in the dish

Braised broccoli

⫯ 25 minutes

Serves 4
350 g /12 oz broccoli heads, trimmed
15 g /½ oz butter
15 ml /1 tbls olive oil
2 garlic cloves, finely chopped
200 ml /7 fl oz dry white wine
salt
freshly ground black pepper

1 Wash the broccoli heads thoroughly in plenty of cold water, drain and pat dry with absorbent paper.
2 In a large saucepan, heat the butter and the olive oil, then add the finely chopped garlic and cook gently for 3–4 minutes until lightly golden. Add the drained broccoli and toss to coat each broccoli head in the butter and olive oil.
3 Pour in the wine and bring to the boil. Reduce the heat and cover the pan. Simmer for about 10 minutes, or until the broccoli is tender, but still firm. Season with salt and freshly ground black pepper.
4 Transfer the cooked broccoli and pan juices to a heated serving dish and serve.

Braised cabbage with tomatoes

🔪 40 minutes

Serves 4
700–900 g /1½–2 lb shredded white cabbage
15 ml /1 tbls olive oil
1 Spanish onion, finely chopped
1 bouquet garni
1 garlic clove, finely chopped
4 large, ripe tomatoes, blanched, skinned, seeded and diced
salt and freshly ground black pepper
15 g /½ oz butter
175 g /6 oz streaky bacon, cut into strips
fresh parsley, to garnish

1 In a saucepan, heat the olive oil. Add the finely chopped onion and cook over a high heat for about 10 minutes, or until soft and golden brown, stirring occasionally.
2 Add the bouquet garni, the finely chopped garlic and the diced tomato flesh. Season with salt and freshly ground black pepper to taste. Simmer over a low heat for 15 minutes, or until the tomatoes are reduced to a purée, stirring occasionally. Reserve and keep warm.
3 Meanwhile, in a flameproof casserole, heat the butter, then add the bacon strips. Cook, tossing frequently with a spatula, for 5 minutes, or until golden.
4 Stir in the shredded cabbage. Season with salt and freshly ground black pepper to taste. Cover and cook for 10 minutes, or until the cabbage is almost tender, stirring with a wooden spoon from time to time.
5 Pour the reserved tomato purée over the cabbage and stir it in gently. Cook for a further 5 minutes, stirring occasionally, until the cabbage is cooked but still crisp and the flavours have blended.
6 Remove the bouquet garni, adjust the seasoning and transfer to a heated serving dish. Garnish with fresh parsley and serve.

Mushrooms in green packets

🔪🔪 1 hour, plus cooling

Serves 4
12 large, unblemished spinach leaves
salt
25 g /1 oz butter
15 ml /1 tbls olive oil
1 Spanish onion, finely chopped
2 small garlic cloves, finely chopped
225 g /8 oz button mushrooms, finely chopped
150 g /5 oz breadcrumbs made from 1-day-old white bread
1 egg, lightly beaten
1.5 ml /¼ tsp freshly grated nutmeg
freshly ground black pepper
butter for greasing
275 ml /10 fl oz chicken stock, home-made or from a cube
1 egg yolk
juice of ½ lemon

1 Wash the spinach leaves and trim away the stalks. Boil the leaves for 2 minutes in salted water. Transfer the leaves with a slotted spoon to a bowl of cold water and leave to cool. Remove the leaves individually and pat dry with absorbent paper.
2 Heat the butter and olive oil in a saucepan. When the foaming subsides, add the

Braised broccoli

finely chopped onion and garlic. Cook over a moderate heat for 7–10 minutes, or until the onion is soft, stirring occasionally with a wooden spoon. Add the finely chopped button mushrooms and cook for 5 minutes, or until the mushrooms are tender. Leave the ingredients to cool.
3 Stir in the breadcrumbs, lightly beaten egg and freshly grated nutmeg. Season with salt and freshly ground black pepper to taste. Place 30 ml /2 tbls of the stuffing in the centre of each of the reserved dried spinach leaves. Fold both sides in and roll up carefully.
4 Lightly butter a shallow, flameproof dish large enough to take the spinach packets in one layer. Lay the spinach packets side by side in the buttered dish. Pour the chicken stock over, bring to the boil, reduce the heat, cover and simmer for 30 minutes. With a slotted spoon, transfer the packets to a heated serving platter and keep warm. Reserve the cooking liquid.
5 In the top pan of a double boiler, whisk the egg yolk and lemon juice until well blended. Strain the cooking liquid into the egg yolk mixture and stir to blend. Over simmering water cook for 2 minutes, or until the sauce has thickened, stirring constantly. Do not allow the sauce to boil or the egg yolk will curdle. Season with salt and freshly ground black pepper to taste. Dribble the sauce over the mushroom packets, or serve it separately. Serve immediately.

Braised chicory with cheese sauce

Serves 4
700 g /1½ lb chicory
25 g /1 oz butter, plus extra
   for greasing
salt
freshly ground black pepper
30 ml /2 tbls lemon juice
a sprig of parsley, to garnish

For the cheese sauce
25 g /1 oz butter
25 g /1 oz flour
425 ml /15 fl oz milk
1 egg yolk, lightly beaten
30 ml / 2 tbls each grated Gruyère
   and Parmesan cheeses
freshly grated nutmeg

1   Heat the oven to 180C /350F /gas 4, if you wish to cook the chicory in the oven.
2   Trim the root ends from the chicory, removing the bitter core at the base. Discard any damaged leaves and wash the chicory well in cold water. Drain thoroughly.
3   In a shallow flameproof casserole, heat the butter. Add the chicory and season to taste with salt and freshly ground black pepper. Sprinkle with lemon juice. Butter a sheet of greaseproof paper and cover the chicory.
4   Cover the casserole and cook until tender over a very low heat for 25–30 minutes. Alternatively, cook in the oven for 35–45 minutes, or until tender.
5   Meanwhile, make the cheese sauce. In a heavy-based saucepan, melt the butter and stir in the flour with a wooden spoon. Cook over a low heat for 2–3 minutes to make a pale roux, stirring constantly. Gradually add the milk, stirring vigorously with a wire whisk to prevent lumps forming. Bring to the boil and simmer for 7–10 minutes, or until the sauce is smooth and thick, stirring frequently.
6   Remove from the heat. Stir in the lightly beaten egg yolk and 15 ml /1 tbls each Gruyère and Parmesan cheeses.
7   Heat the grill to high. Season the sauce lightly with salt (taking into account the saltiness of the cheese), more generously with freshly ground black pepper, and with nutmeg to taste. Keep warm.
8   Using a slotted spoon, transfer the chicory to a flameproof serving dish. Pour over the cheese sauce and sprinkle with the remaining cheese. Place under the grill for 5 minutes, or until well browned. Serve immediately, garnished with a sprig of parsley.

 50 minutes–1 hour

Herby cabbage and celery

Serves 4
350 g /12 oz white cabbage
1 head celery
25 g /1 oz butter
150 ml /5 fl oz white wine
5 ml /1 tsp fresh thyme, chopped
salt and freshly ground black pepper
a sprig of thyme, to garnish

1   Cut the cabbage into quarters. Remove the core and shred the leaves finely.
2   Separate the celery into stalks and cut off any leaves. Reserve the leaves for the garnish. Wipe each stalk with a damp cloth and cut into 5 mm /¼ in thick slices.
3   In a medium-sized saucepan, combine the butter and white wine. Place over a moderate heat until the butter has melted.
4   Add the shredded cabbage, sliced celery, chopped fresh thyme and season to taste with salt and freshly ground black pepper. Cook over a moderate heat for 20 minutes, or until the cabbage is tender but still crunchy, stirring occasionally with a wooden spoon.
5   To serve, adjust the seasoning and transfer to a heated serving dish. Garnish with the reserved celery leaves and a sprig of thyme and serve immediately.

30 minutes

Broccoli au mirepoix

Serves 6
700 g /1½ lb broccoli
90 ml /6 tbls finely diced carrots
90 ml /6 tbls finely diced celery
90 ml /6 tbls finely diced onion
275 ml /10 fl oz chicken stock, home-made or from a cube
15 ml /1 tbls soy sauce
salt and freshly ground black pepper

1   Heat the oven to 180C /350F /gas 4.
2   Wash the broccoli, drain and pat dry with a clean tea-towel. Cut off and discard two-thirds of each stem.
3   In a shallow ovenproof serving dish, combine the finely diced carrots, celery and onion. Arrange the broccoli on top in neat rows if the dish is rectangular, in a circle if it is round.
4   In a bowl, mix together the chicken stock and soy sauce. Pour this over the vegetables. Season to taste with salt and freshly ground black pepper.
5   Cover the dish with foil and bake for 1 hour, or until the broccoli is tender. Adjust the seasoning and serve immediately.

● The term *mirepoix* describes the finely diced vegetables (usually carrots, onions and celery) traditionally used to add extra flavour to braised dishes. Diced ham is sometimes included.

Braised carrots with black olives

Serves 4
500 g /1 lb carrots
24 black olives
25 g /1 oz butter
30 ml /2 tbls olive oil
1 Spanish onion, finely chopped
30 ml /2 tbls wine vinegar
salt and freshly ground black pepper
30 ml /2 tbls finely chopped fresh parsley

1   Peel the carrots and trim off the ends. Cut into 5 cm /2 in segments, then cut each segment into thin, even-sized strips, and reserve.
2   Bring a saucepan of water to the boil and blanch the black olives for 4 minutes. Drain, then rinse under cold, running water, drain again and reserve.
3   In a heavy-based flameproof casserole, heat the butter and the olive oil. When the foaming subsides, add the finely chopped onion and sauté over a moderate heat for 7–10 minutes, or until the onion is soft, stirring occasionally with a wooden spoon.
4   Add the carrot strips, the drained, blanched olives and the wine vinegar. Season to taste with salt and freshly ground black pepper. Cover and simmer gently for 20–25 minutes, or until tender, stirring occasionally.
5   Adjust the seasoning and transfer to a heated serving dish. Sprinkle with finely chopped parsley and serve immediately.

 1½ hours

1 hour

ORIENTAL-STYLE VEGETABLES

It would be impossible, in this book on vegetables, to ignore the influence of the East. The distinctive way of cooking, involving careful preparation, delicate flavours and crisp textures, is well worth trying.

Food is a passport to friendship in the Orient where the ingredients, the presentation of meals and the rituals of hospitality form an important part of the culture of the people. In this section I include vegetable dishes from China, Japan and South-east Asia, and from India too, as many Westerners count it as part of the East.

China

If, traditionally, France has been the home of all that is best in European cooking, China must take that place in the East. How far back good cooking actually goes in China is hard to determine, but certainly the traditions that continue today have been built up over thousands of years, evolving as a delicate blending of tastes and textures.

Chinese cuisine depends on two basic methods of cooking – the one long and slow, the other quick and light. It is the quick method that mainly concerns us for vegetable recipes. For this method the ingredients must always be absolutely fresh, and they are cut into tiny pieces – usually strips rather than dice. They are added to hot oil in a wok or frying-pan and stir-fried with seasonings for 2-3 minutes.

For a braised recipe a little liquid may then be added and the cooking continued at a lower heat for a few minutes more – never for an hour or so as in Europe. The finished dish will be crisp and light, the flavours subtly blended.

Thailand

In Thailand many of the cookery traditions are similar to China, with stir-fried dishes and a constant blending of flavours and textures. But there are other influences in Thailand, too, from the more westerly regions of India and Pakistan.

From here comes a love of pungent and hot food and, above all, of chillies. The Thais also love to decorate their food. They use colour with great skill and then dress the dishes with the intricacy of an artist, carving ginger root or radishes into intriguing shapes and using fresh flowers and shoots for additional contrast and shape.

India

The hottest Asian cuisine comes from India and its neighbouring countries of Pakistan and Bangladesh. Typical dishes from the south of India are bitingly hot, with chillies, coriander, lemon grass, garlic, fenugreek, mustard seed and cumin.

Further north however, though the food is still spiced, the sauces tend to be milder and thicker, with cream or yoghurt added. These spices, and others, are now much more readily available from ethnic grocery shops.

Many Indians are vegetarian, so their cuisine offers a wide choice of vegetable dishes. The Spiced potato cakes (see recipe) that I have chosen appeal as much to the eye as they do to the palate.

Japan

Japanese food is unique among the Oriental countries for its delicacy of flavour and simplicity of presentation. Vegetables are an important feature of Japanese cuisine, served as an accompaniment and as a garnish with seafood, poultry and pork. Soy beans are also used in many ways: as delicious, salted black beans, in bean curd and in *miso* paste, a rich flavouring used both alone and as a seasoning in sauces.

The Japanese do not blend food like the Chinese, but serve it singly, arranged in a sparse and delicate fashion, although several dishes may be served at the same time.

In my selection of Oriental recipes I have aimed to give you the flavour and the feel of the East rather than to reproduce totally authentic dishes. With this concept in mind, I have tried to choose recipes that use our own familiar vegetables in unfamiliar ways. (The special seasonings may be obtained from Oriental grocery shops.) Use these recipes alongside fish or meat recipes with an Eastern influence or mix them with more familiar dishes.

Ingredients

Spices: these are essential in Oriental cooking. Precisely which spices you use is less important than their quality and freshness and the skill with which you blend the flavours. The common spices are, on the whole, familiar to most of us – ginger and coriander are basic (though the fresh leaves and roots of the coriander are often used, which is not so common in the West, where we tend to use the seeds).

Garlic is often mixed with the spices, turmeric is used for colour and fresh chillies appear in many of the dishes. Different varieties of chilli will give you varying degrees of 'heat' in your flavourings. If, on the whole, you find chillies too hot, take care to remove all the seeds and use only the flesh. Lemon grass (sometimes known as sereh powder) is a spice not often used in the West but which characterizes many Oriental dishes. Totally typical of Chinese cooking is star anise; this is a basic part of the much-used 'Chinese five-spice-mix'.

The Indians also have a typical spice blend, known as *garam masala*. It is the forerunner of what we know as curry powder but is incomparably better. My own personal Indian spice blend is less complicated than a true Indian mix but gives pleasing results.

Soy in various forms is an inherent part of most South-east Asian cookery. We are most familiar with it as a fermented sauce for flavouring stews and braises and for adding to Chinese dishes at the table. The Japanese also use soy sauce but theirs is quite a different product; black rather than brown, it has a distinctly different flavour.

When cooking Japanese dishes try to find the authentic soy sauce to prevent your dish taking on too much of a Chinese tinge. Other forms of soy are less common in the West – *tofu* bean curd is typical of Japan as is *miso* paste, a fermented soy bean paste used both on its own and as a flavouring for other sauces. *Nam pla*, also known as fish soy or fish gravy, is used in Thai dishes.

Because soy has a rather salty taste you will find little salt seasoning in dishes that contain it.

Sake and mirin: rice wines are used in many Oriental dishes. Sake is the dry

version, mirin is sweeter; mirin is also easier to obtain in Western shops. As a substitute for sake use dry sherry, for mirin use a half and half mixture of dry sherry and water. When served for drinking rather than cooking, sake is often warmed to just above blood temperature.

Vegetables: some of the vegetables that are typically Oriental are now totally familiar on our tables. Chinese leaves are a case in point; the tender, delicately flavoured, light-green leaves are now seen in many supermarkets, for serving raw in salads or for braising lightly, Oriental-style, to serve as a hot dish. Bean sprouts, too, available only in cans up to a few years ago, are now much easier to find fresh.

Oriental vegetables that are available only in a preserved form are bamboo shoots – these come in cans – and Chinese mushrooms, which are dried. Soak these well and rinse them carefully or they may be tough and gritty; well prepared they are delicious. If all else fails, use ordinary fresh mushrooms. Other of my recipes are dried, black fungus which is frilly, black and has a different flavour from the Chinese mushrooms.

MSG: Monosodium glutamate is a flavour enhancer that brings out the flavour of other food without adding any flavour of its own. Always use it sparingly.

Ginger: for Oriental cooking you will need fresh root ginger – many health food shops stock it. Peeled and sliced it carries a freshness of flavour that makes dried ginger root seem musty by comparison; if dried ginger is all that you can get, then it is better than no ginger at all. For authenticity, powdered ginger is the least desirable.

Oils and fats: Asians tend to like lighter oils than the European olive oil. Peanut oil and sesame seed oil are favourites, adding light flavours of their own. Indians and Pakistanis use *ghee* for frying, which is a purified milk fat. It is possible to buy ghee in Indian shops, or use clarified butter.

Equipment

The basic implement for Oriental cooking is the wok. This is a large, circular, iron pan with a rounded bottom and high sides. It is perfect for every type of cooking except that done in the oven. For stir-frying it holds just a little oil and, as each new ingredient is added, those that are already cooked can be pushed to one side of the pan to keep hot without over-cooking. The best woks also have a lid so they can be used with a steaming rack or basket.

Always dry your wok carefully after washing and store it in a warm place to prevent it rusting. A large frying-pan is the best substitute for a wok. An electric frying-pan gives an excellent simulation of the cooking conditions created in a wok.

Traditionally a mortar and pestle is used for grinding spices, but I find this hard work. I keep a special coffee grinder for the purpose – special because once a grinder has been used for spices it will always smell of them. Or you could blend your spices in a hand grinder, such as a spare pepper mill.

Vegetables in coconut milk

25 minutes

Serves 4
150 g /5 oz very fine desiccated coconut
2 large tomatoes
30 ml /2 tbls peanut or vegetable oil
½ Spanish onion, coarsely chopped
1 garlic clove, finely chopped
125 g /4 oz mange tout
1.5 ml /¼ tsp ground turmeric
a large pinch of chilli powder
salt
225 g /8 oz Chinese cabbage, coarsely
  chopped

1 Place the desiccated coconut in a bowl; add 425 ml /15 fl oz water and knead with your hands for 3 minutes. Strain the liquid through a fine sieve into a bowl, pressing the coconut with a wooden spoon. (You will end up with about 300 ml /10 fl oz.)
2 Cut the tomatoes into thin wedges, cut in half across and reserve.
3 Heat the oil in a wok or large frying-pan and cook the coarsely chopped onion and finely chopped garlic for 2–3 minutes, or until slightly softened. Add the mange tout, turmeric, chilli powder, salt to taste and 150 ml /5 fl oz of the coconut milk. Cook for 3 minutes, stirring constantly. Add the coarsely chopped cabbage and tomatoes and cook for a further 3 minutes.
4 Pour in the remaining coconut milk. Simmer for 1–2 minutes, or until the vegetables are heated through but still crunchy. Adjust the seasoning, transfer to a serving dish and serve immediately.

Thai stir-fried vegetables (page 52)

Chinese-style mushrooms

¶ making the onion flower,
and 10 minutes

Serves 4
225 g /8 oz mushrooms, wiped
30 ml /2 tbls peanut oil
2.5 ml /½ tsp salt
5ml /1 tsp cornflour
1 spring onion flower, to garnish (see below)

1   Heat the oil in a wok or frying-pan. Add the mushrooms and the salt and stir over a moderate heat for 1 minute.
2   Add 150 ml /5 fl oz water. Cover the wok or pan and simmer for 3 minutes, shaking occasionally.
3   Meanwhile, in a small bowl, blend the cornflour with 15 ml /1 tbls cold water to a smooth paste.
4   Pour the cornflour paste onto the mushroom mixture and stir for 1 minute, or until thickened.
5   Pour into a heated serving dish. Garnish with a spring onion flower and serve.

● To make a spring onion flower, remove the bulbous end from the spring onion and cut the stalk to measure 7.5 cm /3 in. Cut the green part lengthways in several places, leaving 25 mm /1 in of the white stalk whole. Leave in iced water for 1 hour, or until the flower opens. Drain and pat dry.

Stir-fried sweet and sour Chinese leaves

¶ 25 minutes

Serves 4–6
700–900 g /1½–2 lb Chinese leaves
20–30 ml /4–6 tsp rice or wine vinegar
20–30 ml /4–6 tsp sugar
20–30 ml /4–6 tsp thin soy sauce
a large pinch of salt
5–7.5 ml /1–1½ tsp tapioca or potato flour
60–75 ml /4–5 tbls groundnut or corn oil
1 large or 2 small chillies, washed, seeded
   and cut into thread-like strips
10–15 ml /2–3 tsp sesame oil for sprinkling

1   Remove any tough leaves from the Chinese leaves, halve the rest lengthways, slice across into 5 cm /2 in strips and reserve. Mix the vinegar, sugar, soy sauce, salt and tapioca or potato flour and then reserve.
2   Heat a wok or large frying-pan until hot. Add 30–45 ml /2–3 tbls of the groundnut or corn oil and swirl it around the pan. Add the leaves and stir and toss continuously for 5–6 minutes. If the pieces begin to burn, lower the heat. The bulk of the leaves will decrease. Transfer the leaves to a colander, drain and reserve.
3   Wipe the wok or frying-pan dry and

Chinese-style mushrooms

reheat it. Add the rest of the oil, swirling it around the pan, then the chilli, stirring twice, and then the reserved sauce. When the sauce bubbles, add the leaves.
4   Stir and toss the leaves so that they absorb the sauce. When thoroughly hot, transfer it to a warm serving plate. Sprinkle the sesame oil over the leaves and serve.

Chinese leaves in cream

¶¶ 30–45 minutes

Serves 6
700–800 g /1½–1¾ lb Chinese leaves
9 ml /1¾ tsp salt
60 ml /4 tbls groundnut or corn oil
25 g /1 oz cooked ham, chopped
For the sauce
15 ml /1 tbls potato or tapioca flour
75 ml /3 fl oz chicken stock, home-made or
   from a cube
150 ml /5 fl oz evaporated milk or thin
   cream

1   Discard any tough outer leaves of the Chinese leaves. Wash the others, halve each one lengthways, then slice them across into strips about 6.5 cm /2½ in long.
2   Bring 1.5 L /2½ pt water to the boil in a large saucepan. Add 5 ml /1 tsp salt and 15 ml /1 tbls oil (this will make the leaves glisten) and plunge in the leaves. When the water returns to a rolling boil, pour everything into a colander.
3   Refresh the leaves thoroughly under cold, running water and leave them to drain in the colander for 15–30 minutes.
4   For the sauce, dissolve the potato or tapioca flour in 30 ml /2 tbls of the stock and then stir in the remainder. Stir in the cream and then add 4 ml /¾ tsp salt.
5   Heat a wok or frying-pan over a medium heat until it is moderately hot. Add the remaining 45 ml /3 tbls oil and whirl it around the pan. Tip in the leaves and stir and turn with a spatula until they are thoroughly hot, taking care, however, not to burn them. Push the leaves to the sides, making a well in the middle.
6   Stir the sauce well and then pour it into the centre of the wok. Stir the sauce continually until it thickens, then fold in the leaves. Tip the mixture onto a warm serving plate.
7   Arrange the top layer of leaves in parallel lines, sprinkle the chopped ham over the top and serve.

Stir-fried mushrooms with mange tout

Serve this crunchy, sweet-sour vegetable dish with grilled pork chops or chicken.

¶ 15 minutes

Serves 4
225 g /8 oz mange tout
salt
225 g /8 oz button mushrooms
15 ml /1 tbls soy sauce
15 ml /1 tbls dry sherry
5 ml /1 tsp clear honey
60 ml /4 tbls sunflower oil
1 garlic clove, chopped
1 small red pepper, washed, cored, seeded
   and cut into matchstick strips
50 g /2 oz cashews

1   Top and tail the mange tout, string if necessary, and cut into 25 mm /1 in pieces. Blanch in boiling, salted water for 1½ minutes; drain, refresh and drain again.
2   Trim, wipe and slice the mushrooms, then reserve. In a small bowl, combine the soy sauce, sherry and honey.
3   Heat the oil and garlic in a Chinese wok or large frying-pan over a moderate heat. When the garlic begins to sizzle, add the sliced mushrooms and strips of pepper and stir-fry for 2 minutes. Add the cashews and stir-fry for 1 minute more.
4   Add a good pinch of salt and 60 ml /4 tbls water and boil over high heat until the liquid has almost evaporated. Give the soy sauce mixture a good stir and pour into the pan. Toss the vegetables and nuts in the sauce, then add the mange tout and stir-fry for 1 minute. Serve immediately.

Stir-fried bean sprouts

¶¶ 2–3 hours chilling,
plus about 15 minutes

Serves 2
225 g /8 oz bean sprouts
30 ml /2 tbls peanut or vegetable oil
1–2 spring onions, cut into 25 mm /1 in
   sections, white and green parts reserved
   separately
2 thin slices of fresh root ginger, peeled
about 1.5 ml /¼ tsp salt
15 ml /1 tbls oyster sauce

1   Do not wash the bean sprouts if they are commercially sealed in a plastic container, but do refrigerate them until they are cooked. (Chilling helps assure they remain crunchy when cooked.) If the beans have to be washed, drain them well and refrigerate for 2–3 hours before cooking them.
2   Heat a wok or frying-pan over high heat until it starts to smoke. Add the oil and whirl it around. Put in the white parts of the spring onion and as soon as they sizzle, add the ginger slices.
3   Add the bean sprouts. Leaving the heat on high, stir-fry by flipping and tossing the bean sprouts evenly and vigorously for about 2 minutes.
4   Sprinkle the bean sprouts with salt towards the end of the cooking time; add the green parts of the spring onion. The bean sprouts should still be crisp. Transfer them to a warm serving plate.
5   Pour over the oyster sauce, mix lightly with a pair of chopsticks or a fork and serve.

Thai stir-fried vegetables

🍴 40 minutes

Serves 4–6
125 g /4 oz carrots, sliced
125 g /4 oz whole green beans, trimmed to
* 5 cm /2 in lengths*
125 g /4 oz mange tout, trimmed and halved
125 g /4 oz broccoli florets
1 red pepper, cut into strips or arrow shapes
1 green pepper, cut into strips or arrow
* shapes*
4 celery sticks, cut diagonally into 15 mm
* /½ in slices*
60 ml /4 tbls peanut or vegetable oil
125 g /4 oz button mushrooms, stems
* removed*
30 ml /2 tbls Thai fish sauce (nam pla)
lemon juice
Tabasco sauce
sugar

1   Put the sliced carrots, trimmed beans and mange tout in a large saucepan, cover with cold water and bring to the boil. Boil for 3 minutes, then remove from the heat and remove the vegetables from the water with a slotted spoon. Refresh under cold, running water, drain well and reserve.
2   Put the broccoli florets, red and green pepper strips or arrow shapes and celery slices into the same water; bring back to the boil. Boil for 2 minutes and drain. Rinse under cold running water, drain well and reserve.
3   Put the oil in a wok or large frying-pan and place over a high heat. When the oil is hot, add all the blanched vegetables, plus the mushrooms. Fry quickly, stirring, for 1–2 minutes, until the vegetables are heated through.
4   Add the Thai fish sauce (nam pla), lemon juice, Tabasco sauce and sugar to taste, toss well and simmer for 1 minute. Serve the dish immediately.

Chinese braised vegetables

🍴 30 minutes

Serves 4
1 head celery
225 g /8 oz button mushrooms
45 ml /3 tbls vegetable or peanut oil
freshly ground black pepper
1.5 ml /¼ tsp monosodium glutamate
* (optional)*
15–30 ml /1–2 tbls soy sauce
5 ml /1 tsp sugar

1   Wash and cut the celery sticks diagonally into 25 mm /1 in lengths. Wipe the mushrooms clean with a damp cloth and cut the stems level with the caps.
2   Heat the oil in a wok or large, heavy frying-pan. Fry the celery lengths for 3

minutes, stirring frequently with a wooden spoon. Add the mushrooms, season with pepper to taste, and continue cooking for a further 3 minutes, stirring frequently.
3   Add monosodium glutamate, if desired, soy sauce and sugar and cook for a further 4–5 minutes, or until the celery is just tender.
4   Transfer the vegetables to a serving dish, pour over the juices and serve.

Spinach with bamboo shoots

🍴 15–45 minutes

Serves 4
450 g /1 lb fresh spinach
4 dried Chinese mushrooms
* or 75 g /3 oz fresh button mushrooms*
30–60 ml /2–4 tbls peanut oil
60 ml /4 tbls sliced bamboo shoots
5 ml /1 tsp sugar
salt
1.5 ml /¼ tsp monosodium glutamate
* (optional)*
30 ml /2 tbls mirin (Japanese wine) or 15 ml
* /1 tbls each dry sherry and water*

Gado gado and Spiced potato cakes

1   Remove the tough stems and any yellow leaves from the spinach.
2   Wash the leaves thoroughly under cold running water and reserve.
3   Place the dried mushrooms in a small bowl, add boiling water to cover and let them stand for about 30 minutes. Drain the mushrooms, wash them thoroughly and then squeeze them to remove excess moisture. Cut off and discard the stems, then slice the mushroom caps thinly. If using fresh mushrooms, remove and discard the stems and slice the caps.
4   Heat the peanut oil in a wok or large frying-pan and add the mushrooms and the bamboo shoots. Cook, stirring, over high heat for 1 minute.
5   Add the spinach and stir-fry for 2–3 minutes more.
6   Add the sugar, salt to taste, monosodium glutamate (if wished) and Japanese wine (or sherry and water). Cook, stirring constantly, for 1 minute more.
7   Transfer the vegetables to a heated serving dish with a slotted spoon and serve.

Fried aubergine in miso sauce

🍴 30 minutes

Serves 6
700 g /1½ lb aubergines
10 ml /2 tsp salt
30 ml /2 tbls vegetable oil
30 ml /2 tbls sesame seed oil
30–60 ml /2–4 tbls miso paste
45 ml /3 tbls sake or dry sherry
15 ml /1 tbls sugar
30 ml /2 tbls lemon juice
tomato wedges, to garnish

1 Cut the aubergines into 5 mm /¼ in slices and cut each slice into strips. Sprinkle with salt and leave to stand for 5 minutes. Rinse under cold running water and dry on absorbent paper, or in a clean tea-towel.
2 In a wok or large frying-pan, heat the oils and add the aubergines. Fry for 2–3 minutes, stirring.
3 Dilute the miso paste with 60 ml /4 tbls water, and add the sake or dry sherry and the sugar. Add the miso mixture to the aubergines, mix well and simmer over a low heat for 3–4 minutes, or until the aubergines are soft. If the sauce begins to dry up, add a little more water. Add the lemon juice, garnish and serve.

Gado gado

 40 minutes,
plus cooling

Serves 4
75 ml /5 tbls sesame seed oil
450 g /1 lb white cabbage, shredded
125 g /4 oz cauliflower florets
75 g /3 oz green beans, cut into 4 cm /1½ in lengths
175 g /6 oz bean sprouts
125 g /4 oz salted peanuts
45–60 ml /3–4 tbls lemon juice
1 garlic clove, finely chopped
1 shallot, finely chopped

1 Heat 30 ml /2 tbls of the sesame seed oil in a wok or deep frying-pan, add the shredded cabbage, cauliflower florets, green beans and bean sprouts and cook over high heat, stirring, for 3–5 minutes until softened but still crisp. Remove the vegetables from the pan with a slotted spoon and arrange decoratively on a serving dish; allow to cool.
2 Meanwhile, heat 30 ml /3 tbls of the sesame seed oil in a small saucepan, add the salted peanuts and fry for 5–6 minutes over high heat until golden, stirring constantly. Drain thoroughly on absorbent paper. Put them in a blender or food processor with 45 ml /3 tbls of the lemon juice and blend to a purée.
3 Add the remaining sesame oil to the saucepan and sauté the finely chopped garlic clove and the shallot for 5 minutes, or until softened. Add the peanut sauce and add more lemon juice if necessary, mixing well.

4 Put the warmed sauce in a small bowl, place this on the serving dish of salad and serve.

Indian spice blend

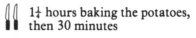 2 minutes

Makes about 20 ml /4 tsp
5 ml /1 tsp cardamom seeds
2.5 ml /½ tsp cumin seeds
1.5 ml /¼ tsp whole cloves
10 ml /2 tsp coriander seeds

1 Grind all the ingredients together to a fine powder in a mill kept especially for spices. Use immediately or keep in a tiny airtight jar.

Spiced potato cakes

1¼ hours baking the potatoes,
then 30 minutes

Serves 4
3 large, hot baked potatoes
5 ml /1 tsp salt
5 ml /1 tsp Indian spice blend
1 egg
30 ml /2 tbls each finely chopped red and green peppers
ghee, vegetable oil or clarified butter, for frying
5 ml /1 tsp coriander seeds
For the sauce
¼ onion, finely chopped
1 garlic clove, finely chopped
3 thin slices of fresh ginger
5–10 ml /1–2 tsp Indian spice blend
ghee, vegetable oil, or clarified butter
2 tomatoes, skinned, seeded and coarsely chopped
150 ml /5 fl oz thick cream
2.5 ml /½ tsp ground turmeric
chilli powder
salt and freshly ground black pepper

1 Remove the flesh from the potatoes — you will need 225 g /8 oz of the flesh. Mash the potato with a fork, mixing in the salt, Indian spice blend and egg. Mix well.
2 Blanch the finely chopped peppers for 1 minute, drain, refresh and add to the potato mixture.
3 To prepare the sauce, sauté the finely chopped onion, garlic, the sliced ginger and Indian spice blend in 5–10 ml /1–2 tsp ghee, oil or clarified butter, until the onion is translucent. Add the tomato, thick cream and turmeric, and season with chilli powder and salt and pepper to taste. Simmer gently for 2–3 minutes and reserve, keeping the sauce warm.
4 Meanwhile, form 8 potato cakes from the spiced mashed potato and fry them in ghee, vegetable oil or clarified butter, until crisp and golden brown.
5 To serve, adjust the seasoning of the sauce and spoon a bed of sauce onto the base of a heated serving dish. Arrange the potato cakes in an overlapping circle on top, sprinkle with coriander seeds and serve.

Chinese fried rice with mushrooms

Serves 4 when accompanied by 2 or more other dishes
60–75 ml /4–5 tbls corn oil
1 medium-sized onion, chopped
100 g /4 oz button mushrooms, coarsely chopped
about 450 g /1 lb cold, cooked long-grain rice (about
  175 g /6 oz uncooked weight)
15 ml /1 tbls soy sauce
freshly ground black pepper
4 tomato roses, to garnish (see below)

1   Heat 30 ml /2 tbls of the corn oil in a large, deep frying-pan and sauté the chopped onion gently for about 10 minutes, or until golden. Add a further 15 ml /1 tbls corn oil and the coarsely chopped mushrooms and continue to sauté, stirring, for 5 minutes.
2   Add 15–30 ml /1–2 tbls more corn oil and the cooked rice and continue to cook, stirring constantly, for 5 minutes, until the rice is hot and thoroughly mixed with the other ingredients.
3   Sprinkle with the soy sauce. Season to taste with freshly ground black pepper and stir over the heat for 1–2 minutes. Serve immediately, in 4 warmed individual dishes and garnish each with a tomato rose.

● To make tomato roses, wind up thinly pared tomato peel.

Spinach with soy

Serves 6–8
1.8 kg /4 lb fresh spinach
45 ml /3 tbls peanut oil
5–10 ml /1–2 tsp salt
30 ml /2 tbls soy sauce

1   Wash the spinach leaves in several changes of water, discarding any damaged or yellowed leaves. If the spinach is young, snap the stems off at the base of the leaves. If it is older, the leaf will come away from the entire stem. Drain the spinach well, shaking off any excess moisture.
2   Heat the peanut oil in a wok or large frying-pan. Add the spinach and the salt to taste and cook over a moderate heat for 3 minutes, stirring constantly. Pour off any water that collects in the pan. Add the soy sauce and stir lightly. Transfer to a heated serving dish and serve immediately.

● It may be necessary to cook the spinach in 2 batches if the frying-pan or wok is not large enough.

cooking and cooling the rice,
then 25 minutes

15 minutes

Chinese courgettes

Serves 4
450 g /1 lb small courgettes
30 ml /2 tbls peanut oil or lard
salt and freshly ground black pepper
15 ml /1 tbls soy sauce
15 ml /1 tbls sake or dry sherry

1   Wipe the courgettes with a damp cloth. Cut off the ends and
slice the courgettes thinly without peeling them.
2   Heat the peanut oil or lard in a large frying-pan or wok. When
hot, add the courgette slices and stir-fry over a medium heat for 3–5
minutes, or until just cooked, constantly turning the courgettes with
a spatula or chopsticks.
3   Season with a little salt and freshly ground black pepper to
taste.
4   Add 90 ml /6 tbls water, the soy sauce and sake or dry sherry.
Bring to the boil and adjust the seasoning. Transfer the courgettes
to a heated serving dish and serve immediately.

● If you are using a wok, which has a narrower base than a frying-
pan, you will need to stir-fry in the Chinese way. Add a few
courgettes to the hot centre of the pan and, as they begin to soften,
push them up the sides of the pan, out of the direct heat, then add
more courgettes to the pan centre.

Chinese mushrooms and broccoli

Serves 4
4 spring onions
125 g /4 oz button mushrooms
4 broccoli spears
30–45 ml /2–3 tbls peanut or vegetable oil
120 ml /8 tbls well-flavoured chicken stock, home-made or from a
*   cube*
30 ml /2 tbls soy sauce
15 ml /1 tbls dry sherry
pinch of monosodium glutamate (optional)

1   Trim the spring onions and slice into 25 mm /1 in lengths. Clean
and thinly slice the mushrooms. Slice the broccoli spears diagonally.
2   Combine the vegetables in a saucepan, cover with cold water
and bring to the boil. Drain.
3   Heat the oil in a frying-pan. Add the blanched, sliced vegetables
and stir-fry, stirring constantly, until the vegetables begin to brown.
4   Add the chicken stock and cover and simmer for 3–4 minutes,
or until the vegetables are tender but still crisp, shaking the pan
occasionally.
5   Add the soy sauce, dry sherry and monosodium glutamate, if
using, to taste. Stir well and serve immediately.

15 minutes

    30 minutes

BAKING & ROASTING VEGETABLES

Whether simply roasting vegetables as an accompaniment to the Sunday joint, or baking them au gratin, this chapter will give you many ideas for side, lunch and supper dishes.

Nearly all vegetables can be oven-cooked by one of the following methods to make tasty, warming dishes.

Roasting

This is a method of cooking food in radiant heat in an oven using just enough hot fat or oil to stop the food from burning. Root vegetables – potatoes, parsnips, swedes and turnips – are most suited to this method.

Preparation: potatoes can be cooked in their skins – this way they retain more of their vitamins. Simply wash the potatoes well, scrubbing them if necessary to get them clean. Cut away any blemishes. If you must peel them before cooking, peel as thinly as possible and immediately place them in a bowl of cold water to avoid discoloration, but do not let them soak too long or they will lose some of their nutrients. It is much better to prepare them just before cooking. Cut large potatoes into even-sized pieces.

For parsnips, turnips and swedes, barely peel young roots so that you keep the nutrients that are immediately beneath the skin, but peel mature roots. Like potatoes, always try to prepare the vegetables just before cooking them, but if they have to be prepared in advance, cover them with cold water.

Cooking: coat potatoes in hot fat or oil, then roast in an oven heated to 200C /400F /gas 6 for 50–60 minutes. Cut down on cooking time by boiling for 10 minutes first, draining, drying, then finishing in the oven.

To roast parsnips, turnips and swedes for 4 people, cut 700 g /1½ lb roots into evenly-sized pieces and parboil for 5 minutes. Drain, then shake them over the heat for a minute to dry. Roast in about 25 g /1 oz hot dripping or butter and oil in a moderate to hot oven for 45–60 minutes, until tender and golden. Turn them once. Check that they are cooked by piercing them right through to the central core.

Baking

This method of cooking is better suited to the softer vegetables – marrows, aubergines, courgettes, tomatoes, cucumbers and avocados. It differs from roasting in that less fat is used.

Preparation: vegetables for baking may be peeled but usually they are washed or wiped and then simply trimmed. They may be left whole, cut in half lengthways, cut into rings or sliced into rounds. Some vegetables which are to be baked with a savoury filling, for

Roast potatoes

example, aubergines or courgettes, are cut in half lengthways and the centres scooped out. **Cooking:** brush with melted butter or oil and cook in the oven at the recommended setting until tender.

Au gratin
This term refers to dishes which have had a topping added. The vegetables are pre-cooked first, moistened with cream, egg or a sauce, put in an ovenproof dish, topped and then baked.

For the simplest topping, sprinkle the vegetables with a light covering of breadcrumbs and dot with butter. Alternatively sprinkle the vegetables with freshly grated cheese, using either a mixture of Gruyère and Parmesan, or Gruyère or Parmesan alone. This gives a moister topping. A combination of breadcrumbs and freshly grated cheese will give you both the cheesy flavour and the crispness of breadcrumbs. This can be varied by adding finely chopped parsley or other fresh herbs. Breadcrumbs, mixed with freshly grated Parmesan cheese and paprika adds a hint of spice, or to really make something of your topping, sauté breadcrumbs in butter together with a little finely chopped onion, parsley (or finely chopped bacon) and paprika. Flaked almonds, as in Celery, almond and Gruyère bake, will add texture.

Pies and tarts
Another way of baking precooked vegetables is in pies and tarts. For small, individual ones the filling may be puréed and then added to cooked pastry cases. For larger tarts and pies the vegetables are often combined with a sauce before being put into a pastry case and baked.

Roast potatoes

1 hour 10 minutes

Serves 4
450 g /1 lb floury potatoes
15 g /½ oz dripping, or 15 ml /1 tbls oil
15 g /½ oz butter
salt and freshly ground black pepper

1   Heat the oven to 200C /400F /gas 6. Peel the potatoes and cut them into even-sized pieces weighing about 50 g /2 oz each. Thoroughly wash and dry them.
2   Combine the dripping or oil with the butter in a roasting tin and melt them together over a low heat. When the fat is almost smoking hot, add the potatoes. Using kitchen tongs, turn the potatoes in the fat until they are evenly and thoroughly coated. Sprinkle them with salt and black pepper.
3   Roast the potatoes in the oven, turning them occasionally, for 50–60 minutes, or until they are crisp and golden and feel soft when pierced with a fork.

● If you like your roast potatoes to have a thick crust, cut the peeled potatoes into large pieces and parboil them for 6–10 minutes. Drain, dry carefully and score them lightly before turning them in the hot fat.

Vegetable gratin

1¼ hours

Serves 4
1 small green cabbage
2 medium-sized potatoes
salt and freshly ground black pepper
4 small turnips
4 small carrots
30 ml /2 tbls chicken stock, home-made or
  from a cube
65 g /2½ oz butter
1 egg yolk
75 ml /5 tbls thick cream
45 ml /3 tbls freshly grated Gruyère cheese
15 ml /1 tbls grated Parmesan cheese
30 ml /2 tbls fresh white breadcrumbs

1   Heat the oven to 190C /375F /gas 5. Halve and quarter the cabbage, remove the core, shred finely, wash and reserve.
2   Bring the potatoes to the boil in a saucepan of salted water. Simmer for 15–20 minutes until cooked.
3   Meanwhile, peel and cut the turnips into fine matchstick strips. Peel and quarter the carrots and then halve the quarters again so the carrots are cut into eighths. Put them in a pan of cold, salted water and bring to the boil; drain. Return to the pan with the chicken stock, 25 g /1 oz butter and the turnip strips. Season with black pepper to taste, and simmer, stirring constantly for 7–8 minutes, or until the vegetables are just tender. Drain and reserve.
4   Bring a saucepan with 10 mm /½ in of salted water to the boil and simmer the cabbage for 10 minutes, or until just tender. Drain and refresh.
5   Mash the hot potatoes with 25 g /1 oz of butter until smooth. In a small bowl, blend the egg yolk and cream together and beat

Vegetable gratin

into the potatoes. Add the cabbage and continue to beat until blended. Season with salt and black pepper to taste.
6   Butter a 1.1 L /2 pt gratin dish with the remainder of the butter and spread half of the potato and cabbage mixture evenly over the bottom with a palette knife. Arrange the drained turnip and carrot strips on top. Cover with the remaining potato and cabbage mixture, smoothing the top.
7   Sprinkle the dish with the cheese and breadcrumbs and bake in the oven for 30 minutes, or until golden brown.

Celery, almond and Gruyère bake

40–50 minutes

Serves 4 as a main dish, 6–8 as a starter
1.2 kg /2¾ lb canned celery hearts
575 ml /1 pt thin cream
1 medium-sized egg
50 g /2 oz freshly grated Gruyère cheese
50 g /2 oz freshly grated Parmesan cheese
salt and freshly ground black pepper
50 g /2 oz flaked almonds

1   Heat the oven to 180C /350F /gas 4. Drain the celery hearts and place them in a shallow casserole.
2   Whisk together the cream and egg; add half the Gruyère cheese and all of the Parmesan cheese. Season to taste.
3   Pour the cream mixture over the celery hearts and sprinkle with the flaked almonds and remaining cheese.
4   Bake in the oven for 30–40 minutes, until the custard is lightly set and the nuts golden brown and crisp. Serve at once.

the centres with a sharp spoon, taking care not to break the skins and leaving a shell about 5 mm /¼ in thick. Sieve or thoroughly mash the potato in a large bowl and then beat in the butter and the soured cream mixture. Season with salt and freshly ground black pepper to taste.

6   Arrange 4 of the best potato shells on a metal tray, discarding the rest. Spoon the potato mixture into these shells, mounding them slightly, and sprinkle with paprika.

7   Cut the bacon slices in half and roll each one up. Place 1 roll on each potato-filled shell and bake in the oven for 20–25 minutes, or until golden brown. Garnish with a sprig of parsley, and serve.

Cauliflower and cream tarts

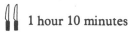 1 hour 10 minutes

Serves 6
40 g /1½ oz butter, plus extra for greasing
175 g /6 oz made-weight shortcrust pastry,
   defrosted if frozen
2 medium-sized carrots, finely diced
½ small cauliflower, divided into small florets
1 small onion, finely chopped
1 garlic clove, finely chopped
50 g /2 oz button mushrooms, thinly sliced
15 ml /1 tbls flour
225 ml /8 fl oz thin cream
a pinch of freshly grated nutmeg
2 bay leaves
salt and freshly ground black pepper
15 ml /1 tbls chopped fresh marjoram, or 5
   ml /1 tsp dried marjoram
flat-leaved parsley, to garnish

Marrow au gratin

 1 hour

Serves 4
1 medium-sized marrow, about 1 kg /2 lb
15 ml /1 tbls olive oil
25 g /1 oz butter
1 Spanish onion, finely chopped
1 fat garlic clove, finely chopped
4 ripe tomatoes, blanched, skinned, seeded
   and chopped
15 ml /1 tbls tomato purée
30 ml /2 tbls finely chopped fresh parsley
2.5 ml /½ tsp dried oregano
salt and freshly ground black pepper
90 ml /6 tbls grated Cheddar cheese
30 ml /2 tbls grated Parmesan cheese
60 ml /4 tbls breadcrumbs

1   Heat the oven to 190C /375F /gas 5.
2   Peel the marrow and cut it in half lengthways. Remove the seeds and membranes. Cut the flesh into 25 mm /1 in dice.
3   In a large frying-pan, heat the olive oil and half the butter. Add the finely chopped onion and garlic and cook over a low heat for 5–7 minutes, or until soft and transparent, stirring occasionally.
4   Add the chopped tomatoes and tomato purée and cook for a further 2 minutes, stirring constantly.
5   Add the diced marrow, parsley and oregano and season with salt and pepper to taste. Cook over a moderate heat for 10 minutes, or until the marrow begins to soften, stirring occasionally.
6   Transfer the marrow mixture to an

Marrow au gratin

ovenproof dish. In a small bowl combine the grated Cheddar and Parmesan cheeses with the breadcrumbs. Mix well, and sprinkle over the top. Dot with the remaining butter and bake for 30 minutes, or until the marrow is tender and the topping crisp. Serve immediately.

Baked potatoes with soured cream

 1¾–2 hours

Serves 4
3 large potatoes
150 ml /5 fl oz soured cream
30 ml /2 tbls finely chopped fresh chives
2.5 ml /½ tsp ground cumin
1 egg, lightly beaten
25 g /1 oz butter
salt and freshly ground black pepper
a pinch of paprika
2 slices of bacon
sprigs of parsley, to garnish

1   Heat the oven to 220C /425F /gas 7.
2   Scrub the potatoes with a stiff brush until absolutely clean. Pat dry and prick all over with a fork. Bake in the oven for 1–1¼ hours, or until cooked through.
3   In a bowl blend the soured cream, finely chopped chives, cumin and beaten egg.
4   Remove the potatoes from the oven and reduce temperature to 190C /375F /gas 5.
5   Cut the potatoes in half and scoop out

1 Heat the oven to 220C /425F /gas 7. Thoroughly grease a 12-hole deep bun or muffin tin.
2 Roll out the pastry 3 mm /⅛ in thick and line the tins. Prick the bases with a fork, line with foil and beans and bake blind for 10 minutes. Remove from the oven and remove the foil and beans. Reduce the heat to 190C /375F /gas 5.
3 Steam the carrots and cauliflower separately over boiling water until they are just tender.
4 Melt 25 g /1 oz butter in a small pan and sauté the onion and garlic over moderate heat for 4 minutes, stirring once or twice. Add the mushrooms, stir and sauté for a further 2 minutes. Stir in the carrots and cauliflower, remove from the heat and then spoon the vegetables into the pastry cases.
5 Melt 15 g /½ oz butter in a saucepan, stir in the flour and gradually pour in the cream, stirring. Add the nutmeg and bay leaves and bring to the boil, stirring. Simmer for 5 minutes. Remove the bay leaves, season with salt and pepper and stir in the marjoram.
6 Pour the sauce over the vegetables and return the tarts to the oven. Bake for 15 minutes, arrange on a warmed serving plate, garnish with flat-leaved parsley and serve at once.

Serve these tarts as a substantial first course, or as a light lunch or supper dish.

Gratin of aubergines

Gratin of aubergines

1 hour's salting,
then 1 hour

Baked potatoes with soured cream

Serves 4
2 medium-sized aubergines, peeled and diced
salt
60–75 ml /4–5 tbls fresh breadcrumbs
45 ml /3 tbls olive oil
40 g /1½ oz butter
½ Spanish onion, finely chopped
15 ml /1 tbls tomato purée
225 g /8 oz canned tomatoes
1 garlic clove, finely chopped
15 ml /1 tbls finely chopped fresh parsley
freshly ground black pepper
generous pinch each of allspice, cinnamon
*   and sugar*

1 Liberally sprinkle the diced aubergines with salt and leave them to drain in a colander for 1 hour.
2 Heat the oven to 190C /375F /gas 5. Rinse the aubergines very thoroughly in cold water, then drain and gently press them dry in a cloth. Roll the aubergine cubes in 30 ml /2 tbls of the fresh breadcrumbs.
3 Heat 30 ml /2 tbls olive oil and 15 g /½ oz butter in a frying-pan. Add the aubergine cubes and sauté until golden. Remove the aubergines from the pan and, in the same oil, fry the finely chopped onion until soft and just turning gold, adding more oil if necessary. Add the tomato purée, tomatoes, finely chopped garlic and parsley, and season to taste with salt and freshly ground pepper, allspice, cinnamon and sugar. Simmer the mixture, stirring occasionally, for 5 minutes.
4 Add the aubergine cubes to the tomato mixture and pour into a buttered gratin dish. Sprinkle the dish with the remaining breadcrumbs. Dot with the remaining butter and bake in the oven for 30 minutes.

Creamed button onions

peeling the onions,
then 45 minutes

Serves 4–6
450 g /1 lb small, white onions, peeled
salt
65 g /2½ oz butter
45 ml /3 tbls flour
425 ml /15 fl oz milk, hot
freshly ground black pepper
5–10 ml /1–2 tsp dry mustard
45–60 ml /3–4 tbls fresh breadcrumbs

1 To peel the onions without releasing any irritating juice, drop a batch into boiling water and turn off the heat. Remove, one by one, slicing off the top and bottom and slipping the skins off. Repeat in batches. Cook the peeled onions in boiling, salted water for 15 minutes, then drain. Heat the oven to 180C /350F /gas 4.
2 Melt 50 g /2 oz butter in a saucepan. Add the flour and cook, stirring constantly, until the roux is smooth. Add the hot milk and cook for about 5 minutes, stirring constantly, until the sauce is thick and smooth. Season with salt, pepper and dry mustard to taste.
3 Add the boiled onions to the white sauce and turn the mixture into a shallow, heatproof casserole. Top with the breadcrumbs, dot with the remaining butter and bake for 20 minutes.

Courgette soufflé

The egg yolk courgette mixture in this recipe can be prepared in advance and the egg whites beaten and added just before baking.

🔪🔪 1 hour

Serves 4
butter for greasing
450 g /1 lb small courgettes
50 g /2 oz butter
1 garlic clove, chopped
3 spring onions, finely chopped
200 ml /7 fl oz sweet white wine
juice of ½ lemon
a large pinch of nutmeg
2.5 ml /½ tsp salt
a pinch of freshly ground black pepper
15 ml /1 tbls freshly chopped parsley
1 large pimento, finely chopped
30 ml /2 tbls grated Parmesan
5 egg yolks
6 egg whites

1 Butter a 1.4 L /2½ pt soufflé or baking dish and chill it. Top and tail the courgettes and cut them into pencil-thin strips 25 mm / 1 in long.
2 Melt the butter in a saucepan over medium heat and cook the garlic and spring onions for 3 minutes. Add the courgettes and stir for 2 minutes to coat each piece with butter.
3 Add the wine, lemon juice, nutmeg, salt, pepper and parsley. Cook for 15 minutes over high heat until most of the liquid has evaporated, stirring occasionally. The courgettes should be tender but firm. Stir in the chopped pimento and set aside to cool.
4 Heat the oven to 200C /400 F /gas 6. Beat the Parmesan into the yolks until well blended and then stir them into the vegetable mixture.
5 Beat the egg whites until stiff but not dry and fold them carefully into the vegetable mixture. Pour it into the soufflé or baking dish and bake for 25 minutes, or until well risen and golden. Serve at once.

Little potato loaves

These 'loaves' of puréed potato go well with any meat or egg dish, or serve them with a buttered cooked green vegetable and grilled tomatoes for a light lunch.

🔪🔪 1 hour

Makes 12 loaves, serves 6
700 g /1½ lb floury potatoes
salt and freshly ground black pepper
50 g /2 oz butter
45 ml /3 tbls freshly grated Parmesan cheese
2 eggs
15 ml /1 tbls stale white breadcrumbs

1 Heat the oven to 220C /425F /gas 7. Thinly peel the potatoes and, if they are very large, cut them into even-sized pieces. Drop

Pea tarts

These elegant little tarts are made from a crisp cheese pastry filled with a creamy pea purée.

🔪🔪 1 hour for pastry, including chilling time, then 25 minutes

Makes about 12
175 g /6 oz flour
salt
freshly ground black pepper
a pinch of cayenne pepper
50 g /2 oz finely grated Gruyère or Parmesan cheese, or a mixture of both
100 g /4 oz butter, diced
1 medium-sized egg, separated
For the filling
700 g /1½ lb fresh peas in the pod, or 225 g / 8 oz frozen peas, defrosted
a pinch of sugar
30 ml /2 tbls thick cream or mayonnaise
salt and freshly ground black pepper

1 Make the pastry. Sift the flour with a pinch of salt, black pepper and a pinch of cayenne pepper into a chilled mixing bowl. Stir in the cheese. Rub the butter into the flour and cheese with your fingertips until the mixture resembles breadcrumbs
2 Beat the egg yolk with 5 ml /1 tsp water and mix it into the rubbed-in mixture with a fork. Continue mixing until the ingredients

Pea tarts

begin to cling together, then gather the pastry into a ball with your fingers.
3 Tip the pastry onto a lightly floured surface and knead briefly until smooth. Wrap in cling film and chill for 30 minutes.
4 On a lightly floured surface, thinly roll out the pastry and use it to line 12 or more tartlet tins or small barquette (boat-shaped) moulds. Chill for about 10–15 minutes. Meanwhile, heat the oven to 200C /400F / gas 6.
5 Place the moulds on a baking sheet and line them with foil and beans. Bake blind for 10 minutes. Remove the foil and beans and lightly brush the insides of the pastry cases with the beaten egg white. Bake for a further 5 minutes. Cool the pastry cases slightly, then carefully unmould them and leave them on a wire rack.
6 Meanwhile, cook the peas in a saucepan of simmering, lightly salted water, with a pinch of sugar added, until tender. Drain the peas and refresh them in cold water for 3–4 minutes, then drain thoroughly again.
7 Combine 100 g /4 oz of the drained peas with the cream or mayonnaise and reduce to a smooth, thick purée in a blender. Season with salt and pepper to taste.
8 Spread the purée evenly in the cold pastry cases. Divide the remaining whole peas among the tarts, arranging them neatly over the purée. Serve within 2 hours of filling as an appetizer or garnish.

the potatoes into boiling, salted water and simmer them for about 20 minutes, or until they feel soft when pierced with a fork.

2 As soon as the potatoes are cooked, drain them thoroughly, then return them to a dry pan and toss the potatoes briefly over a low heat so that all the remaining moisture is evaporated away. (This prevents the purée from becoming soggy in texture.) Remove the pan from the heat.

3 Mash the potatoes to a smooth purée or rub them through a wire sieve into a bowl. Add the butter and 30 ml /2 tbls of the grated Parmesan cheese to the potato purée and beat in with a wooden spoon. Season to taste with salt and black pepper.

4 Vigorously whisk 1 egg, add it to the purée and then beat with the wooden spoon until thoroughly blended.

5 Divide the purée into 12 equal portions. Roll each portion into a fat, oval shape and pat it into a small loaf shape. With a sharp knife, cut diagonal slashes on the top of each 'loaf'.

6 Transfer the potato loaves to a buttered, large baking sheet. Beat the remaining egg and brush it over the tops of the loaves. Mix the breadcrumbs with the remaining grated Parmesan cheese and sprinkle the mixture over the tops of the loaves.

7 Bake the loaves in the oven for about 20 minutes, until puffed and golden brown. Serve immediately.

Rich leek and onion double-crust pie

Rich leek and onion double-crust pie

This rich double-crust pie is a version of a French leek tart known as a *flaniche,* which is popular in the Burgundy and Picardy regions of France.

🔪🔪 30 minutes, plus 20 minutes chilling, then 1 hour

Serves 6
450 g /1 lb flour
7.5 ml /1½ tsp salt
1.5 ml /¼ tsp freshly ground white pepper
225 g /8 oz butter, diced
2 medium-sized eggs
flour for sprinkling
For the filling
700 g /1½ lb leeks, white and pale-green parts only
75 g /3 oz butter
450 g /1 lb onions, sliced
2 medium-sized egg yolks
75 ml /5 tbls thick cream
20 ml /4 tsp flour
salt and freshly ground black pepper

1 First make the filling. Slice the leeks and put them in a colander. Rinse them well under cold, running water, shaking the colander to drain them well.

2 Melt the butter in a large saucepan over a low heat, add the onion and leek and stir until they are well coated. Cover and sweat the vegetables over a medium-low heat for about 10 minutes, or until soft, stirring occasionally.

3 Combine the egg yolks and cream and reserve 15 ml /1 tbls for brushing. Sprinkle the flour over the vegetables in the pan and stir well. Add the egg yolk mixture, stir briskly, then remove the pan from the heat. Season generously and leave to cool.

4 Meanwhile, make the pastry. Sift the flour, salt and pepper into a bowl and rub in the butter until the mixture resembles breadcrumbs. Whisk the eggs lightly with 30 ml /2 tbls water, then add this to the dry ingredients. Mix with a round-bladed knife or pastry blender until a firm dough forms which leaves the sides of the bowl clean. Chill for 20 minutes.

5 Heat the oven to 200C /400F /gas 6. Roll out slightly more than half the pastry on a floured surface and use it to line a 23 cm /9 in deep flan tin. Transfer the vegetables to the pastry case. Roll out the remaining pastry to make a lid and lay it over the filling. Dampen, seal and flute the edges and cut a steam vent in the centre. Decorate the top of the pie with leaf shapes cut from the pastry trimmings.

6 Brush the top of the pastry with the rest of the egg yolk mixture and then bake the pie in the oven for about 50 minutes, or until a deep golden brown. Serve the pie hot from the oven or leave until cold.

Baked potato croquettes

Serves 4
450 g /1 lb potatoes
salt
30 ml /2 tbls softened butter
1 egg yolk
15 ml /1 tbls thick cream
freshly ground black pepper
cayenne pepper
flour for dusting
1 egg, beaten
50 g /2 oz fresh white breadcrumbs
50 g /2 oz butter
15 ml /1 tbls finely chopped parsley, and 1 sprig of parsley to garnish

1   Peel the potatoes and cut them into medium-sized even pieces. Put them in a saucepan, cover with cold water, add a pinch of salt and bring to the boil. Cook for about 15 minutes, or until just cooked through but not mushy.
2   Drain the potatoes and mash them to a smooth purée, or press them through a fine wire sieve. Beat in the butter until melted. Stir in the egg yolk and the thick cream. Season to taste with salt and freshly ground black pepper and a pinch of cayenne pepper. Chill for 1 hour.
3   Heat the oven to 190C /375F /gas 5.
4   Divide the chilled potato mixture into 12 even-sized balls. With lightly floured hands, roll a ball of potato into a croquette shape, 4 cm /1½ in long and 20 mm /¾ in wide. Repeat with the remaining potato balls.
5   Place the beaten egg in a shallow dish and the breadcrumbs on a plate. Coat each croquette in beaten egg, drain and roll in the breadcrumbs, shaking off the excess.
6   Butter an ovenproof dish large enough to take the potato croquettes in one layer. Lay them side by side in the dish. Dot with the remaining butter. Bake them in the oven for 20 minutes, or until the potato croquettes are golden brown, turning them once halfway through cooking. Sprinkle them with finely chopped parsley, garnish with a sprig of parsley and serve immediately.

 55 minutes, plus chilling

Aubergine soufflés

Serves 8
4 medium-sized aubergines
salt
275 ml /10 fl oz milk
1 small onion, peeled and studded with 10 cloves
1 bay leaf
4–5 black peppercorns
30 ml /2 tbls olive oil
30 ml /2 tbls chicken stock, home- made or from a cube
50 g /2 oz butter
1 small onion, finely chopped
225 g /8 oz tomatoes, blanched skinned, seeded and chopped
1 garlic clove, finely chopped
30 ml /2 tbls finely chopped fresh parsley
10 ml /2 tsp tomato purée
15 ml /1 tbls lemon juice
30 ml /2 tbls flour
2 eggs, separated
freshly ground black pepper
60 ml /4 tbls grated Parmesan
tomato wedges, to garnish
chilli 'flowers', to garnish

1   Halve the aubergines lengthways. Make deep slashes in the cut surfaces, without breaking the skins. Rub with salt and leave upside down in a colander for 1 hour so the bitter juices drain away.
2   Bring the milk to the boil with the onion, bay leaf and peppercorns. Turn off heat, cover and leave to infuse for ½ hour.
3   Heat the oven to 170C /325F /gas 3. Rinse and wipe the aubergines with absorbent paper. Arrange the halves in a baking dish, cut sides up. Combine the oil and stock and pour over the aubergines. Bake, turning the halves now and then to keep them moist, for 40–50 minutes, or until the flesh is very soft. Remove from the oven, cool slightly and scoop out the flesh with a spoon – do not damage the shells. Chop the flesh finely.
4   Increase the oven temperature to 190C /375F /gas 5.
5   Melt 25 g /1 oz butter in a heavy saucepan and sauté the finely chopped onion for about 10 minutes. Add the chopped aubergine flesh, tomatoes, garlic, parsley, tomato purée and lemon juice. Cook for 2 minutes. Remove from the heat and leave to cool.
6   Melt the remaining butter in a small saucepan, stir in the flour and cook over a low heat for 1 minute. Strain the milk and gradually stir in, until smooth. Bring to the boil and cook, stirring, for 2 or 3 minutes.
7   Mix the sauce into the vegetable mixture. Beat the egg yolks in a small bowl and beat into the mixture. Stir over a medium heat for about 5 minutes. Remove from the heat and allow to cool.
8   Season the sauce. Whisk the whites until stiff but not dry and fold into the sauce. Place the aubergine shells in a buttered ovenproof dish and pile in the mixture. Sprinkle with cheese and bake until golden and set. Garnish and serve hot.

 1 hour salting, then 2¼ hours

Gratin of baby turnips

Serves 4–6
700 g /1½ lb baby turnips
25 g /1 oz butter
1 egg
150 ml /5 fl oz thick cream
salt and freshly ground black pepper
50 g /2 oz freshly grated Gruyère cheese
60 ml /4 tbls freshly grated Parmesan cheese

1   Heat the oven to 170C /325F /gas 3.
2   Grease a gratin dish with 15 g /½ oz butter.
3   Peel the turnips and slice them very thinly.
4   Whisk the egg and thick cream together lightly until they are well blended.
5   Arrange a quarter of the turnip slices in overlapping rows in the prepared gratin dish. Season with salt and freshly ground black pepper. Pour over a quarter of the cream mixture. Sprinkle with 30 ml /2 tbls grated Gruyére cheese and 15 ml /1 tbls grated Parmesan cheese, then dot with butter. Repeat, to make 3 more layers as above, until all the ingredients have been used.
6   Cover the gratin with foil and bake for 1 hour. Remove the foil and bake, uncovered, for a further 20–30 minutes, or until the turnips are tender and the cheesy topping is golden brown.

 1¾ hours

Brussels sprouts au gratin

Serves 4–6
700 g /1½ lb small Brussels sprouts
salt and freshly ground black pepper
butter for greasing
25 g /1 oz butter
15–25 g /½–1 oz walnuts, chopped
30 ml /2 tbls fresh breadcrumbs
For the cheese sauce
40 g /1½ oz butter
5 ml /1 tsp French mustard
40 g /1½ oz flour
425 ml /15 fl oz warm milk
100 g /4 oz Gruyère cheese, grated
salt and white pepper

1   Heat the oven to 200C /400F /gas 6. Remove any wilted or damaged outer leaves from the Brussels sprouts and trim the stem ends. (If the sprouts are older, remove the tough outer leaves entirely.) Cut a small cross in the stems as this helps the sprouts to cook evenly.
2   Meanwhile, make the cheese sauce. In a heavy-based saucepan melt the butter over a low heat. Remove the pan from the heat and stir in the mustard and the flour. Return the pan to a low heat and cook the roux, stirring constantly, for 2–3 minutes. Remove the pan from the heat and gradually blend in the warm milk. Return the pan to the heat and bring to the boil; boil the sauce for 2 minutes. Remove the pan from the heat and stir in the grated cheese; season with salt and white pepper to taste. Return the pan to the heat and simmer gently for about 1 minute until thick and smooth.
3   Drop the sprouts into a large pan of boiling, salted water and simmer, uncovered, for 5 minutes. Cover the pan and continue to cook for 5–15 minutes more, depending on the age and size of the sprouts. When they are just tender drain them thoroughly, season generously with salt and freshly ground black pepper and place in a well-buttered ovenproof dish. Gently reheat the cheese sauce, stirring constantly until it is smooth, and pour over the sprouts.
4   Melt the butter in a small saucepan, add the chopped walnuts and fresh breadcrumbs, sauté for 1–2 minutes, then sprinkle over the cheese sauce. Bake the gratin in the oven for 15 minutes.

1 hour

VEGETABLE CASSEROLES

Cooked alone, or in delicious combinations, both hard and softer vegetables taste remarkably good simmered slowly with a little liquid and a variety of flavourings and aromatics.

A good way to appreciate vegetables is to eat them as a separate course. They need not be a main course, they simply need to be eaten as a delicious dish in their own right, rather than as an afterthought to something else. The French, for instance, usually eat their meat on its own and then follow it with the vegetables, however simple.

Now, you may feel odd eating a helping of plain, steamed beans or buttered garden peas as a separate course. A vegetable casserole, being slightly more substantial, may be just the thing to get you started.

A glance at the following recipes will show you just how many vegetables are suitable for casseroling. Some, like carrots, onions, shallots, celery and mushrooms, are chosen for their flavour. Mushrooms, in particular, bring out and complement the other flavours in a casserole. Others, such as aubergines, courgettes and peppers, are chosen for their texture, as well as their taste.

Potatoes or rice (see Shallot casserole and Kitchri) are added to make the casserole more substantial. Herbs and spices form an important part of the casserole, too.

For vegetable casseroles which have a lot of liquid and ingredients, use a flameproof casserole with a tightly-fitting lid. It can be used on top of the stove to sauté the vegetables before the liquid is added and then, once the lid is put on, the flavours are sealed in. But for recipes such as Italian baked asparagus, in which the vegetable is arranged in one layer, use a shallow, ovenproof dish covered with foil.

Cooking a vegetable casserole
Vegetable casseroles can be cooked in varying amounts of liquid, from 300 ml /10 fl oz of stock (see Shallot casserole) to just a little olive oil, but the basic methods remain the same. Well prepared vegetables are important both for taste and appearance. They may be sliced, diced or cubed, according to the recipe, but whichever method is called for, make sure they are equally-sized pieces.

Sautéeing the vegetables: some of the vegetables, usually the flavouring ones such as onions and carrots, should be sautéed first. This is done in butter or olive oil. It softens the vegetables and gives them a delicious flavour before the liquid and other flavourings are added.

Adding the liquid: I use chicken stock in many of my vegetable casseroles, although another favourite is beef stock and, for a special taste, wine. Or you can simmer the vegetables in a white sauce – it gives a lovely creamy flavour. Another 'liquid' is oil – in my recipe for Ratatouille the vegetables are stewed, rather than fried, in the oil and the juices they produce.

Timing: unlike meat-based casseroles, which tend to improve in taste and

succulence with lengthy cooking, vegetable casseroles need careful timing.

I never like to overcook my vegetables and this rule holds true for casseroled ones, too. Cook them until they are just *al dente* and they will be perfect.

Serving suggestions
If the casserole dish is attractive, serve the vegetables straight from it. I prefer doing it this way as it seems to me to defeat the purpose to transfer them to a serving dish.

Where appropriate, a dish of freshly grated Parmesan cheese is the ideal accompaniment for a vegetable casserole, otherwise I suggest you serve it just as it is.

Vegetable hotpot

🍴 2 hours 10 minutes

Serves 4
50 g /2 oz butter
2 large carrots, sliced
1 small turnip, diced
2 celery sticks, thinly sliced
12 small leeks, including green tops, thickly sliced
25 g /1 oz flour
425 ml /15 fl oz chicken stock, home-made or from a cube
salt and freshly ground black pepper
5 ml /1 tsp Worcestershire sauce
30 ml /2 tbls chopped fresh parsley
500 g /1 lb potatoes, peeled and sliced
50 g /2 oz grated Cheddar cheese
finely chopped fresh parsley, to garnish

1   Heat the oven to 180C /350F /gas 4.
2   Melt the butter in a frying-pan and fry the carrots, turnip and celery over a low to medium heat for 7–8 minutes, stirring often to prevent them from browning. Remove the vegetables with a slotted spoon and put them into a 1 L /2 pt ovenproof casserole.
3   Add the leeks to the fat in the pan and fry them for 2–3 minutes, turning often so that they do not brown. Add them to the casserole.
4   Stir the flour into the butter remaining in the pan, then gradually pour on the stock, stirring. Bring to the boil, stirring, then season with salt, pepper and Worcestershire sauce. Simmer for 3 minutes, then mix in the parsley. Pour the sauce over the vegetables and toss carefully to mix.
5   Arrange the sliced potatoes in overlapping circles on top of the vegetables. Cover the casserole with a lid or with foil, stand it on a baking sheet and cook for 1½ hours, or until the potatoes are tender.
6   Heat the grill to high. Sprinkle the cheese over the potatoes and grill until well browned. Garnish with parsley and serve.

Chakchouka

🔪 40 minutes

Serves 4
45–60 ml /3–4 tbls olive oil
1 large onion, chopped
2 garlic cloves, crushed
1 medium-sized cauliflower, cut into florets
1 green or red pepper, cut into small pieces
450 g /1 lb tomatoes, blanched, skinned and coarsely chopped
salt and freshly ground black pepper
10 ml /2 tsp paprika
a large pinch of cayenne or chilli pepper
4 eggs

1   Heat the oil in a large frying-pan and cook the onion for 5 minutes, or until it is soft.
2   Add the garlic, cook for 2 minutes, then add the cauliflower, pepper and tomatoes.
3   Season with salt, pepper, paprika and cayenne and moisten with a little water. Cook gently for about 20 minutes, or until the vegetables are tender, adding more water if the mixture becomes too dry.
4   Drop the eggs into the vegetable mixture and cook gently until they set, stirring them with a fork if wished. Transfer to a heated serving dish and serve immediately.

Curried aubergines

🔪 40 minutes

Serves 4
25 g /1 oz butter
1 garlic clove, finely chopped
3 cm /1¼ in fresh root ginger, finely chopped
6 black peppercorns
1.5 ml /¼ tsp caraway seeds
4 cardamom pods
3 cloves
15 ml /1 tbls ground coriander
10 ml /2 tsp turmeric
2.5 ml /½ tsp ground cinnamon
2 large onions, sliced
400 g /14 oz potatoes, cut into chunks
500 g /1 lb aubergines, cut into chunks
salt
125 ml /4 fl oz chicken stock, home-made or from a cube
4 tomatoes, quartered
juice of ½ lemon

1   In a flameproof casserole, melt the butter and fry the garlic, ginger and whole spices for 2–3 minutes. Add the powdered spices and the onions and cook for a further 5 minutes.
2   Add the potatoes and aubergines, salt and stock and stir well.
3   Cover and cook on a low heat for 20 minutes, stirring once or twice. Add the tomatoes and continue cooking for a further 5 minutes. Add the lemon juice, then pile the curried aubergines into a warmed serving dish and serve at once.

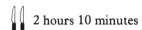

Vegetable hotpot

Kitchri

This dish, which originated in India, is the forerunner of kedgeree.

overnight soaking, then 1¼–1½ hours

Serves 4
45 ml /3 tbls olive oil
1 Spanish onion, finely chopped
4 garlic cloves, finely chopped
2.5 ml /½ tsp ground turmeric
2.5 ml /½ tsp ground ginger
2.5 ml /½ tsp curry powder
5 ml /1 tsp cumin seeds
a pinch of chilli powder
1 potato, cubed
2 tomatoes, quartered
225 g /8 oz mung beans, soaked overnight
225 g /8 oz long-grain brown rice
425 ml /15 fl oz milk
freshly ground black pepper
salt
15–30 ml /1–2 tbls lemon juice

1   In a flameproof casserole, heat the oil. Add the chopped onion and garlic and cook for 10 minutes, stirring, or until softened and golden but not browned.
2   Add the ground turmeric and ginger, the curry powder, cumin seeds and chilli powder and fry for a further 3–4 minutes, stirring occasionally.
3   Add the cubed potato, tomato quarters, drained mung beans and brown rice to the mixture. Fry gently for 5 minutes, stirring, and then stir in the milk with 425 ml /15 fl oz water. Season with freshly ground black pepper. Bring to the boil, then cover and simmer gently for 40–50 minutes, until the rice and the beans are cooked, stirring occasionally.
4   Turn off the heat and leave the pan to stand, covered, for 15 minutes, by which time all the liquid should have been absorbed. Season with salt and lemon juice to taste, stirring the mixture gently with a fork. Turn the Kitchri into a heated serving dish and serve at once.

Kitchri

Ratatouille

1¼ hours, including draining

Serves 4
2 aubergines, quartered and cut into 5 mm / ¼ in slices
salt
120 ml /8 tbls olive oil
1 Spanish onion, sliced
2 green peppers, seeded and cut into 25 mm /1 in squares
2 small courgettes, cut into 15 mm /½ in slices
4 tomatoes, blanched, skinned, seeded and chopped
1 large garlic clove, crushed
15 ml /1 tbls finely chopped fresh parsley
2.5 ml /½ tsp dried marjoram
2.5 ml /½ tsp dried basil
freshly ground black pepper

1   Sprinkle the aubergine slices generously with salt. Place in a colander and leave for 30 minutes, so that the bitter juices drain away. Rinse the slices in cold water and drain thoroughly on absorbent paper.
2   Heat the olive oil in a flameproof casserole, add the sliced onion and sauté for 2–3 minutes, or until transparent.
3   Add the green peppers and the aubergine slices, cover and cook for 5 minutes.
4   Add the sliced courgettes, chopped tomatoes, garlic, parsley, marjoram and basil and season with salt and freshly ground black pepper to taste. Cook, covered, for a further 30 minutes. Serve hot from the casserole, or cold as a starter.

Italian baked asparagus

1¼ hours

Serves 4
500 g /1 lb fresh asparagus
25 g /1 oz butter
30 ml /2 tbls finely chopped onion
1 celery stick, finely chopped
400 g /14 oz canned tomatoes, chopped
2.5 ml /½ tsp dried oregano
2.5 ml /½ tsp dried thyme
salt and freshly ground black pepper
30 ml /2 tbls freshly grated Parmesan cheese

1   Trim the ends from the asparagus and scrape off any woody parts on the stems.
2   Heat the oven to 180C /350F /gas 4.
3   Melt the butter in a small frying-pan and cook the finely chopped onion and celery for 2–3 minutes, stirring, until transparent.
4   Place the asparagus in one layer in a casserole or rectangular baking dish. Scatter the sautéed onion and celery over the asparagus and cover with the chopped tomatoes and their juices. Add the dried herbs and season to taste with salt and freshly ground black pepper. Sprinkle with Parmesan cheese. Cover with foil and bake in the oven for 45–50 minutes, then serve.

Shallot casserole

 40 minutes

Serves 4–6
50 g /2 oz butter
125 g /4 oz streaky bacon in one piece, diced
500 g /1 lb shallots
500 g /1 lb carrots, sliced
225 g /8 oz button mushrooms
225 g /8 oz potatoes, cut into 25 mm /1 in
   cubes
300 ml /10 fl oz chicken stock, home-made
   or from a cube
bouquet garni
2.5 ml /½ tsp dried thyme
2.5 ml /½ tsp dried basil
5 ml /1 tsp tomato purée
salt and freshly ground black pepper
2 courgettes, quartered lengthways and cut
   into 5 cm /2 in lengths

1 In a flameproof casserole, melt the butter. Add the diced bacon and sauté for 5 minutes, stirring, or until golden.
2 Add the vegetables, cook for 10 minutes.
3 Add the chicken stock, bouquet garni, thyme, basil and tomato purée. Season to taste with salt and freshly ground black pepper. Bring to the boil, add the courgettes and mix well. Cover and simmer for 10–15 minutes, until the vegetables are cooked but still *al dente*. Serve immediately.

Crécy potatoes

Serve this rich casserole with plainly cooked meat or poultry.

 1 hour 10 minutes

Serves 4
225 g /8 oz carrots, sliced
salt and freshly ground black pepper
350 g /12 oz waxy new potatoes, sliced
6 spring onions, sliced
200 ml /7 fl oz milk, more if necessary
150 ml /5 fl oz thick cream
50 g /2 oz Emmental cheese, grated

1 Heat the oven to 190C /375F /gas 5. Drop the carrots into lightly salted, boiling water and simmer for 10 minutes, then drain. Meanwhile, boil the potatoes and spring onions in the milk with a little black pepper for 5 minutes. Drain, reserving the milk.
2 Layer the carrots, potatoes and spring onions in a small, ovenproof dish, seasoning each layer with salt. Pour in the milk and the cream, and sprinkle the top with grated cheese.
3 Bake, uncovered, for 45 minutes, or until tender, checking from time to time to make sure that it is not drying out. If so, add a little hot milk. Serve immediately, straight from the dish.

Shallot casserole

Mexican corn and courgette casserole

50 minutes

Serves 6–8
25 g /1 oz butter
1 Spanish onion, chopped
1 green pepper, chopped
700 g /1½ lb courgettes, thinly sliced
2 firm tomatoes, skinned, seeded and
   chopped
350 g /12 oz frozen sweet corn kernels
salt and freshly ground black pepper

1 Heat the oven to 180C /350F /gas 4. Melt the butter in a medium-sized casserole and sauté the chopped onion and pepper over a low heat until soft.
2 Add the thinly sliced courgettes to the casserole, stirring frequently until coated in the butter.
3 Remove the casserole from the heat and add the skinned, seeded and chopped tomatoes and the frozen sweetcorn kernels. Season generously with salt and freshly ground black pepper. Sprinkle over 60–90 ml /4–6 tbls water. Cover the pan and cook in the oven for 20 minutes. Serve the casserole immediately.

Baked barley and mushroom casserole

Serves 4

150 g /5 oz pearl barley
25 g /1 oz butter, plus extra
   for greasing
salt
30 ml /2 tbls finely chopped
   onion

350 g /12 oz button mushrooms,
   thinly sliced
freshly ground black pepper
1 medium-sized egg, beaten
about 125 ml /4 fl oz thin cream
50–75 g /2–3 oz cheese, grated

1   Measure the barley in a measuring jug and make a note of its volume, then measure out double that volume of water into a heavy saucepan, and set aside. Put the barley in a sieve and rinse it under running, cold water until the water runs clear. Place it in a bowl and add enough water to cover. Soak for about 4 hours, until soft. Drain well.
2   Add 15 g /½ oz of the butter to the measured water in the pan. Add salt to taste and bring to the boil. Stir in the soaked barley, cover and lower the heat. Barely simmer the barley until the liquid has been absorbed and the barley is cooked but not mushy. This will take about 30 minutes.
3   Meanwhile, in a large frying-pan which has a lid, sauté the finely chopped onion in the remainder of the butter until soft and golden. Add the thinly sliced mushrooms and toss gently over a moderate heat for a few minutes. Season to taste with salt and freshly ground black pepper. Moisten with 30–45 ml /2–3 tbls water and simmer, tightly covered, until the mushrooms are soft.
4   Heat the oven to 170C /325F /gas 3. Butter a 1 L /2 pt ovenproof dish and spread half the barley evenly over the bottom. Cover with the sautéed onion and mushroom mixture and top with the remaining barley.
5   Beat the egg lightly and add a pinch of salt and enough cream to make 150 ml /5 fl oz. Pour this over the barley in the casserole and sprinkle the surface with grated cheese.
6   Bake the dish for 20 minutes. While the casserole is cooking, heat the grill to maximum.
7   Remove the casserole from the oven and cook it under the grill until it is golden brown. Serve very hot.

● Here is a dish, of Polish origin, which uses barley rather as we use rice. If you have never served barley before, it is worth trying this.

4 hours soaking,
then 1 hour

Quick corn and bacon casserole

Serves 4–6

5–6 corn on the cobs or 580 g /1¼ lb canned or frozen sweetcorn
   kernels
15 ml /1 tbls oil
4 lean bacon slices
40 g /1½ oz butter
1 large Spanish onion, finely chopped
4 tomatoes, blanched and skinned
1 green pepper, seeded and diced
60 ml /4 tbls finely chopped fresh parsley
freshly ground black pepper
1.5 ml /¼ tsp freshly grated nutmeg
a large pinch of cayenne pepper

1   Heat the oven to 180C /350F /gas 4. Cook the corn on the cobs in boiling, salted water for 5–8 minutes, then drain. With a sharp knife, cut the kernels from the corn cobs and discard the latter. Drain canned corn kernels if using, or defrost frozen corn kernels.
2   Heat the oil in a frying-pan and cook the bacon slices until they are crisp. Remove from the frying-pan with a slotted spoon. Dice the bacon and transfer it to a large ovenproof casserole, then reserve.
3   Pour off all but 15 ml /1 tbls fat from the frying-pan. Add the butter and sauté the finely chopped onion in the fat and butter until it is transparent. Transfer it to the casserole with the diced bacon.
4   Remove all the seeds and juice from the tomatoes (reserve for another dish) and dice the flesh. Add this to the casserole with the corn kernels, diced green pepper, finely chopped parsley, freshly ground black pepper to taste, grated nutmeg and cayenne pepper. Mix well, cover the casserole and cook for about 15 minutes, or until the corn is tender.

50 minutes

Broccoli alla siciliana

Serves 4

550 g /1¼ lb fresh broccoli, trimmed, with the larger heads cut into 3
  lengthways
60 ml /4 tbls olive oil
½ Spanish onion, finely chopped
125 g /4 oz Gruyère cheese, thinly sliced
12 black olives, stoned and sliced
6 canned anchovy fillets, drained and slivered
salt and freshly ground black pepper
300 ml /10 fl oz dry red wine

1 Heat 15 ml /1 tbls of the olive oil in a frying pan. Sauté the
finely chopped onion over low heat for 1–2 minutes, or until the
onion is transparent, stirring occasionally with a wooden spoon.
Transfer the onion to a shallow flameproof dish.
2 Put a layer of broccoli in the dish, cover with the cheese, the
sliced black olives and the slivered anchovy fillets, sprinkle with the
remainder of the olive oil and season with a little salt and a generous
amount of black pepper.
3 Pour in the wine, bring to the boil, cover and simmer for 20–30
minutes, or until the broccoli is cooked but *al dente*. Transfer to a
serving dish, if wished, and serve immediately.

Red cabbage campagnard

Serves 4–6

1 kg /2 lb red cabbage
25 g /1 oz butter
450 g /1 lb smoked streaky bacon, diced
2 onions, finely chopped
2 carrots, sliced
bouquet garni
2 cloves
10 ml /2 tsp wine vinegar
salt and freshly ground black pepper
600 ml /1 pt beef stock, home-made or from a cube

1 Heat the oven to 180C /350F /gas 4. Cut the cabbage in
quarters with a sharp knife and remove the hard central core. Shred
the cabbage finely. This is easy to do with a food processor or with
an electric mixer which has a shredder attachment.
2 Melt the butter in a large flameproof casserole of about 3.5 L /6
pt capacity. Sauté the diced bacon until it releases its fat. Add the
finely chopped onion and cook for 5 minutes. Add the sliced carrots,
bouquet garni, cloves, shredded cabbage and wine vinegar, and stir
until the vegetables are all well coated in the bacon fat. Season with
salt and freshly ground black pepper to taste.
3 Pour in the stock and mix well. Cover and bake in the oven for 1
hour, or until the cabbage is tender.

● Serve this rich, red country cabbage dish as an accompaniment to
pork or gammon

45 minutes

1½ hours

TERRINES & MOULDED VEGETABLES

For a novel way to serve vegetables, try an elegant terrine, sliced to reveal layers of colourful vegetables, or a moulded vegetable mousse, hot from the oven or glistening in an aspic coating.

Moulded vegetable dishes look elegant and impressive, yet they are surprisingly simple to accomplish. As well as being an attractive focus for a meal, they also save the busy cook time because they can be made in advance and then cooked or unmoulded at the last minute.

Types of vegetable moulds
Cold mousses: these are based on a purée of vegetables thickened with mayonnaise or cream and set with gelatine. Whisked egg whites may be folded in to add an extra lightness to the mousse. For extra sophistication, the mould can be lined with aspic, giving the turned-out dish a glistening and clear coating.
Hot moulds: a thick vegetable purée, bound with eggs and baked until set, forms the base of most hot moulds. Or, more simply, the vegetables can be sliced and used to line and fill a large mould or individual moulds. A hot, moulded mousse is delicious served masked with a complementary sauce, such as hollandaise.
Vegetable terrines: these are attractive layers of whole or sliced vegetables which offer contrasts of colour and texture. They are either set in a cold gelatine sauce or baked with an egg binding.

Which vegetables to use
Nearly all vegetables can be puréed and therefore used as the base for a cold mousse or hot mould. Different types of vegetables produce different consistencies of purée and this will affect what other thickening ingredients are added to the mousse before it is moulded.

For vegetable terrines, choose crisp, colourful vegetables which complement each other. Carrots, celery, mange tout, whole green beans, avocado and green and red peppers are all successful. A popular way to serve a vegetable terrine is to line the terrine with a green leaf such as spinach or sorrel to give the unmoulded pâté an unusual and attractive green casing.

Moulds
Moulds can be made of porcelain, plastic or metal. Porcelain moulds are attractive, but they can be expensive and have the disadvantage of being breakable.

Plastic moulds are cheap and lightweight, although not particularly pretty to look at. As they are semi-transparent, they have the advantage that you can see if the mousse is unmoulding successfully or not.

Of all moulds, a metal ring mould is probably the most useful; it can be used for both hot and cold mousses and also, of course, for cakes.

Whatever mould you choose, make sure that it is the correct capacity for the amount of mixture you are using. If the mould is too large, the mixture will have a long way to fall when turned out and may break.

Using aspic
One of the most elegant ways of presenting a cold mould is to first line the mould with a layer of aspic. A perfect aspic should be absolutely clear; it is made from clarified stock, with added gelatine. There are, however, short-cut methods of making aspic. A good-quality, canned consommé can easily be substituted for your own clarified stock or, for the quickest results, use aspic granules or powder – see Tomato and cucumber mould.

It is safest to chill an aspic before using it to make sure it will set – if not, add more aspic powder. Melt it again before using.
Lining a mould with aspic: to line a small mould, fill the mould with syrupy aspic, then stand it in a bowl of ice and watch it carefully. As soon as a 3 mm /$\frac{1}{8}$ in layer is set around the edge, pour off the remaining syrupy aspic into a bowl. There should be an even thickness of aspic lining the mould – if it is too thick on the base, scoop it out with a spoon dipped in hot water.

Lining a larger mould with aspic is more difficult. Prepare a bowl of ice and stand the mould in it, then add the aspic, a tablespoonful at a time. Tilt the mould to coat the base evenly. Lay the mould on its side on the ice and coat a strip from base to rim by tilting the mould. Gradually turn and coat the mould until the inside is covered. Continue adding aspic, by the spoonful, until a 3 mm /$\frac{1}{8}$ in layer is built up. Chill until set. Dip decorations in syrupy aspic and arrange on the set aspic. Spoon over another layer of aspic, then chill until set.

Lining a mould

Lay the mould on its side and coat a strip from base to rim, then continue round.

Vegetable terrine

🕐 🍴 1¾ hours, plus overnight chilling

Serves 12
6 medium-sized carrots
2 young turnips
2 celery sticks
12 large spinach or sorrel leaves
salt and freshly ground black pepper
175 g /6 oz green beans, topped and tailed
2 red peppers, halved and seeded
2 avocados
700 g /1½ lb cooked ham
2 egg whites
juice of 1 lemon
30 ml /2 tbls peanut oil

1 Peel the carrots and leave them whole. Peel the turnips and cut them into sticks 15 mm /$\frac{1}{2}$ in square and 5 cm /2 in long.
2 Remove the strings from the celery.
3 Remove the spinach or sorrel stalks, and wash the leaves well. Bring a large saucepan of salted water to the boil, blanch the spinach or sorrel leaves for 10 seconds, then plunge them immediately into cold water to arrest the cooking, taking great care not to tear them. Drain the leaves and spread on a cloth or absorbent paper.
4 Wash the carrots, turnips, green beans, red pepper and celery. Cook in boiling salted water, one after the other in the same saucepan, until all the vegetables are *al dente*. It is not necessary to change the water. Whole carrots take 8 minutes; celery 5 minutes; halved red peppers 3 minutes; green beans 2 minutes; and the turnip sticks 1 minute. Drain, refresh and drain again.
5 Peel and halve the avocados. Halve each piece again, cutting parallel to the first cut.
6 Put the ham and egg whites in a blender or food processor and blend to a fine purée. Add the lemon juice and peanut oil, season with black pepper and blend again.
7 Heat the oven to 170C /325F /gas 3.
8 Line the bottom and sides of a 1.7 L /3 pt terrine or loaf tin with the spinach or sorrel leaves and, using your fingers, add a thin layer of ham mousse. Continue layering the vegetables in the following order, with a layer of ham mousse in between each: whole carrots, turnip sticks, green beans, red pepper, celery and avocado. The whole carrots, turnip sticks and the beans are laid lengthways and close together in the terrine. Finish with a layer of ham mousse and press down the surface, then smooth the top.
9 Cover the terrine with the remaining spinach or sorrel leaves and seal with foil. Place in a roasting tin, add hot water to come half way up the sides of the dish and cook in the oven for 30 minutes.
10 Remove the terrine from the roasting tin. Place a 500 g /1 lb weight on top and allow to cool, then chill overnight.
11 To serve, unmould the terrine and slice.

Vegetable terrine

Tomato and cucumber mould

Serve this elegant mould as a starter with mayonnaise or vinaigrette dressing, or to accompany a cold main course.

¶¶ 30 minutes, plus chilling

Serves 6–8
225 ml /8 fl oz boiling water
15 ml /3 tsp aspic granules or powder
15 thin slices of cucumber
575 ml /1 pt cold chicken stock, home-made
    or from a cube
60 ml /4 tbls powdered gelatine
575 ml /1 pt tomato juice
freshly ground black pepper
½ iceberg lettuce, shredded

1   Pour the boiling water over the aspic granules or powder and stir until it is completely dissolved.
2   Prepare a bowl of ice and stand a 1.1 L / 2 pt mould in it. Add the aspic a tablespoonful at a time, tilting the mould to coat the base evenly. Put the mould on its side and gradually coat the sides, until a 3 mm /⅛ in layer is built up. Chill until set.
3   Dip the cucumber slices in aspic and arrange 3 of them on the base of the mould. Arrange the remaining slices around the sides. Cover all the slices with another layer of aspic and chill until set.
4   Measure 90 ml /6 tbls of the chicken stock into a small bowl and sprinkle the gelatine over the top. Leave to soften for a few minutes, then stand it in a pan of simmering water until completely dissolved.
5   In a saucepan, combine the remaining chicken stock with the tomato juice and freshly ground black pepper to taste. Warm through gently. Strain the dissolved gelatine into this mixture and stir well. Leave until cool and then pour the mixture into the mould and chill until set.
6   Turn the mould out onto a large serving platter; hold a hot, damp tea-towel around the mould to loosen it. Invert the plate over the mould and then reverse the two. Shake firmly once or twice to release the jelly. Garnish the platter with shredded lettuce and then serve.

Hot celeriac mousse

¶ about 1¼ hours

Serves 4–6
1 kg /2 lb celeriac
salt
3 medium-sized eggs
1 medium-sized egg yolk
150 ml /5 fl oz thick cream
freshly ground black pepper
freshly grated nutmeg
butter, for greasing
275 ml /10 fl oz Hollandaise sauce (page 74)
sprigs of fresh thyme, to garnish
lemon slices, to garnish

1   Heat the oven to 170C /325F /gas 3. Peel the celeriac, cut it into chunks and cook it in boiling salted water for 10–15 minutes, until very soft. Drain the cooked celeriac, then rub it through a fine sieve to make a purée.
2   Beat the eggs, egg yolk and thick cream into the puréed celeriac and then season generously with freshly ground black pepper and freshly grated nutmeg. Add a little salt.
3   Transfer the mousse mixture to a well-buttered 575 ml /1 pt mould or soufflé dish. Place the mould or dish in a large saucepan of shallow hot water on top of the stove. Bring the water to the boil, then remove the mould or dish and put it in the oven. Cook for 45–50 minutes, or until set. (Make the hollandaise sauce at this point.)
4   Turn the mousse onto a heated serving dish and mask it with the hollandaise sauce. Garnish with sprigs of fresh thyme and lemon slices.

Italian bean mould

This sophisticated, delicious dish is popular in northern Italy, although it is rarely found in restaurants. It can also be made with spinach, cauliflower, peas or fennel; whatever the vegetable, the basic recipe remains the same.

¶¶ 1½ hours

Serves 6
1 kg /2¼ lb French beans, topped and tailed
salt and freshly ground white pepper
50 g /2 oz butter
½ small onion, very finely chopped
125 ml /4 fl oz thick cream
25 g /1 oz flour
250 ml /9 fl oz milk
2.5 ml /½ tsp freshly grated nutmeg
25 g /1 oz Parmesan cheese, freshly grated
3 medium-sized eggs
1 medium-sized egg yolk
butter for greasing
30 ml /2 tbls dried breadcrumbs
For the tomato sauce
900 g /2 lb fresh tomatoes, blanched and
    peeled, or canned tomatoes
1 medium-sized onion, quartered
1 celery stick, chopped
1 large or 2 small garlic cloves
1 bay leaf
5 ml /1 tsp sugar
salt
freshly ground black pepper

1   Cook the beans in plenty of boiling salted water until tender. Drain them well and press them through a food mill at the coarsest setting, or purée them very coarsely in a food processor.
2   Heat half the butter in a frying-pan, add the onion and sauté until golden. Add the bean purée and cook for 3–4 minutes. Add the cream, mix well, then turn the mixture into a large bowl and reserve.
3   Heat the oven to 190C /375F /gas 5. Melt the rest of the butter in a small saucepan over medium-low heat and stir in the flour. Cook for 1 minute, then stir in the

milk until the sauce thickens. Season with salt, pepper and nutmeg and add the sauce to the bean purée with the Parmesan and the eggs and egg yolk. Mix very thoroughly, taste and adjust the seasoning.
4   Thoroughly butter a 1 L /1¾ pt ring mould and sprinkle it with the breadcrumbs, discarding the excess. Transfer the purée to the mould, smoothing the top with a palette knife.
5   Stand the mould in a roasting tin and pour enough boiling water into the tin to come three-quarters of the way up the ring mould. Bake for 50–60 minutes, or until a skewer inserted in the middle of the vegetable mixture comes out dry.
6   Meanwhile, make the tomato sauce. Put the ingredients in a saucepan over medium heat and simmer, uncovered, for 30 minutes, stirring frequently. Remove the bay leaf and purée the sauce in a blender or through a food mill or fine sieve. Leave the sauce to cool slightly.
7   Allow the mould to cool for 5 minutes, then turn it out onto a deep, round serving plate. Pour the warm tomato sauce into the centre of the mould and around its edge.

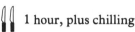

onto a plate. Remove the mould. (If the potatoes are not quite golden enough, you can return them to the moulds and cook them for a little longer).

7 Transfer the potato moulds to a heated serving dish and serve immediately.

Creamy vegetable terrine

Try this creamy, layered terrine as an impressive start to your dinner party.

 1 hour, plus chilling

Serves 6
900 g /2 lb small courgettes
150 ml /5 fl oz chicken stock, home-made or from a cube
450 g /1 lb carrots, cut lengthways into 10 mm /⅓ in batons
90 ml /6 tbls aspic powder
425 ml /15 fl oz boiling water
105 ml /7 tbls thick cream
105 ml /7 tbls mayonnaise
15 ml /1 tbls white wine vinegar
5 ml /1 tsp lemon juice
30 ml /2 tbls finely chopped fresh parsley
salt and freshly ground black pepper
2 canned pimentos, drained and thinly sliced
parsley sprigs, to garnish
sliced tomatoes, to garnish

1 Steam the courgettes, whole, for 10 minutes. Cool them quickly and slice them lengthways into 10 mm /⅓ in thick batons.
2 Bring the chicken stock to the boil in a saucepan, add the carrots and simmer for 5–6 minutes, or until they are just tender. Drain, discarding the stock, and cool the carrots quickly.
3 Put the aspic into a bowl, pour on the boiling water and stir to dissolve. Leave to stand for 10 minutes.
4 Stir in the cream, mayonnaise, vinegar, lemon juice and finely chopped parsley. Season with salt and freshly ground black pepper. Beat the mixture until all the ingredients are well blended. Chill in the refrigerator for about 20–25 minutes, until it has the consistency of unbeaten egg white.
5 Rinse a 1.5 L /3 pt loaf tin with cold water. Arrange a layer of courgette strips on the base, along the length of the tin. Then place a layer of carrot strips across the tin. Add four layers of courgettes and three of carrots in the same way. Then add all the pimentoes in one layer. Finish with one more layer each of courgettes and carrots.
6 Pour the aspic cream over the vegetables and rap the sides of the tin so that the cream penetrates all the layers and there are no air bubbles trapped inside. Cover the tin and refrigerate for at least 2 hours so that the aspic cream firms up.
7 To turn out, run a knife around the edges of the terrine. Invert a serving platter over the top, turn over the tin and platter together and give a sharp shake. Garnish the serving platter with parsley sprigs and sliced tomatoes. Slice the terrine into individual portions to serve.

Pommes Anna in darioles

The traditional Pommes Anna is one large potato cake. This novel way of presenting them as individual portions makes a super garnish for a dish such as roast game. Make sure that you take great care when you transfer the hot oil from the top of the cooker to the oven.

1¼ hours

Serves 4
450–700 g/1–1½ lb floury potatoes
oil
butter for greasing
salt and freshly ground black pepper

1 Heat the oven to 190C /375F /gas 5.
2 Peel the potatoes and trim them to roughly the width of a 150 ml /5 fl oz dariole mould. Cut them into even slices about 3 mm /⅛ in thick.

Tomato and cucumber mould

3 Pour oil into a flameproof gratin dish until 25 mm /1 in deep and place over a low heat until hot but not smoking. Add the potato slices a few at a time and cook for 1–2 minutes, until soft but not coloured. Remove them from the oil with a slotted spoon and drain them on absorbent paper.
4 Butter four 150 ml /5 fl oz dariole moulds. Line the base and sides of each mould with potato slices, season well with salt and freshly ground black pepper and fill the centres with the remaining slices. The potatoes should be packed down and the top slightly domed as they will shrink slightly during cooking.
5 Place the dariole moulds in the dish of hot oil, making an oil bain-marie, and carefully transfer the dish to the oven. Cook for 20 minutes, or until the sides are golden brown where they start to shrink away from the mould.
6 Remove the dish from the oven and, using an oven cloth, remove the moulds from the oil. Run a knife around the edge of each mould to free the potato and invert it

Cauliflower loaf

Serves 8

2 × 500 g /1 lb cauliflowers
salt
3 medium-sized egg yolks, well
   beaten
75 g /3 oz butter, softened
freshly ground black pepper

pinch of freshly grated nutmeg
For the hollandaise sauce
10–15 ml /2–3 tsp lemon juice
salt and white pepper
100 g /4 oz softened butter
4 medium-sized egg yolks

1 Bring a large saucepan of salted water to the boil. Add the
cauliflowers, cover and simmer gently for about 20 minutes, or until
the cauliflowers are just tender when pierced at the stem end with a
fork.
2 Heat the oven to 190C /375F /gas 5. Drain the cauliflowers well
and press through a fine sieve.
3 Beat the egg yolks and butter a little at a time into the
cauliflower purée. Season with salt, pepper and nutmeg.
4 Pour into a well-buttered small loaf tin or 575 ml /1 pt soufflé
dish. Stand the tin or dish in a pan of hot water in the oven and
bake for 25 minutes. Meanwhile, to make the hollandaise sauce,
combine 5 ml /1 tsp lemon juice, 15 ml /1 tbls water and salt and
white pepper to taste in the top of a double saucepan (or a bowl over
a pan of hot water). Put hot, but not boiling, water in the bottom
pan.
5 Divide the butter into quarters. Add the egg yolks and a quarter
of the butter, diced small, to the liquid in the saucepan. Use a wire
whisk to stir the mixture rapidly and constantly over hot, but not
boiling, water until the butter is melted and the mixture begins to
thicken. Add the second quarter of butter, diced small, in the same
way. Do not allow the water over which the sauce is cooking to boil
and make sure that you beat the mixture continually from the sides
and bottom of the pan. Continue until all the butter portions have
been used up.
6 Remove the sauce from the heat and continue to beat for 2–3
minutes. Replace the sauce over the hot, but not boiling, water for 2
minutes more, beating constantly. By this time the emulsion should
have formed and the sauce will be rich and creamy. If, at any time,
the mixture should curdle, beat in 15–30 ml /1–2 tbls cold water to
rebind the emulsion. Add 5–10 ml /1–2 tsp of the remaining lemon
juice to the sauce.
7 To serve, turn the cauliflower loaf out onto a heated dish and
mask with the hollandaise sauce.

 1 hour

Avocado and watercress mousse

Serves 8

900 g /2 lb ripe avocados
juice of 1 lemon
150 ml /5 fl oz chicken stock,
   home-made or from a cube,
   chilled
salt and ground black pepper
a few drops of Tabasco
25 g /1 oz gelatine
60–90 ml /4–6 tbls
   mayonnaise

150 ml /5 fl oz thick cream
90–120 ml /6–8 tbls finely
   chopped watercress
For the garnish
½ bunch watercress, washed
   and dried
100 g /4 oz button mushrooms,
   thinly sliced
50 ml /2 fl oz vinaigrette
spring onions, trimmed

1 Halve and peel the avocados and remove the stones. Put the
flesh in a blender with the lemon juice, chicken stock, salt, freshly
ground black pepper and Tabasco, to taste. Blend to a purée, then
sieve.
2 In a small bowl, sprinkle the gelatine over 90 ml /6 tbls cold
water and leave to soften for a few minutes. Place the bowl in a
saucepan of simmering water until the powder is completely
dissolved. Remove from the heat and leave to cool slightly.
3 Wet a 1.1 L /2 pt ring mould and chill it for 10 minutes.
4 Meanwhile, add the cooled gelatine and the mayonnaise to the
avocado mixture and mix well. Whip the thick cream to soft peaks
and fold it gently into the mixture with the finely chopped
watercress, using a large metal spoon. Adjust the seasoning.
5 Spoon the avocado mixture into the mould, tapping the mould a
few times, to prevent air pockets from forming. Refrigerate until set.
6 Meanwhile, prepare the garnish. Trim the watercress,
discarding any yellow or damaged leaves, and cut off the stems.
Reserving a sprig, put the remainder of the watercress in a bowl
with the thinly sliced mushrooms and the vinaigrette. Toss until
well coated.
7 To unmould, turn the ring mould upside down on a wet serving
dish slightly larger in diameter than the mould. Soak a tea-towel in
hot water and wrap it around the mould, then shake the dish and
mould together until the mousse slides out.
8 Spoon the mushroom and watercress salad into the centre of the
avocado ring, garnish with the spring onions and the reserved sprig
of watercress and serve immediately.

 45 minutes, plus chilling

French aubergine mould

Serves 4

3 medium-sized aubergines
salt
120 ml /8 tbls olive oil, plus
extra for greasing
7.5 ml /½ tbls brandy
60 ml /4 tbls beef stock, home-
made or from a cube
2 × tomato sauce (page 72)
watercress, to garnish
For the filling
15 g /½ oz butter
15 ml /1 tbls olive oil

1 medium-sized onion, finely
chopped
1 garlic clove, crushed
75 g /3 oz cooked pork, finely
chopped
50 g /2 oz cooked ham, finely
chopped
2 large tomatoes, blanched,
skinned, seeded and chopped
15 ml /1 tbls finely chopped parsley
salt and ground black pepper
1 large egg, lightly beaten

1 Wipe the aubergines with a damp cloth. Slice them thinly without peeling them. Sprinkle with salt and leave to drain.
2 Meanwhile, prepare the filling. In a small saucepan, heat the butter and olive oil. When the foaming subsides, sauté the finely chopped onion for 5 minutes, stirring occasionally with a wooden spoon. Stir in the garlic, finely chopped pork and ham, tomatoes and parsley. Season with salt and pepper and sauté for 5 minutes.
3 Remove the pan from the heat. Leave to cool a little and stir in the beaten egg. Rinse the aubergine slices and pat them dry.
4 In a large frying-pan, heat one-third of the olive oil and sauté one-third of the aubergines for 2 minutes each side, or until golden, turning them over with a spatula. Remove and drain on absorbent paper. Repeat with the remaining 2 batches.
5 Heat the oven to 180C /350F /gas 4.
6 Oil a 600 ml /1 pt ovenproof pudding bowl and line the bowl with sautéed aubergine slices. Cover the aubergines at the bottom with a layer of the meat mixture. Top it with a layer of aubergines and continue until all the ingredients are used up, ending with an aubergine layer.
7 Stir the brandy into the beef stock and moisten the mould with the liquid. Cover with an ovenproof plate or piece of foil. Place the bowl in a roasting pan and pour in hot water to come halfway up the bowl. Bake for 1 hour. Meanwhile, make the tomato sauce.
8 Turn the aubergine mould out carefully onto a large, flat dish. Pour over the hot tomato sauce. Garnish with watercress and serve.

 2 hours

Little vegetable towers

Serves 4

butter
225 g /8 oz button mushrooms,
finely chopped
3 spring onions, finely chopped
salt

freshly ground black pepper
200 g /7 oz frozen spinach
½ medium-sized cauliflower, cut
into florets
2 large egg yolks, lightly beaten

1 In a small saucepan, melt 15 g /½ oz butter. Add the finely chopped mushrooms and spring onions to the hot butter. Cook over a high heat for 7–10 minutes until all the moisture from the mushrooms has evaporated, stirring constantly. Season to taste with salt and freshly ground black pepper. Leave to cool.
2 Meanwhile, in a clean saucepan, melt 15 g /½ oz butter. Add the frozen spinach and cook for 7 minutes, or until tender, stirring occasionally. Strain the cooked spinach, squeezing out any excess moisture, and purée in a blender or push through a sieve using the back of a wooden spoon. Season to taste with salt and freshly ground black pepper. Leave to cool.
3 Bring a saucepan of salted water to the boil and cook the cauliflower florets for about 7 minutes, or until tender. Drain, rinse under cold running water and drain again. Push the cauliflower through a sieve, using the back of a wooden spoon. Season to taste with salt and freshly ground black pepper.
4 In a clean saucepan, heat 15 g /½ oz butter. Add the cauliflower purée and cook over a high heat for 2–3 minutes to remove excess moisture. Leave to cool.
5 Heat the oven to 180C /350F /gas 4.
6 Beat 7 g /¼ oz butter and one-third of the lightly beaten egg yolks into each separate vegetable mixture. Adjust the seasoning.
7 Butter four 150 ml /5 fl oz dariole moulds. Cut four rounds of greaseproof paper to fit the bottom of each mould and butter them. Divide the spinach purée among the moulds and level the surface. Carefully spoon the cauliflower purée on top and level the surface again. Finally, spoon in the mushroom mixture to make a third layer. Cover each mould with a piece of foil.
8 Place the moulds in a roasting tin and add enough boiling water to come halfway up the sides of the moulds. Cook in the oven for 30 minutes, or until set.
9 When ready to serve, turn the moulds out onto a heated serving platter. Serve immediately.

 30 minutes, cooling,
then 45 minutes

COLD VEGETABLE DISHES

Cold vegetables combine to make dishes that will make your mouth water; try crunchy broccoli and carrot with juicy, brandy-soaked raisins, or a Sicilian vegetable stew for a summer hors d'oeuvre.

Cold dishes made with cooked or raw vegetables are much more versatile than just the classic combination of salad vegetables. They can make a delicious appetizer for a dinner party or an unusual accompaniment to the main course. Some dishes in the following chapter benefit from being made in advance so the flavours have an opportunity to mingle, others can be prepared well ahead, just needing to be combined at the last minute; both these methods are handy for the cook who is planning a menu.

With good-quality produce it is possible to add only a few simple ingredients or just herbs and spices to what you may consider to be a very ordinary vegetable to create an elegant dish. Moroccan carrot appetizer (see recipe) combines hot, African-style spices with the cool, sweet crunch of carrot for an unusual but easy starter. Assiette verte (see recipe), a classic combination of green vegetables, is similar in that the vegetables are cooked briefly to retain their maximum

flavour and texture and then simply combined with a yoghurt and garlic dressing.

An unusual variation on a vegetable salad is to serve it warmed through. A hot vinaigrette dressing will add a distinctive touch to the dish and, if bacon is first fried in the oil which is to be part of the dressing, it will add extra flavour. A dressing which has been brought to the boil can either be poured over already warm salad ingredients (see recipe for Belgian warm salad) or over cold ingredients which will then be heated through by the dressing (see Country red cabbage with bacon). This is a delicious way to serve a winter salad, especially as an accompaniment to Christmas cold meats.

As well as delicious appetizers and side dishes, there are cold vegetable dishes which also make a substantial main course. Stuffed aubergines (see recipe) make a delightful vegetarian dish or, well chilled before serving, they make another dish handy for preparing ahead.

Broccoli and raisin platter

Begin the day before by marinating the raisins in brandy for a very special blend of flavours.

 overnight marinating, then 30 minutes

Serves 4
100 g /4 oz seedless raisins
45 ml /3 tbls brandy
450 g /1 lb broccoli, cut into florets
salt
2 large carrots, cut into matchstick strips
lettuce leaves, to serve
50 g /2 oz walnut halves, to garnish
For the dressing
60 ml /4 tbls mayonnaise
30 ml /2 tbls soured cream
15 ml /1 tbls cider vinegar
5 ml /1 tsp clear honey
salt and freshly ground black pepper

1 Put the raisins and brandy in a lidded jar, cover, shake well and leave the raisins to marinate overnight (or longer). Shake the

Broccoli and raisin platter

...ar from time to time, if it is convenient.
2 Steam the broccoli florets over boiling water for 6–7 minutes, or until they are barely tender, cool quickly and dry them on absorbent paper.
3 To make the dressing, combine the mayonnaise, soured cream, vinegar, honey and salt and freshly ground black pepper to taste and blend together well.
4 Just before serving, drain the raisins and toss them with the broccoli and carrots. Stir in the dressing. Line a serving dish with lettuce leaves, pile the salad onto the lettuce and garnish with the walnut halves.

Cabbage and olive appetizer

 10 minutes,
plus 30 minutes standing

Serves 4
1 small, white cabbage, finely shredded
125 ml /4 fl oz olive oil
100 g /4 oz Feta cheese, crumbled
100 g /4 oz large black olives, stoned
100 g /4 oz anchovy-stuffed green olives
freshly ground black peppper

1 Place the cabbage into a large salad bowl and dress with the oil. Crumble the cheese over the cabbage and add all the olives.
2 Season with freshly ground black pepper – you will not need any salt as the cheese is quite salty – and toss everything 2 or 3 times. Let the salad stand for 30 minutes so the flavours blend, then serve.

Belgian warm salad

🍴 35 minutes

Serves 4–6
350 g /12 oz new potatoes, in their skins
salt and freshly ground black pepper
350 g /12 oz green beans, topped and tailed
25 g /1 oz butter
225 g /8 oz streaky bacon, cut into strips
1 Spanish onion, finely chopped
60 ml /4 tbls wine vinegar
30 ml /2 tbls finely chopped parsley

1 Cook the potatoes for 15–20 minutes in boiling, salted water until tender.
2 Meanwhile, cook the beans in boiling salted water for 8–10 minutes, or until tender. Drain and keep warm.
3 Drain the potatoes. Allow them to cool slightly, then cut them into 6 mm /$\frac{1}{4}$ in slices. Keep warm.
4 Meanwhile, melt the butter in a medium-sized frying-pan. Sauté the streaky bacon strips and the finely chopped onion over a high heat for 7 minutes, or until lightly golden, tossing the mixture frequently with a spatula. Reduce the heat.
5 Pour in the wine vinegar and simmer over a low heat for 3 minutes, stirring occasionally. Season with the black pepper.
6 In a salad bowl, combine the drained beans and sliced new potatoes. Pour over the bacon dressing and toss gently until well mixed; do not break up the potato slices.
7 Adjust the seasoning, sprinkle with finely chopped parsley and serve lukewarm.

Cabbage and olive appetizer

Sauerkraut

🕐 🍴 $\frac{1}{2}$ hour,
then 4–4$\frac{1}{2}$ weeks fermenting

Makes about 1.5 kg /3$\frac{1}{4}$ lb
2 kg /4$\frac{1}{2}$ lb white cabbage, finely shredded
75 g /3 oz coarse salt
4 bay leaves, crumbled
5 ml /1 tsp caraway seeds

1 Use a large, deep earthenware or porcelain container and sprinkle a layer of salt in the base. Add a layer of cabbage, sprinkle with pieces of bay leaf and a few caraway seeds, then add another layer of salt. Continue adding the layers to the dish, finishing with salt.
2 Scald a piece of muslin or cheesecloth in boiling water and use it to cover the container. Top with a plate and then a heavy weight to keep the cabbage immersed in the brine formed from the juices and the salt.
3 Leave it in a warm place with a steady temperature (about 20C /68F) for a few days until bubbles start to rise, then transfer it to a cooler place (about 10C /50F) for 3–4 weeks until the fermentation has stopped (when the bubbles have stopped rising).
4 During this time skim off the scum every 1–2 days. Replace the cloth each time with a freshly sterilized one and also wash the plate.
5 The sauerkraut will keep for 3–4 days in a covered container in the refrigerator. Drain well before using it.

Country red cabbage with bacon

30 minutes,
plus 3 hours marinating

Serves 4–6
1 small, firm red cabbage
salt
225 g /8 oz streaky bacon, thickly sliced
60 ml /4 tbls olive oil
45 ml /3 tbls wine vinegar
5 ml /1 tsp French mustard
5 ml /1 tsp sugar
lemon juice
freshly ground black pepper
100 g /4 oz shelled walnuts, halved

1   Halve the cabbage. Cut out the hard central core and shred the cabbage very thinly. Put the cabbage in a bowl. Sprinkle with 15 ml /1 tbls salt, working it in well with your fingers. Leave to marinate for 3 hours.
2   Rinse the cabbage thoroughly under cold running water. Drain thoroughly, wrap in muslin or a clean tea-towel and squeeze out the excess moisture. Put the cabbage in a salad bowl.
3   Cut the bacon slices into 25 mm /1 in lengths. Sauté the bacon in the olive oil until crisp and golden. Remove from the pan with a slotted spoon, add to the cabbage and toss.
4   To the oil remaining in the frying-pan, add the wine vinegar, French mustard, sugar and a few drops of lemon juice. Bring this to the boil over a high heat, stirring constantly, and immediately pour over the salad. Mix well.
5   Season lightly with salt, if necessary, and a little pepper. Add the halved walnuts and give the salad a final toss before serving.

Green bean, lettuce and asparagus bowl

20 minutes

Serves 4
1 lettuce
175 g /6 oz young green beans
350 g /12 oz asparagus
salt
½ × vinaigrette (see Stuffed courgette appetizer)

1   Wash and dry the lettuce, wrap in a tea-towel and chill. Top and tail the beans. Trim the stems from the asparagus so you are left with just the tips. Use the stems for soup.
2   Bring 2 saucepans of salted water to the boil. Blanch the beans for 4–5 minutes in one pan, then drain and refresh them under cold, running water. In the other pan simmer the asparagus tips for 5–6 minutes (according to the size of the heads) until just tender. Drain and refresh them.
3   Line a large salad bowl with the lettuce. Scatter the beans over the lettuce and arrange the asparagus heads decoratively on top. Spoon over the vinaigrette and serve.

Country red cabbage with bacon

Stuffed aubergines

10 minutes, 1 hour draining,
then 1½ hours, plus chilling

Serves 4
2 large aubergines
salt
60 ml /4 tbls olive oil
2 medium-sized onions, chopped
2 garlic cloves, crushed
500 g /1 lb tomatoes, skinned, seeded and chopped
freshly ground black pepper
15 ml /1 tbls chopped fresh basil, or 5 ml /1 tsp dried basil
45 ml /3 tbls freshly chopped parsley
60 ml /4 tbls grated Parmesan cheese
15 ml /1 tbls lemon juice
freshly chopped parsley, to garnish

1   Trim the aubergines, halve them lengthways and scoop out the flesh, leaving a shell about 5 mm /¼ in thick. Sprinkle the insides of the shells thickly with salt and leave them cut side down in a colander to drain. Chop the scooped-out flesh coarsely and add to the colander. Sprinkle with salt and leave both the shells and the flesh to drain for about 1 hour.
2   Rinse the salt off the aubergines and dry the chopped flesh and the shells on absorbent paper. Heat the oven to 180C /350F / gas 4.
3   Heat 30 ml /2 tbls of the olive oil in a frying-pan, add the onion and garlic and cook for about 10 minutes, until the onion is soft and transparent. Add the chopped aubergine flesh and the chopped tomatoes, with any juice they may have made. Season the mixture well and cook gently for about 15 minutes, until the aubergine is soft. Stir in the chopped or dried basil and the chopped parsley and remove the mixture from the heat.
4   Put the aubergine shells in an ovenproof dish and spoon the cooked mixture into them. Sprinkle with the Parmesan cheese.
5   Sprinkle the remaining 30 ml /2 tbls olive oil and the lemon juice over the filling and bake for about 1 hour, until the flesh on the shells is tender.
6   Remove the aubergines from the oven and allow them to cool, then chill for about 1 hour before serving. Garnish the tops of each one with chopped parsley.

Sicilian vegetable hors d'oeuvre

This Sicilian vegetable stew is usually served as an hors d'oeuvre. If you omit the tuna fish, it is a good accompaniment to sausages or egg-based dishes. It is also excellent with pasta. Prepare the dish at least 24 hours before required so that the sweet-sour flavour of the sauce permeates the vegetables. Good quality, fruity olive oil is essential.

 1¾ hours,
then 24 hours marinating

Serves 4

2 large aubergines, diced
salt
90 ml /6 tbls olive oil for frying
1 small onion, peeled and chopped
400 g /14 oz canned tomatoes
45 ml /3 tbls red wine vinegar
15 ml /1 tbls sugar
freshly ground black pepper
½ head of celery, trimmed, chopped and
*   blanched*
15 ml /1 tbls capers
25 g /1 oz black olives, stoned and coarsely
*   chopped*
30 ml /2 tbls pine nuts, toasted
200 g /7 oz canned tuna fish, drained
freshly chopped parsley, to garnish

1 Layer the diced aubergine in a colander and sprinkle with salt. Cover with a plate, weight it and leave to drain for 30–40 minutes, then rinse the pieces and squeeze them dry in absorbent paper. Sauté the aubergine in 75 ml /5 tbls of olive oil and then drain and reserve.

2 Heat 15 ml /1 tbls olive oil in a large, heavy-based saucepan. Add the onion and cook, stirring, for 5–7 minutes until soft. Add the tomatoes with about one-third of their juices. (Reserve the remaining juices.) Simmer for 5 minutes, then stir in the vinegar and sugar and season to taste. Simmer the sauce for 15–20 minutes until it is well reduced and richly coloured.

3 Add the blanched celery to the pan, together with the aubergine, capers, olives and pine nuts, stirring well to mix. Cover the pan with a tight-fitting lid and cook gently for 30 minutes, stirring regularly. If the mixture appears too dry and the vegetables show signs of sticking, add a little of the reserved tomato juices, but avoid making the stew too wet.

4 Remove the pan from the heat and turn the stew into a bowl. Allow it to cool, then cover it tightly and chill it for at least 24 hours.

5 To serve, bring the stew to room temperature, adjust the seasoning and turn into a serving dish. Flake the tuna into fairly large chunks and scatter these around the edge, then garnish with plenty of the freshly chopped parsley.

Assiette verte

🔪 30 minutes

Serves 4

50 g /2 oz mange tout, or courgettes
salt
50 g /2 oz green beans
125 g /4 oz broccoli florets
12 green asparagus spears
½ cucumber, seeded
50 g /2 oz celery
freshly ground black pepper
15 ml /1 tbls chopped, mixed herbs
For the dressing
45 ml /3 tbls olive oil
15 ml /1 tbls yoghurt
15 ml /1 tbls wine vinegar
1 garlic clove, crushed

1 Bring a large saucepan of salted water to the boil and blanch the mange tout or courgettes for 2 minutes. Remove with a slotted spoon and refresh under cold running water. Drain the mange tout or courgettes and dry with a clean tea-towel.

2 In the same water, blanch the green beans for 2 minutes, the broccoli and asparagus for 4 minutes. Drain and refresh under cold running water. Drain again and pat dry.

3 Cut the cucumber and celery into batons 8 mm /¼ in square and 5 cm /2 in long.

4 To make the dressing, in a bowl stir the olive oil into the yoghurt. Add the wine vinegar and crushed garlic, and then season with salt and freshly ground black pepper to taste.

5 In another bowl, combine the mange tout, green beans, cucumber and celery with 60 ml /4 tbls of the dressing. Divide the dressed vegetables among 4 individual serving plates. Season with salt and freshly ground black pepper.

6 Coat the asparagus and broccoli in the remaining dressing and arrange around the edges of the plates. To finish, sprinkle each serving with a generous pinch of chopped, mixed herbs.

Moroccan carrot appetizer

Moroccan carrot appetizer

🔪 35 minutes, including cooling

Serves 4–6

900 g /2 lb carrots, quartered and cut into 5
*   cm /2 in lengths*
salt
2 garlic cloves, finely chopped
15–30 ml /1–2 tbls lemon juice
1.5 ml /¼ tsp cayenne pepper
1.5 ml /¼ tsp paprika
2.5 ml /½ tsp cumin powder
15–30 ml /1–2 tbls freshly chopped parsley

1 Cook the carrots in boiling salted water for 5–8 minutes, or until *al dente*, tender but still firm. Drain and refresh under cold running water, drain again and cool.

2 When the carrots are cold, toss with the finely chopped garlic, lemon juice, cayenne pepper, paprika, cumin powder and salt to taste. Sprinkle with parsley and serve.

Mixed bean salad with tomatoes

Serves 6
175 g /6 oz green beans
salt
200 g /7 oz canned haricot beans, drained
225 g /8 oz small tomatoes, quartered
10 black olives, stoned
4 canned anchovy fillets, drained and finely chopped
For the vinaigrette
90 ml /6 tbls olive oil
30 ml /2 tbls red wine vinegar
1 small garlic clove, finely chopped
30 ml /2 tbls finely chopped parsley
coarse salt and freshly ground black pepper

1   Top and tail the green beans. Bring a saucepan of salted water to the boil and blanch the beans for 3–4 minutes, or until lightly cooked but still crisp. Drain, rinse under cold running water and drain again.
2   In a serving dish, combine the blanched beans, drained haricot beans, quartered tomatoes, stoned black olives and finely chopped anchovy fillets. Toss lightly but thoroughly until well mixed.
3   Make the vinaigrette: in a small bowl, combine the olive oil, red wine vinegar, finely chopped garlic and parsley. Season to taste with coarse salt and freshly ground black pepper. Beat with a fork until the mixture emulsifies. Pour the vinaigrette over the salad, toss lightly to coat and serve immediately.

 20 minutes

Cucumber with fresh dill

Serves 4
2 medium-sized cucumbers
50 g /2 oz butter
salt and freshly ground black pepper
3 sprigs of fresh dill
25 g /1 oz cold, diced butter
chopped fresh dill, to serve
dill sprigs, to garnish

1   Peel the cucumbers. Cut each in half lengthways and remove the seeds with a teaspoon. Cut each half into 25 mm /1 in chunks and then slice these lengthways to make batons each 6 mm /¼ in wide.
2   Put the butter and 120 ml /8 tbls water in a saucepan. Bring to the boil and stir to blend. Add the cucumber batons. Season with salt and freshly ground black pepper to taste. Add the sprigs of fresh dill, cover and simmer gently for 20 minutes, shaking the pan occasionally.
3   Transfer the cucumber batons to a heated serving dish with a slotted spoon. Arrange the batons in neat rows and keep warm.
4   Discard the sprigs of dill and, over a moderate heat, whisk the diced butter, a piece at a time, into the liquids remaining in the saucepan.
5   Adjust the seasoning and pour over the cucumber batons. Serve the cucumber immediately sprinkled with fresh dill and garnished with dill sprigs.

50 minutes

Leeks and carrots vinaigrette

Serves 4
6 medium-sized young leeks
6 medium-sized carrots
salt
For the vinaigrette
90 ml /6 tbls olive oil
30 ml /2 tbls red wine vinegar
1 garlic clove, finely chopped
5 ml /1 tsp Dijon mustard
15 ml /1 tbls finely chopped fresh parsley
coarse salt
freshly ground black pepper

1   Trim the leeks. Cut them into 5 cm /2 in lengths, and then lengthways into quarters. Wash carefully in several changes of water to remove any dirt and grit.
2   Peel the carrots, cut off and discard the tops. Cut into 5 cm /2 in lengths and then lengthways into quarters.
3   Put the carrots in a saucepan of cold salted water. Bring to the boil and boil for 8–10 minutes, or until tender. Drain the carrots well and leave them until lukewarm.
4   Meanwhile, bring a saucepan of cold salted water to the boil. Add the leeks and cook for 4–5 minutes, or until just tender. Drain well and leave until lukewarm.
5   Make the vinaigrette dressing: in a bowl, combine the olive oil, red wine vinegar, finely chopped garlic, Dijon mustard and finely chopped parsley. Season to taste with coarse salt and freshly ground black pepper. Beat the dressing with a fork until the vinaigrette mixture emulsifies.
6   Arrange the carrots and leeks neatly in a serving dish. Dress with the vinaigrette and serve at room temperature.

🍴 25 minutes, plus cooling

Stuffed courgette appetizer

Serves 8
8 courgettes, 10–12.5 cm /4–5 in long
salt and freshly ground black pepper
1½ Spanish onions, finely chopped
1 garlic clove, finely chopped
lettuce leaves
6 medium-sized tomatoes, skinned, seeded and chopped
2 green peppers, finely chopped
30 ml /2 tbls chopped gherkins
10 ml /2 tsp finely chopped fresh parsley
10 ml /2 tsp finely chopped fresh basil
sprigs of parsley, to garnish
For the vinaigrette
45 ml /3 tbls wine vinegar or lemon juice
salt and freshly ground black pepper
pinch of mustard powder or 5 ml /1 tsp French mustard
135–180 ml /9–12 tbls olive oil

1   Wipe the courgettes and trim off the ends. Drop the courgettes, unpeeled, into salted boiling water and simmer for about 5 minutes. Drain and cool.
2   Meanwhile, to make the vinaigrette, stir the wine vinegar or lemon juice with a generous pinch of salt, freshly ground black pepper and dry or French mustard to taste. Beat in the olive oil with a fork until the dressing thickens and emulsifies.
3   Cut the cooled courgettes in half lengthways and carefully scoop out the seeds. Lay the courgettes, cut sides up, in a flat dish.
4   Combine one-third of the finely chopped onion and the garlic; cover the courgettes with this mixture. Sprinkle one-third of the vinaigrette over them, cover with foil and allow to marinate in this mixture in the refrigerator for at least 4 hours.
5   When ready to serve, remove the courgettes from the marinade, discard the onion and garlic and the marinade and wipe the courgettes dry. Arrange the courgette halves on crisp lettuce leaves. Combine the remaining vinaigrette with the chopped tomatoes, finely chopped green peppers and remaining onion, gherkins, parsley and basil, and season with salt and freshly ground pepper.
6   Spoon the tomato mixture into the hollowed-out courgettes, garnish with sprigs of parsley and serve.

🍴 40 minutes, plus 4 hours marinating

VEGETABLE SOUPS

Although cans of soups are an excellent store-cupboard stand-by, there is nothing to beat a good home-made soup. Here is a selection – from warming family dishes to more exotic ones.

Hot or chilled, chunky or creamy in texture, vegetable soups are the most versatile of dishes and lend themselves to a variety of occasions. By adding substantial ingredients – pulses, pasta shapes or thick rounds of French bread and cheese – they become nourishing, filling meals in themselves. More delicate ingredients – cucumbers, avocados and lettuce – make lighter, puréed soups which are excellent as starters. Pretty in colour, a swirl of cream or yoghurt, fresh garnishes or shaped croûtons make them even more eye-catching.

A big advantage of soup is that it is both easy and economical to make. It is important, though, to use only good-quality ingredients as the soup will be only as good as what goes into it. Preparation is best done just before you are ready to start cooking. If possible, leave the vegetables unpeeled, this way you retain their vitamins, as well as adding texture and colour to your soup. Never leave vegetables to soak in water as this robs them of nutrients, and don't overcook them so that they lose their shape and 'bite'.

Minestrone

🕐 🍴 soaking beans overnight, 1½ hours cooking, then 1 hour

Serves 4
40 g /1½ oz dried haricot beans, soaked overnight in cold water to cover
30 ml /2 tbls olive oil
1 medium-sized onion, chopped
1 garlic clove, chopped
1 small leek, trimmed, washed and sliced
1 L /1¾ pt well-flavoured stock, home-made or from a cube
bouquet garni
1 medium-sized carrot, sliced
2 celery sticks, sliced
10 ml /2 tsp tomato purée
¼ small cabbage, shredded
2 slices bacon, rind removed, cut into strips
40 g /1½ oz pasta shapes or broken spaghetti
30 ml /2 tbls freshly grated Parmesan cheese
salt and freshly ground black pepper
30 ml /2 tbls freshly chopped parsley
Parmesan cheese, freshly grated, to serve

1 Drain the beans, put them in a saucepan and cover generously with fresh, cold water. Bring slowly to the boil, cover and simmer for about 1½ hours until tender.
2 Heat the oil in a large, flameproof casserole over low heat. Add the onion, garlic and leek and stir well. Cover the pan and cook gently for 5 minutes, shaking the pan occasionally.
3 Drain the beans and add to the pan. Pour in the stock and bring to the boil. Add the bouquet garni, carrot and celery and stir well. Cover the pan and simmer for 15 minutes. Stir in the tomato purée and cabbage and simmer, covered, for a further 10 minutes.
4 Meanwhile, fry the bacon strips gently until cooked, drain and add to the soup. Bring back to the boil and add the pasta. Reduce the heat and simmer, uncovered, for about 8 minutes, or until the pasta is cooked.
5 Remove and discard the bouquet garni. Stir in the 30 ml /2 tbls Parmesan cheese and season carefully with salt and freshly ground black pepper. Just before serving, stir in the chopped parsley. Serve the soup with extra grated Parmesan cheese handed separately in a small bowl.

● Beef, chicken or vegetable stock are all suitable, and the vegetables can be varied according to season.

Minestrone

French mushroom soup

🍴 45 minutes

Serves 4

6 dried mushrooms
50 g /2 oz butter
45 ml /3 tbls flour
700 ml /1¼ pt chicken stock, home-made or
*   from a cube*
500 g /1 lb mushrooms, wiped and thinly
*   sliced*
juice of ¼–½ lemon
150 ml /5 fl oz thick cream
30 ml /2 tbls freshly chopped parsley
salt and freshly ground black pepper
freshly grated nutmeg

1   Place the dried mushrooms in a bowl, pour over 150 ml /5 fl oz boiling water and leave them to soak for 10 minutes. Drain and press dry, then slice them thinly and reserve.
2   Melt the butter in a fairly large saucepan, stir in the flour and cook for 3–4 minutes. Remove the pan from the heat and gradually stir in the chicken stock. Return to the heat and bring slowly to the boil, stirring all the time.
3   Add the sliced dried mushrooms to the pan, half of the sliced fresh mushrooms and lemon juice to taste, and simmer for 5 minutes. Purée the soup in an electric blender, or rub it through a fine sieve.
4   Return the soup to a clean saucepan, stir in the thick cream, chopped parsley and remaining sliced mushrooms and season to taste with salt, pepper and nutmeg. Reheat the soup gently and serve immediately.

Greek vegetable soup

🍴 30 minutes

Serves 4

¼ green pepper
white part of 1 leek
1 celery stick
½ Spanish onion
250 g /8 oz potatoes
3 carrots
¼ head fennel
600 ml /1 pt well-flavoured beef stock,
*   home-made or from a cube*
salt and freshly ground black pepper
3 large mushrooms, sliced
3 tomatoes, blanched, skinned, seeded and
*   coarsely chopped*
30 ml /2 tbls olive oil
30 ml /2 tbls very coarsely chopped fresh
*   parsley*

1   Thinly slice the first 7 ingredients. Place them in a saucepan with the stock and season to taste with salt and pepper.
2   Bring slowly to the boil, skim if necessary, then lower the heat and simmer

for 15–20 minutes, adding the sliced mushrooms and coarsely chopped tomatoes for the last 5 minutes of the cooking time.
3   Just before serving, add the olive oil and coarsely chopped parsley.

Cucumber soup

🍴 50 minutes

Serves 4

2 medium-sized cucumbers, peeled
75 g /3 oz butter
1 small onion, chopped
50 g /2 oz flour
300 ml /10 fl oz milk
600 ml /1 pt chicken stock, home-made or
*   from a cube*
salt and white pepper
60 ml /4 tbls thin cream

1   Set aside a 10 cm /4 in length from one of the cucumbers and slice the rest thinly. Blanch by dropping the slices into boiling water for 2 minutes, then drain.
2   Melt 25 g /1 oz of the butter in a saucepan. Add the cucumber slices, cover the pan and sweat gently for 15 minutes.
3   Meanwhile, make a roux in another saucepan by melting the rest of the butter, softening the chopped onion in it, and gradually stirring in the flour to make a smooth paste. Stir in the milk gradually and bring to the boil to make a thick, smooth sauce. Add the blanched cucumber and the

Red lentil soup

stock. Season and simmer for 15 minutes.
4   Purée in a blender or sieve and return to the rinsed pan. Reheat and garnish each serving with a swirl of cream and the reserved cucumber, cut into very thin slices.

Red lentil soup

🍴 1 hour

Serves 4

25 g /1 oz butter
1 large onion, peeled and chopped
1 stick celery, chopped
150 g /5 oz dried red lentils
1 L /1½ pt chicken stock, home-made or
*   from a cube*
1.5 ml /¼ tsp ground cloves
1.5 ml /¼ tsp ground allspice
salt and freshly ground black pepper
finely chopped fresh parsley, to garnish

1   Melt the butter in a large saucepan and fry the onion and celery lightly for 10 minutes, but do not brown.
2   Add the lentils, stock and spices to the saucepan. Bring up to the boil, then turn down the heat and simmer the lentils gently for 30–35 minutes, or until they are soft.
3   Liquidize the soup, then reheat it and season to taste with salt and black pepper. Garnish the soup with the freshly chopped parsley and serve immediately.

the beans are soft. Allow to cool slightly.
3 Blend the beans and their cooking liquid to a purée – blend in batches and add a little of the milk if the purée is too stiff in consistency and therefore hard to work.
4 Return the purée to a clean pan and gradually stir in the milk. Reheat gently, stirring frequently, but do not allow the soup to come to the boil. Season to taste with salt, pepper and a grating of nutmeg.
5 To serve, ladle the soup into warmed individual bowls, swirl 15 ml /1 tbls sour cream into each portion and garnish with the reserved green spring onion stalks.

Fennel soup

This soup has a most delicate and unusual taste and is equally delicious served hot or cold. The aniseed flavour of the fennel is enhanced by adding a touch of Pernod just before serving.

1 hour, plus chilling
if serving cold

Serves 4–6
2 medium-sized bulbs of fennel
60 ml /4 tbls walnut oil
1.7 L /3 pt chicken stock, home-made or
  from a cube
salt
freshly ground black pepper
150 ml /5 fl oz thick cream
5 ml /1 tsp Pernod

1 Trim any feathery fronds of fennel from the top of the bulbs, chop them finely and reserve them for the garnish.
2 Wash and finely chop the bulbs, discarding the outer layers if bruised or discoloured.
3 Put the oil in a large saucepan over moderate heat and add the chopped fennel. Cook for 1–2 minutes, then lower the heat and let the fennel sweat gently for 10 minutes.
4 Add the chicken stock, bring to the boil and then simmer for 20–25 minutes, or until the fennel is tender. Remove from the heat and cool.
5 Put the cooled liquid into a liquidizer and blend. Return to the pan and reheat gently.
6 Add salt and freshly ground black pepper to taste and, just before serving, stir in the cream and the Pernod. Pour into a warmed soup tureen or individual bowls, garnish with the reserved feathery fronds, and serve immediately. If you are serving the soup cold, let it cool, then chill it for a few hours before garnishing and serving.

Pea-pod soup

This soup, which is a Swiss recipe, is a good way of using up the humble pea-pod after the spring peas have been enjoyed as a vegetable. It can be served either hot with croûtons or cold sprinkled with chives.

50 minutes,
plus 2 hours chilling if serving cold

Watercress and onion soup

30 minutes

Serves 4
25 g /1 oz butter
2 medium-sized onions, finely chopped
15 ml /1 tbls flour
600 ml /1 pt chicken stock, home-made or
  from a cube
1.5 ml /¼ tsp ground mace
salt
freshly ground black pepper
1 bay leaf
300 ml /10 fl oz dry, white wine
75 g /3 oz watercress, stems and leaves,
  finely chopped
4 slices of French bread, toasted
125 g /4 oz Gruyère cheese, finely grated

1 Melt the butter in a saucepan over a low heat. Add the onions and cook, stirring occasionally, until they are golden.
2 Stir in the flour and cook for 1 minute. Stir in the stock, bring to the boil, stirring, then add the mace, salt and pepper and bay leaf. Simmer the soup, uncovered, for 10 minutes.
3 Remove the bay leaf and discard. Pour in the wine and add the watercress. Bring the soup to just below boiling point and then remove it from the heat.
4 Put a slice of toasted French bread in the

Watercress and onion soup

bottom of each of 4 hot, deep soup bowls. Top them with the cheese, pour the soup over and serve at once.

Broad bean and parsley soup

40 minutes

Serves 4
50 g /2 oz butter
1 bunch spring onions, trimmed and
  chopped
15 g /½ oz freshly chopped parsley
500 g /1 lb shelled or frozen broad beans
425 ml /15 fl oz creamy milk
salt
freshly ground black pepper
freshly grated nutmeg
60 ml /4 tbls soured cream

1 Melt the butter in a medium-sized pan over low heat. Reserve a handful of tender, chopped green stalks from the spring onions and add the remainder to the pan. Cover and cook them gently for about 5 minutes until softened.
2 Stir in the chopped parsley and the shelled or frozen broad beans. Pour in enough water to barely cover the beans, add a pinch of salt and then bring the liquid to the boil. Cover the pan, and simmer until

Serves 5–6
15 g /½ oz butter or margarine
30 ml /2 tbls chopped onion
500 g /1 lb pea-pods, topped and tailed
3–4 large outside leaves of lettuce
850 ml /1½ pt chicken stock, home-made or
*   from a cube*
150 ml /5 fl oz thin cream
salt
freshly ground black pepper
croûtons or finely chopped fresh chives, to
*   serve*

1 Melt the butter or margarine in a large saucepan over very low heat, add the chopped onion, cover and leave the onion to sweat for 8–10 minutes. Do not allow it to brown.
2 Add the pea-pods, lettuce leaves and stock to the pan and bring the mixture to the boil. Reduce the heat and simmer, covered, for 20 minutes, or until tender.
3 Purée the mixture in a blender or press it through a sieve. To serve the soup hot, return it to the rinsed-out saucepan, season with salt and pepper, add the cream and reheat it without boiling. Serve in warmed bowls with croûtons.
4 To serve cold, chill the soup in the refrigerator for 2 hours, then skim off any fat. Divide the soup among 5–6 bowls, swirl a little cream into the top of each bowl of soup, sprinkle with chopped chives and serve.

Brussels sprouts soup

 30 minutes

Serves 4
25 g /1 oz butter
1 medium-sized onion, sliced
700 g /1½ lb Brussels sprouts, trimmed
850 ml /1½ pt chicken stock, home-made or
*   from a cube*
salt and freshly ground black pepper
grated nutmeg
150 ml /5 fl oz thick cream
To garnish
2 slices of lean bacon, rind removed and
*   diced*

1 Melt the butter in a large saucepan, add the onion and cook over a moderate heat for 3–4 minutes, until the onion is soft but not brown.
2 Cut any very large Brussels sprouts in half. Add the sprouts to the pan with the stock, bring to the boil, cover the pan and simmer for 20 minutes. Remove the pan from the heat and purée the contents in a blender or through a food mill.
3 Return the purée to the rinsed pan, season to taste with salt, pepper and nutmeg, and stir in the cream. Heat gently.
4 To prepare the garnish, fry the bacon in a non-stick pan over a moderate heat until it is crisp and dry. Remove it from the pan with a slotted spoon and set it aside.
5 Pour the soup into a heated tureen and garnish with the bacon. Serve immediately.

Provençal vegetable soup

 50 minutes

Serves 4–6
salt
bouquet garni
1 large potato, diced
1 large onion, chopped
1 celery stick, finely sliced
2 carrots, scraped and sliced
225 g /8 oz French beans
225 g /8 oz runner beans
2 courgettes, topped and tailed but unpeeled
100 g /4 oz pasta shells
For the pistou sauce
3–4 large garlic cloves
60 ml /4 tbls freshly chopped sweet basil
*   leaves*
50 g /2 oz freshly grated Parmesan cheese
2 medium-sized tomatoes, skinned, seeded
*   and coarsely chopped*
60 ml /4 tbls olive oil

1 Bring 1.7 L /3 pt water with 5 ml /1 tsp salt to the boil in a large flameproof casserole. Add the bouquet garni, potato, onion, celery and carrots. Bring back to the boil, then cover the pan, and simmer for about 10 minutes, or until the vegetables are tender.
2 Top and tail the beans and remove any fibrous strings. Slice the French beans in half, slice the runner beans into 15 mm /½ in lengths, and slice the courgettes fairly thickly. Add the beans, courgettes and pasta to the casserole and simmer, uncovered, for 10–15 minutes until tender.
3 While the soup is cooking, prepare the pistou. Pound the garlic and basil, with salt and pepper to taste, to a paste using a mortar and pestle. Gradually work in the cheese, alternating with the tomatoes. Then slowly work in the olive oil, a few drops at a time to start with, to make a thick sauce.
4 Remove the bouquet garni from the soup and discard. Blend 60 ml /4 tbls of the hot soup into the sauce, then stir this into the rest of the soup and serve.

Provençal vegetable soup

Soufflé onion soup

Serves 6

40 g /1½ oz butter
45 ml /3 tbls olive oil
2.5 ml /½ tsp caster sugar
525 g /1¼ lb onions, thinly sliced
1.4 L /2½ pt beef stock, home-
    made or from a cube
60 ml /4 tbls brandy
2.5 ml /½ tsp French mustard
salt
freshly ground black pepper
6 rounds of toasted and
    buttered French bread

For the soufflé mixture
20 g /¾ oz butter
22.5 ml /1½ tbls flour
150 ml /5 fl oz milk
2 egg yolks
60 ml /4 tbls grated Gruyère
    cheese
30 ml /2 tbls freshly grated
    Parmesan cheese
a pinch each of nutmeg,
    cayenne pepper, dry mustard
3 egg whites

1   In a large saucepan, heat the butter, olive oil and caster sugar.
Add the onions and cook over moderately low heat for 15–20
minutes, stirring to brown them evenly. When the onions are soft
and golden, stir in the beef stock gradually. Bring to the boil, lower
the heat, cover and simmer gently for 1 hour. The soup should
reduce to 1.1 L /2 pt.
2   Meanwhile, begin to make the soufflé mixture. Melt the butter
in a saucepan. Blend in the flour and stir over a low heat for 2–3
minutes to make a pale roux. In another saucepan, heat the milk,
then gradually add it to the roux, stirring to make a smooth sauce.
Bring to the boil and simmer over low heat, stirring with a whisk,
for 4–5 minutes until the sauce is thick and smooth. Remove the
pan from the heat. Cool the sauce slightly and beat in the egg yolks
1 at a time with a wooden spoon. Allow the sauce to cool.
3   Heat the oven to 230C /450F /gas 8.
4   Beat the grated Gruyère and Parmesan cheeses smoothly into
the tepid sauce and season generously with salt and black pepper
and a pinch each of nutmeg, cayenne pepper and dry mustard.
5   When the soup is cooked, stir in the brandy and French mustard
and season with salt and freshly ground black pepper to taste.
6   In a clean bowl, whisk the egg whites with a pinch of salt until
stiff but not dry. Stir about 30 ml /2 tbls beaten egg white into the
cheese sauce to soften it, then fold in the remainder.
7   Put a round of prepared French bread in the bottom of each of 6
ovenproof soup bowls. Divide the hot soup among them and when
the bread rises to the top, spoon over the soufflé mixture. Bake for
10 minutes in the oven, or until the soufflé toppings are well risen
and golden. Serve at once.

 1¾ hours

Chilled avocado and cucumber soup

Serves 8

4 large avocados
juice of ½ lemon
1.5 L /2½ pts well-flavoured chicken stock, home-made or from a
    cube, chilled thoroughly
salt and ground white pepper
8 drops of Tabasco sauce
150 ml /5 fl oz thick cream
a small piece of cucumber, trimmed
croûton shapes, to garnish

1   Peel and halve the avocados, then remove the stones. Brush the
avocados generously with lemon juice to prevent discoloration.
2   Purée the avocado halves with the chilled chicken stock until
smooth, either in an electric blender, or by rubbing through a very
fine sieve. Season to taste with salt and white pepper.
3   Add the Tabasco and thick cream to the avocado soup. Blend
thoroughly again, adjust the seasoning to taste and chill for 2 hours.
4   Cut the cucumber into thin slices and then quarter each slice.
Stir the cucumber into the soup and serve this in small, individual
bowls. Garnish with croûton shapes.

●   Freshly fried croûtons make a pretty garnish; cut them into
different shapes with aspic cutters, if you own them, tiny biscuit
cutters or an apple corer. Fry them in butter over a medium heat
until golden.

20 minutes,
plus 2 hours chilling time

Watercress vichyssoise

Serves 6
6 large leeks, trimmed
50 g /2 oz butter
4 medium-sized potatoes, sliced
1 L /1¾ pt chicken stock, home-made or from a cube
salt and freshly ground black pepper
a pinch of freshly grated nutmeg
425 ml /15 fl oz thick cream
60 ml /4 tbls finely chopped watercress leaves
sprigs of watercress, to garnish

1 Trim the green tops from the leeks. (Reserve them for another dish.) Cut the white part into 25 mm /1 in thick slices and rinse them thoroughly in cold water to remove all grit. Drain them well and pat dry with absorbent paper.
2 In a large, heavy-based saucepan, melt the butter over a medium-low heat. Add the sliced leeks and sauté until soft, without allowing them to colour. Add the sliced potatoes and the chicken stock to the pan and season to taste with salt, freshly ground black pepper and a pinch of freshly grated nutmeg. Simmer for 15–20 minutes, or until the vegetables are quite tender. Remove the pan from the heat.
3 Using a wooden spoon, press the vegetables and stock through a fine nylon sieve. Blend the thick cream into the resulting purée, then chill the soup in the refrigerator for 2–3 hours.
4 Just before serving, stir in 60 ml /4 tbls finely chopped watercress leaves. Pour the soup into individual bowls and garnish with the watercress sprigs.

● Leek soup was transformed from humble to grand status by Louis Diat, when he served it chilled at the Ritz-Carlton hotel in New York. He called his new creation Vichyssoise, in honour of the French spa town of Vichy, near to where he was born.

 45 minutes
plus 2–3 hours chilling

Fresh lettuce soup

Serves 6
2 medium-sized lettuces
50 g /2 oz butter
2 shallots, finely chopped
100 g /4 oz frozen leaf spinach
600 ml /1 pt well-flavoured chicken stock, home-made or from a cube
salt and ground black pepper
150 ml /5 fl oz thick cream
15 ml /1 tbls finely chopped fresh parsley
15 ml /1 tbls finely chopped fresh chervil
For the bechamel sauce (makes 300 ml /10 fl oz)
425 ml /15 fl oz milk
½ bay leaf
6 white peppercorns
a good pinch of freshly grated nutmeg
40 g /1½ oz butter
30 ml /2 tbls flour, sieved

1 Wash the lettuces and dry well. Remove any discoloured leaves and hard stalks, shred the remaining leaves and reserve.
2 Melt the butter in a saucepan and add the finely chopped shallots. Cook over a medium heat for 5–7 minutes, or until just soft, stirring occasionally with a wooden spoon. Add the shredded lettuce and leaf spinach and simmer for 10 minutes, stirring frequently.
3 Add the chicken stock and bring to the boil. Reduce the heat, cover and simmer gently for 15 minutes.
4 Meanwhile, make the bechamel sauce. Add the milk, bay leaf, peppercorns and nutmeg to a saucepan and bring almost to the boil, then leave to infuse.
5 Melt the butter in another saucepan and when it just begins to bubble add the sieved flour. Stir it with a wooden spoon or wire whisk for 2–3 minutes until the mixture is smooth but has not changed colour.
6 Strain the infused milk. Add ¼ of the milk into the roux, off the heat. Return it to a low heat and bring to the boil, stirring.
7 As the sauce begins to thicken, add the remainder of the milk, a little at a time, stirring briskly between additions. Continue stirring until the sauce bubbles, and so is cooked, then simmer it until it reduces to 275 ml /10 fl oz.
8 Season the soup with salt and freshly ground black pepper to taste, then stir in the bechamel sauce and simmer for a further 5 minutes. Leave to cool for a few minutes, then purée the soup in a blender until smooth and return it to a clean saucepan. Stir in the thick cream, finely chopped parsley and chervil and reheat. Adjust the seasoning and serve immediately.

making the bechamel sauce,
then 50 minutes

COOKING PULSES

The popularity of wholefood and vegetarian cookery in recent years has highlighted the possibilities of nutritious dried pulses. Learn all about the different varieties of bean, pea and lentil and how to cook them whole.

Pulses — peas, beans and lentils — are the seeds of pod-bearing or leguminous plants and are used in cooking in dried form. High in protein, they are an important part of a well-balanced vegetarian diet, but since they are inexpensive and make nutritious, easily-prepared and delicious meals, they well deserve more general use.

Buying and storing pulses

Most supermarkets stock a good range of the most popular dried pulses such as peas, butter beans, haricot beans and lentils. A choice of more unusual beans and lentils are available in ethnic, health food and buy-in-bulk wholefood shops.

Dried pulses can, in theory, be stored almost indefinitely in covered containers in dry, cool conditions. But, in fact, the older they are, the tougher they get, and the longer they take to cook. For freshness, it is best to buy pulses from a store with a quick turnover, and in quantities you can reasonably expect to use within six months or so.

Cooked butter beans, flageolets, red kidney beans and other pulses are available canned but are less economical than those bought dry.

Preparing pulses

Washing: even packaged dried pulses should be thoroughly washed. Put them in a colander in a bowl of cold water and then discard any that are discoloured and any grit.

Soaking: most dried pulses need to be soaked before cooking, to replace some of the moisture that has been processed out of them. Use either of the following methods.

For long soaking: put the pulses in a large bowl, cover them with about three times their volume of water and leave to soak for 4–6 hours, or overnight, if more convenient.

For short soaking: bring the pulses to the boil in a large saucepan of unsalted water and boil for 3–5 minutes. Remove from the heat, cover and soak for 40–60 minutes.

Cooking pulses whole

Pulses may be cooked in the soaking liquid, which will contain the vitamins given off during soaking, but also some gases which

From top centre, diagonally in rows: mung beans, soya beans and puy lentils; butter beans, red lentils and chick-peas; pinto beans, yellow lentils, black-eyed beans and flageolets; fava beans, adzuki beans and black beans

can cause indigestion. So, if you prefer, drain the pulses after soaking, rinse them thoroughly in cold, running water, and cook in fresh water or stock.

Cooking on top of the stove: put the soaked pulses in a large saucepan and cover them with cold water, vegetable or meat stock. Add flavourings such as celery, herbs, bay leaf, onion or garlic, and a few grindings of black pepper. Bring the liquid to the boil, reduce the heat and simmer the pulses gently. Add salt to taste at the end of the cooking time.

Pressure cooking with the same additions reduces cooking times by well over half.

Casseroling: all pulses can be cooked successfully with meat and other vegetables in casseroles, but remember to add extra liquid as the pulses soak up a great deal. Check from time to time during cooking in case more liquid is needed.

Electric slow-cooking: boil all pulses except split lentils for 2–10 minutes before adding to the pot.

Dried peas

Chick-peas are light golden brown, like small, round nuts, and very tough. They need long soaking and cooking and can be served in stews, soups or salads, or ground as the base of Greek Hummus.

Dried beans

Adzuki or Aduki are tiny, round, dark red beans with a strong, sweet, slightly nutty flavour, making them ideal to serve with game and rich meat dishes.

Black beans are kidney beans which are white inside and have black, shiny skins. Also called turtle beans, they figure prominently in the cooking of African and West Indian countries.

Black-eyed beans: these small, cream-coloured kidney beans with black spots come mainly from California. They are more easily digested than most other pulses.

Butter beans are also known as Madagascar or Calico beans and are very similar to Lima beans. Large, flat and white, they are popular in soups, stews and casseroles and as a vegetable accompaniment. They are available cooked in cans.

Flageolet beans are considered by many to be the finest of all pulses, since they are harvested when very young and small. They are white or pale green, and are delicious cooked with lamb, or in salads. They are also available cooked in cans.

Haricot beans, which are small, oval and cream in colour, are the dried seeds of French beans. They are the main ingredient in Boston baked beans and feature, too, in French cassoulet, and in mixed salads also containing cooked fresh French beans.

Mung beans, which are small, round and an attractive bright green, are the seeds of Chinese bean sprouts. They cook quickly and do not need pre-soaking. They have a sweetish flavour and hold their shape well.

Pinto beans are pink, speckled kidney beans which make eye-catching side dishes or salads.

Red kidney beans are traditionally served in hot, spicy dishes, soups and salads. After soaking in cold water, they should be boiled

fast for 15 minutes before they are simmered. This is particularly important, to destroy a poisonous enzyme present in the bean. Red kidney beans are also available cooked in cans.

Soya beans are the most important of all the pulses because they contain first-class protein and in greater quantity, weight for weight, than fish, meat or dairy products.

Soya beans are the toughest of the pulses, and need long soaking and cooking, though a variety called 'soya splits', which is partly precooked, can be fully cooked in 30 minutes. Soya beans have little taste, and are better cooked with plenty of added flavourings.

Dried lentils

Lentils are available both whole and split. Soaking is not essential for either type, but cuts down on cooking time.

Whole lentils may be white, green, brown, pink, yellow or grey. They do not disintegrate in cooking and are served as an accompanying vegetable and are good in soups and casseroles. Puy, or French, lentils do not have the earthy taste of other types, and are popular in Italian salads with onion, mint, garlic, olive oil and hard-boiled eggs.

Split lentils, or Egyptian lentils, are red and do not have any flavour of their own. They disintegrate in cooking, so are usually served as a purée.

Falafel

overnight soaking, then 65 minutes

Falafel

Serves 6
225 g /8 oz chick-peas
1 slice of white bread, crusts removed
2 garlic cloves, chopped
30 ml /2 tbls freshly chopped parsley
25 g /1 oz burghul (cracked wheat), rinsed and drained
2.5 ml /½ tsp freshly ground coriander seeds
2.5 ml /½ tsp ground cumin
1.5 ml /¼ tsp freshly ground black pepper
1.5 ml /¼ tsp cayenne pepper
5 ml /1 tsp salt
oil for deep frying
mixed salad, to serve
6 pitta breads, to serve

1 Soak the chick-peas in water to cover for 8 hours, or overnight.
2 Drain and rinse the chick-peas and blend them in a food processor or blender, putting them through twice, if necessary.
3 Soak the bread in water and squeeze it dry. Chop the bread with the garlic and parsley and add it to the chick-peas. Add the wheat, spices and salt, mix thoroughly and leave in a cool place for at least 15 minutes.
4 Shape the mixture with wet hands into small balls about 25 mm /1 in in diameter.
5 In a deep-fat frier, preferably with a frying basket, heat the oil until it is very hot, about 180C /350F, or until a cube of bread browns in 60 seconds. Deep fry the balls, a few at a time, for 2–3 minutes, keeping the finished falafel warm as you continue frying. Serve in pitta bread with mixed salad.

Spiced lentils

🔪 1½ hours

Serves 4
225 g /8 oz continental lentils or split peas
6 cauliflower florets
3 radishes, cut in 15 mm /½ in slices
1 small courgette, cut in 25 mm /1 in slices
5 ml /1 tsp sugar
salt
15 ml /1 tbls ghee or clarified butter
2.5 ml /½ tsp onion seeds
1 green chilli, slightly slit
1 dried red chilli, slightly slit
25 mm /1 in fresh root ginger, peeled and
     chopped
boiled rice, to serve

1   Wash the pulses and place them in a
saucepan. Cover with 5 cm /2 in water,
bring to the boil and simmer for 50–60
minutes, until the pulses begin to be tender.
Top up the water to keep them covered.
2   Add the vegetables and cook until both
the pulses and vegetables are tender, about
10 minutes. Add the sugar and salt to taste
and remove the pan from the heat.
3   Heat the ghee or butter in a frying-pan
over medium heat, add the onion seeds and,
when they begin to pop up, add the prepared
chillies and chopped ginger. Stir the spices
for 1 minute. Remove the chillies, if wished,
and mix the spices thoroughly into the
pulses. Serve hot with plain boiled rice.

Split pea purée

🕐🍴 overnight soaking,
     then 1 hour 10 minutes

Serves 4
125 g /4 oz green split peas, soaked
     overnight
2 slices back bacon, finely diced
25 g /1 oz butter
salt and freshly ground black pepper
1 large bulb of fennel

1   Drain the split peas and place them in a
small saucepan. Add enough fresh, cold
water to cover them by 25 mm /1 in. Bring
to the boil, lower the heat and simmer for
30–40 minutes, until the peas are soft.
Strain the peas, reserving the liquid.
2   Let the peas cool a little, then purée
them in an electric blender or food
processor, adding enough of the cooking
liquid to make a soft purée. Transfer the
purée to a saucepan and reserve.
3   In a frying-pan, sauté the finely diced
bacon in its own fat until golden but still
soft. With a slotted spoon, transfer the
bacon to the saucepan, with the purée. Add
the butter and reheat the purée over a low
heat. Season to taste with salt and pepper.
4   Remove 4 large leaves from the fennel
bulb and blanch them in boiling, salted
water for 3 minutes. Drain well and place on
a heated serving plate. Fill each leaf with
split pea purée and serve immediately, as a
garnish to pork, gammon or smoked meats.

Haricot beans in tomato sauce

In Bordeaux, France, haricot beans are a
regional alternative to potatoes, to serve
with roast meat, particularly lamb.
Haricot beans in tomato sauce can also
be served as an unusual and substantial
first-course.

🕐🍴 soaking the beans,
     then 2 hours

Serves 4
200 g /7 oz dried haricot beans, rinsed and
     soaked overnight in cold water
60 ml /4 tbls oil
salt
100 g /4 oz onions, chopped
5 ml /1 tsp tomato purée
225 g /8 oz canned, or blanched, skinned,
     fresh tomatoes
a pinch of thyme
a pinch of crumbled bay leaf
a pinch of freshly grated nutmeg
1.5 ml /¼ tsp freshly chopped parsley
freshly ground black pepper

1   Drain the beans and dry them with a
tea-towel. Heat 45 ml /3 tbls of the oil in a
saucepan over a medium heat and tip the
beans in. Stir them well to coat with oil.
2   Barely cover the beans with boiling
water and simmer them gently, covered, for
1½ hours, adding more water when
necessary. Five minutes before they are
done, add salt to taste.
3   Meanwhile, heat the rest of the oil in
another saucepan over a low heat and sauté
the onions until soft but not coloured. Add
the tomato purée, stir, and add the
tomatoes, thyme, bay leaf and nutmeg.
Cover and cook over a very low heat for
about 45 minutes.
4   Drain the beans, return them to their
pan and strain the tomato sauce over them.
Cook them gently for a further 10 minutes,
check the seasoning and serve.

Butter beans in hot yoghurt sauce

🕐🍴 overnight soaking,
     then 3 hours

Serves 4
250 g /9 oz butter or lima beans, soaked
     overnight in cold water
850 ml /1½ pt stock, home-made or from a
     cube (see below)
bouquet garni
2 medium-sized potatoes
1 large carrot
1 large onion
2 celery sticks
25 g /1 oz butter
15 ml /1 tbls wholemeal flour
60 ml /4 tbls natural yoghurt
60 ml /4 tbls freshly chopped parsley
juice of ½ lemon
salt and freshly ground black pepper

1   Drain the soaked beans and place them
in a saucepan with the stock and bouquet
garni. Bring to the boil, cover and simmer
them for 1 hour.
2   Dice the vegetables, add them to the
pan, cover and continue to simmer for
another half an hour, or until the beans are
completely tender.
3   Remove the bouquet garni from the pan.
Strain off and reserve the stock. Return the
beans and vegetables to the pan.
4   In a small saucepan, melt the butter over
a moderate heat. Stir in the flour and cook
for 1 minute. Stir in the stock and bring to
the boil, stirring. Simmer for 2–3 minutes,
until you have a thick sauce.
5   Take the pan from the heat and stir in
the yoghurt, parsley and lemon juice. Season
well and stir into the beans.
6   Reheat gently to serve, but do not allow
the mixture to boil or it will curdle because
of the combination of the yoghurt and the
lemon juice.

●   Either vegetable or chicken stock may be
used in this dish.
●   Serve this dish as a main course or as a
vegetable accompaniment; it will go
particularly well with pork.

90

Parslied flageolets

 soaking the flageolets, then 35 minutes

Serves 4
225 g /8 oz dried flageolets, soaked
600 ml /1 pt chicken stock, home-made or from a cube
1 Spanish onion, finely chopped
25 g /1 oz butter
2 garlic cloves, finely chopped
30–45 ml /2–3 tbls finely chopped fresh parsley
salt and freshly ground black pepper

1 Drain the flageolets and place them in a large saucepan, add the chicken stock and finely chopped onion. Bring to the boil, then simmer gently for about 30 minutes, or until the flageolets are tender.
2 Heat the butter in a saucepan, add the finely chopped garlic and the finely chopped parsley and cook for 1 minute. Add the flageolets and the cooking stock and toss well. Season with salt and freshly ground black pepper to taste. Transfer to a heated serving dish and serve immediately.

Marrow rings with lentil stuffing

1 hour 30 minutes

Serves 4
125 g /4 oz split red lentils
45 ml /3 tbls oil, plus extra for greasing
1 small marrow
1 small onion, finely chopped
1 carrot, finely chopped
1 celery stick, thinly sliced
2 tomatoes, blanched, skinned, seeded and chopped
5 ml /1 tsp dried basil
2.5 ml /½ tsp ground coriander
45 ml /3 tbls fresh breadcrumbs
1 medium-sized egg, lightly beaten
175 ml /6 fl oz chicken stock, home-made or from a cube
50 g /2 oz Cheddar cheese, grated
salt
freshly ground black pepper
15 ml /1 tbls tomato purée

Spiced lentils

1 Cook the lentils in boiling water until soft, about 35 minutes, then drain.
2 Meanwhile, heat the oven to 180C / 350F /gas 4. Grease a shallow baking dish.
3 Cut a slice from each end of the marrow. Cut the marrow into 4 slices about 5 cm /2 in thick and cut away and discard the seeds and tough centre fibres. Arrange the marrow slices in a single layer in the dish.
4 Heat the oil in a frying-pan and sauté the onion, carrot, celery and tomatoes over a moderate heat, stirring frequently, for 3 minutes. Remove from the heat and stir in the lentils, basil, coriander, breadcrumbs, egg, 30 ml /2 tbls from the stock and three-quarters of the cheese. Season and mix very thoroughly.
5 Divide the filling among the marrow slices, pushing it well down into the cavity of each and piling it into a mound on top.
6 Mix together the rest of the chicken stock and tomato purée and add salt and pepper to taste. Pour this around, not over, the marrow slices and sprinkle the remaining cheese over the marrow.
7 Bake for 35–45 minutes, until tender. Serve hot, with the juices as a sauce.

Hummus

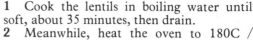 soaking the peas, then 1½ hours

Serves 6–8
225 g /8 oz dried chick-peas, soaked
3–4 garlic cloves
salt
60 ml /4 tbls peanut oil
juice of 3–4 lemons
225 g /8 oz jar of tahini
freshly ground black pepper
a pinch of cumin powder
a pinch of paprika or cayenne pepper
5–10 ml /1–2 tsp olive oil

1 Drain the chick-peas. Cover with twice their volume of water and bring to the boil, reduce the heat and simmer until very soft, 45 minutes–1 hour, depending on the age and the quality of the chick-peas. Drain them thoroughly.
2 Peel the garlic cloves. Using the side of a strong-bladed knife, crush the cloves to a smooth paste with 1.5 ml /¼ tsp salt.
3 Put the chick-peas in a blender. Add the crushed garlic, the peanut oil, the juice of 3 lemons, tahini (add 60 ml /4 tbls water to any remaining paste in the jar, shake well and add to blender) and 150 ml /5 fl oz cold water. Blend to a smooth purée, gradually adding up to 150 ml /5 fl oz cold water, until the purée is of a thick, creamy consistency. Flavour with more lemon juice, if wished, and freshly ground black pepper, cumin powder and paprika or cayenne pepper to taste.
4 Pour the hummus into a shallow serving dish. Just before serving, dribble a little olive oil over the top, and then sprinkle with cumin powder and paprika or cayenne pepper.

● Buy *tahini* (sesame seed paste) from Greek and Oriental food shops.

VEGETABLES A LA GRECQUE

Vegetables served *à la grecque* are cooked in a flavourful mixture of white wine, olive oil and aromatics. They make a wonderful cold – or warm – appetizer.

One of the most enchanting cold appetizers that I know is a selection of vegetables, or just one vegetable, simmered in a highly flavoured bouillon 'in the Greek manner'. Although this method of cooking vegetables is Greek in origin, it has a strong French influence. The vegetables are simmered in a mixture of wine, oil and flavourings and then cooled in the liquid so the maximum amount of flavour is absorbed.

For a true Greek effect, sprinkle the dish liberally with fresh coriander leaves or flat-leaved parsley, or failing these delicious but difficult-to-come-by herbs, ordinary freshly chopped parsley.

The bouillon
The bouillon in which the vegetables are cooked becomes the marinade in which they are cooled and then the sauce in which they are served. This is wonderfully economical in terms of time and money and, more importantly, it is the key to the success of the finished dish.

There is no one definitive recipe for the bouillon; oil and dry white wine are always included, and that typically Greek flavouring, coriander seeds, is usually used. Of the three recipes for bouillon which follow, the first two are based on tomatoes. These may be chopped, fresh or canned tomatoes, but for ease use tomato purée. In my first tomato-based bouillon, Classic à la grecque, the flavour of this base is heightened by a positive spice – cayenne pepper, ginger or saffron, and the sharpness is accentuated by lemon juice.

The second tomato-based bouillon gives an altogether softer flavour. Though the hint of cayenne is retained, the raisins make a fruitier sauce, while added sugar, instead of lemon juice, has a mellowing effect. Onion, included only in the background of the first two types of sauce, comes to the fore in the third bouillon, which is sharpened by more lemon juice.

Choosing the vegetables
Almost any vegetable of your choice can be used, either individually or in interesting combinations. Specially good are aubergines, celeriac, celery, peppers, leeks, carrots, fennel, mushrooms and button onions. The vegetables must, however, be cut into even-sized pieces, so that they cook in the same time. This does not necessarily mean that they should be cut small – whole small leeks are delicious, and celery hearts or fennel can be quartered lengthways.

Harder vegetables are usually blanched briefly in boiling water before the long, slow cooking in the bouillon, which permeates the vegetables and flavours them deliciously.

Experiment with combinations of vegetables and different bouillons until you find your favourites.

Bouillons for à la grecque vegetables

Classic à la grecque bouillon
425 ml /15 fl oz water
75 ml /5 tbls tomato purée
75 ml /5 tbls olive oil
75 ml /5 tbls dry white wine
1 Spanish onion, finely chopped
1 garlic clove, finely chopped
12 coriander seeds, lightly crushed
salt and freshly ground black pepper to taste
a pinch of cayenne pepper, ginger or saffron powder

Celery hearts and carrots à la grecque

To serve
30 ml /2 tbls olive oil
15 ml /1 tbls lemon juice
30 ml /2 tbls finely chopped fresh coriander leaves, flat-leaved parsley or parsley

Tomato-based bouillon with raisins
60 ml /4 tbls tomato purée
225 ml /8 fl oz water
100 g /4 oz raisins, plumped up by soaking overnight in water
60 ml /4 tbls olive oil
90 ml /6 tbls dry white wine
30 ml /2 tbls wine vinegar
½ Spanish onion, finely chopped
1 garlic clove, finely chopped
8 whole coriander seeds
sugar to taste
salt and freshly ground black pepper to taste
a pinch of cayenne pepper

To serve
30 ml /2 tbls chopped fresh coriander leaves, flat-leaved parsley or parsley

Onion and garlic bouillon

juice of 1 lemon
1 Spanish onion, finely chopped
1 garlic clove, finely chopped
8 coriander seeds
8 black peppercorns
12 small button onions, peeled
1 strip lemon zest
120 ml /8 tbls olive oil
300–500 ml /11–18 fl oz dry white wine or
wine and water mixed
salt and freshly ground black pepper to taste
To serve
15–30 ml /1–2 tbls olive oil
lemon juice to taste
30 ml /2 tbls finely chopped fresh coriander
leaves, flat-leaved parsley or parsley

1 The method for making vegetables à la grecque is the same whichever bouillon you decide to use. First wash and trim the vegetables of your choice and cut them into even-sized pieces. Blanch if necessary.
2 Combine all the ingredients for the bouillon in a saucepan. Bring the mixture to the boil. Reduce the heat and simmer for 20 minutes.

3 Add the blanched vegetables, making sure the liquid just covers the vegetables. Simmer, uncovered, for 20–30 minutes, or until the vegetables are tender. Transfer the vegetables and bouillon to a serving dish, leave to cool, then chill, if wished, until needed.
4 To serve, stir in the olive oil and lemon juice, if included in the recipe, and spinkle with finely chopped fresh coriander leaves, flat-leaved parsley or parsley.

Mushrooms à la grecque

50 minutes, plus chilling

Serves 4
450 g /1 lb button mushrooms, thickly sliced
For the bouillon
60 ml /4 tbls tomato purée
60 ml /4 tbls olive oil
90 ml /6 tbls dry white wine
½ Spanish onion, finely chopped
1 garlic clove, finely chopped
8 whole coriander seeds
1.5 ml /¼ tsp saffron powder
salt
freshly ground black pepper
To serve
30 ml /2 tbls chopped fresh coriander leaves,
flat-leaved parsley or parsley

1 Combine the tomato purée and 225 ml / 8 fl oz water in a saucepan with the olive oil, dry white wine, finely chopped onion and garlic, whole coriander seeds, saffron and salt and freshly ground black pepper to taste. Mix well, cover the pan and bring to the boil. Then simmer gently over the lowest possible heat for 20–30 minutes, stirring from time to time.
2 Add the sliced button mushrooms to the bouillon and simmer, uncovered, for 20 minutes, or until the mushrooms are tender. Transfer the mushrooms and reduced bouillon to a serving dish. Leave to cool, then chill in the refrigerator until needed. Serve sprinkled with chopped fresh coriander, flat-leaved parsley or parsley.

Cauliflower florets à la grecque

1 hour, plus chilling

Serves 4–6
1 large cauliflower, cut into florets
For the bouillon
75 ml /5 tbls tomato purée
75 ml /5 tbls olive oil
75 ml /5 tbls dry white wine
1 Spanish onion, finely chopped
1 garlic clove, finely chopped
12 coriander seeds, lightly crushed
salt and freshly ground black pepper
a pinch of cayenne pepper
a pinch of ground ginger

To serve
30 ml /2 tbls olive oil
15 ml /1 tbls lemon juice
30 ml /2 tbls finely chopped fresh coriander
leaves, flat-leaved parsley or parsley

1 Blanch the cauliflower florets by cooking them in boiling salted water for 5 minutes. Drain and refresh.
2 Place the tomato purée, olive oil, dry white wine, finely chopped onion and garlic and the coriander seeds in a saucepan with 425 ml /15 fl oz water. Season to taste with salt and freshly ground black pepper and add the cayenne pepper and ground ginger. Bring the mixture to the boil, skim the surface, then reduce the heat and simmer for 20 minutes, stirring occasionally.
3 Add the blanched cauliflower to the pan and simmer for a further 10–15 minutes, until the cauliflower is tender.
4 Transfer the cauliflower and reduced bouillon to a serving dish and leave to cool completely. Chill until ready to serve.
5 Just before serving, stir in the 30 ml /2 tbls olive oil, the lemon juice and finely chopped coriander leaves, flat-leaved parsley or parsley.

Button onions à la grecque

overnight soaking, 1 hour, plus chilling

Serves 4
900 g /2 lb small button onions
For the bouillon
150 g /5 oz raisins, soaked overnight in
water
150–300 ml /5–10 fl oz dry white wine
100 g /4 oz sugar
60 ml /4 tbls tomato purée
60 ml /4 tbls olive oil
30–60 ml /2–4 tbls wine vinegar
salt and freshly ground black pepper
a pinch of cayenne pepper
To serve
coarsely chopped parley

1 To peel the onions, bring a large pan of water to the boil and drop in half of the button onions. Remove the pan from the heat. Lift out the onions one by one with a slotted spoon and slip off the skins. Repeat with the remaining onions.
2 Place the peeled button onions in a saucepan with 600 ml /1 pt fresh water. Drain the plumped-up raisins and add them to the pan with 150 ml /5 fl oz dry white wine, the sugar, tomato purée, olive oil and wine vinegar. Season to taste with salt, freshly ground black pepper and cayenne pepper.
3 Bring the mixture to the boil, then reduce the heat and simmer for 30–45minutes, until the button onions are tender but still quite firm. Add the remaining wine to the bouillon during the cooking, if necessary.
4 Transfer the onions and bouillon to a serving dish. Leave to cool and then chill. Garnish with parsley just before serving.

Celery hearts and carrots à la grecque

**30 minutes,
plus chilling**

Serves 4–6
225 g /8 oz celery hearts, quartered
*450 g /1 lb carrots, cut into 5 cm /2 in strips,
    about 10 mm /¼ in thick*
For the bouillon
75 ml /5 tbls tomato purée
75 ml /5 tbls olive oil
75 ml /5 tbls dry white wine
1 Spanish onion, finely chopped
1 garlic clove, finely chopped
12 coriander seeds, lightly crushed
salt and freshly ground black pepper
To serve
30 ml /2 tbls olive oil
15 ml /1 tbls lemon juice
finely chopped fresh coriander leaves
sprig of coriander, to garnish

1   To prepare the bouillon, mix 425 ml /15
fl oz water with the first 6 bouillon
ingredients in a saucepan. Add salt and
freshly ground black pepper to taste, bring
to the boil, then reduce the heat and simmer
very gently for 20 minutes. Meanwhile,
blanch the vegetables in boiling salted water
for 5 minutes. Drain and reserve.
2   Add the parboiled vegetables to the
bouillon and simmer for about 8 minutes,
until tender. Transfer the vegetables and
bouillon to a serving dish and leave to cool
completely. Chill until ready to serve.
3   To serve, season again if wished, add the
olive oil and lemon juice, sprinkle with
chopped coriander and garnish with a
coriander sprig.

Courgettes à la grecque

**1 hour,
plus chilling**

Serves 4–6
700 g /1½ lb small courgettes, trimmed
For the bouillon
90 ml /6 tbls olive oil
1 large Spanish onion, finely chopped
1 large garlic clove, finely chopped
150 ml /5 fl oz dry white wine
30 ml /2 tbls tomato purée
bouquet garni
12 coriander seeds
12 black peppercorns
salt to taste
sprig of parsley, to garnish
To serve
30 ml /2 tbls olive oil
30–60 ml /2–4 tbls finely chopped parsley
lemon juice to taste

1   First prepare the bouillon: heat the olive
oil in a heavy frying-pan or flameproof
casserole. Add the finely chopped onion and
garlic and sauté gently for 10–15 minutes,
until transparent. Add 150 ml /5 fl oz water
and the remaining bouillon ingredients.
Bring to the boil, then simmer gently for 5
minutes.
2   Quarter the courgettes lengthways. Cut
into 5 cm /2 in pieces.
3   Add the courgettes to the bouillon and
simmer for 30–35 minutes, stirring
occasionally until tender but still firm.
4   Transfer the courgettes and bouillon to a
serving dish, cool completely, then chill.
5   Before serving, stir in the oil, parsley
and lemon juice. Garnish with parsley.

Artichoke hearts à la grecque

**1 hour,
plus chilling**

Serves 6
6 tender globe artichokes
juice of 1–2 lemons
For the bouillon
1 Spanish onion, finely chopped
1 garlic clove, finely chopped
8 coriander seeds
8 black peppercorns
12 small button onions, peeled
1 strip lemon peel
*175–275 ml /6–10 fl oz dry white wine or
    wine and water mixed*
120 ml /8 tbls olive oil
salt and freshly ground black pepper
lemon juice
To serve
15–30 ml /1–2 tbls olive oil
30 ml /2 tbls finely chopped parsley

1   First, prepare the artichokes. Fill a small
bowl with cold water and acidulate it with
lemon juice. Lay each aritchoke on its side,
slice off the leaves level with the choke (the
fibrous centre) and discard them. Hold each
artichoke firmly and use a sharp knife to
peel around the base and remove all the
remaining leaves. (Reserve them to serve
separately.) As soon as the leaves of each
artichoke have been removed, drop the heart
into the acidulated water. This keeps it from
turning black. Then scrape the fibrous choke
from each heart, dipping the heart into the
acidulated water from time to time to keep it
white.
2   Cut each artichoke heart into 4–6 slices
and arrange all the slices in one layer in a
shallow saucepan. Add the finely chopped
onion and garlic and the coriander seeds and
black peppercorns.
3   Add the button onions to the pan and
the strip of lemon peel, and add enough dry
white wine to barely cover. Bring the
mixture to the boil, reduce the heat, cover
the pan and simmer gently for 15–20
minutes, until the artichoke hearts and
onions are tender.
4   Remove the lid from the pan, pour in the
olive oil and raise the heat. Boil hard for
about 10 minutes, or until the liquid has
reduced to about half its original quantity,
basting the artichokes from time to time.
5   Transfer the vegetables and bouillon to a
serving dish. Cool slightly, season to taste
with salt and freshly ground black pepper
and sprinkle with lemon juice. Leave to cool
completely, then chill until ready to serve.
6   Just before serving, sprinkle with the
15–30 ml /1–2 tbls olive oil, and the finely
chopped parsley.

● Only the hearts of the artichokes are used
in this dish, but the leaves are far too good
to waste. Boil them in salted, acidulated
water until tender, then serve them with a
bowl of melted butter or vinaigrette.

Courgettes à la grecque

Runner beans à la grecque

This is an unusual treatment for runner beans and it's a useful recipe to bear in mind if you have a glut of beans in the summer. Serve it as a salad selection or to accompany a plain cooked main course – it will go well with barbecued chicken.

40 minutes,
plus chilling

Serves 4
450 g /1 lb runner beans topped, tailed and
strings removed
For the bouillon
1 small onion, finely chopped
60 ml /4 tbls olive oil
60 ml /4 tbls dry white wine or lemon juice
6 parsley sprigs, finely chopped
1 celery stick, finely chopped
1 bay leaf
1.5 ml /¼ tsp dried thyme
6 black peppercorns, lightly crushed
6 coriander seeds, lightly crushed
1.5 ml /¼ tsp salt
celery sprigs, to garnish

1   Put the finely chopped onion, olive oil, dry white wine or lemon juice, parsley, finely chopped celery, bay leaf, thyme, black peppercorns, coriander seeds and salt in a medium-sized saucepan with 400 ml /14 fl oz water. Bring to the boil, then cover and simmer for 20–30 minutes. Slice the beans into 25 mm /1 in lengths.
2   Add the beans to the pan and stir well. Bring to the boil, then cover and simmer for 5–10 minutes, until just tender.
3   Transfer the beans and the bouillon to a serving dish and leave to cool. Put in the refrigerator and chill until needed.
4   To serve, garnish the beans with sprigs of celery.

● Whole French beans can be substituted for runner beans.

Fennel à la grecque

The distinctive flavour of fennel combines well with the à la grecque bouillon. In this recipe it is cooked with a tomato-based bouillon but it is equally good with an onion and garlic one. Reserve any of the fine 'frondy' leaves on the fennel bulbs to garnish the dish.

1 hour,
plus chilling

Serves 6
3 large fennel bulbs, trimmed

Runner beans à la grecque

For the bouillon
60 ml /4 tbls tomato purée
60 ml /4 tbls olive oil
90 ml /6 tbls dry white wine
30 ml /2 tbls wine vinegar
½ Spanish onion, finely chopped
1 garlic clove, finely chopped
8 whole coriander seeds
sugar to taste
salt and freshly ground black pepper
a pinch of cayenne pepper
30 ml /2 tbls finely chopped fresh coriander
*   leaves, flat-leaved parsley or parsley*

1   Quarter the fennel bulbs and blanch in boiling salted water for 5 minutes. Drain, refresh and drain again.
2   Combine the tomato purée, olive oil, white wine, wine vinegar, finely chopped onion and garlic and the coriander seeds in a saucepan with 225 ml /8 fl oz water. Season to taste with sugar, salt, freshly ground black pepper and cayenne pepper. Bring to the boil and simmer for 20–30 minutes, stirring occasionally.
3   Add the quartered fennel to the reduced bouillon and simmer for a further 20 minutes, or until the fennel is tender.
4   Transfer to a serving dish and allow to cool, then chill until required. Sprinkle the fennel with the coriander, flat-leaved parsley or parsley and serve.

VEGETABLE SAUCES

Ring the changes to many a dish by adding a tasty vegetable sauce. Versatile and flexible, they make excellent garnishes or, with pasta, delicious, economical meals in themselves.

Vegetable sauces are an ideal way to add extra flavour and colour to a whole variety of dishes. As an addition to other vegetables, meat, fish, eggs, poultry, game and, in particular, pasta, their possibilities are endless.

Making: most sauces are quick and easy to make and require the minimum of ingredients. Usually tender vegetables are used – tomatoes are a favourite – or ones with a distinctive flavour such as garlic, watercress or red peppers, as in Rouille. The vegetables are combined with seasonings and usually a liquid – stock, cream or milk – or something that liquifies easily, for example, cream cheese.

The consistency and texture of the sauce varies according to how it is prepared. For a smooth, pouring sauce, purée the ingredients in a blender or put them through a fine nylon sieve. For chunkier sauces, slice, dice or cut the vegetables into florets and cook them with just enough liquid ingredients to coat them.

Using: sauces will enhance the flavour of foods or add it to ones that are bland. Use the smoother sauces as a garnish, in which case the texture and colour contrast are all-important. A rich, red tomato sauce looks perfect with green beans and a green sauce will look impressive with chicken or white fish. Use the more substantial sauces as the main interest of a dish, particularly with pasta, as in Pasta with green sauce.

Creamy tomato sauce

Creamy tomato sauce

🔪 20 minutes

Makes about 225 ml /8 fl oz
500 g /1 lb ripe tomatoes
25 g /1 oz butter
30 ml /2 tbls tomato purée
125 ml /4 fl oz thick cream
salt and freshly ground black pepper

1 Skin the tomatoes; place the tomatoes in a bowl, cover with boiling water and leave to stand for 10 seconds. Remove them from the water and make a tiny cut in the stalk end of each tomato. Slip off the skins. Cut the tomatoes in half, squeeze out the seeds and juice and discard. Chop the flesh finely.
2 Melt the butter in a frying-pan, add the chopped flesh and tomato purée and cook, stirring constantly, for about 5 minutes, or until smooth.
3 Add the thick cream and season to taste with salt and freshly ground black pepper. Simmer, uncovered, for about 10 minutes, stirring occasionally, until the sauce is slightly thickened. Taste and adjust the seasoning, then serve hot.

● Rich and thick, smooth and creamy, this sauce tastes good with green vegetables, cooked veal, chicken or fish.

Standby tomato sauce

Here's a quick emergency tomato sauce to make when you have neither fresh nor canned tomatoes. It is smooth in texture and delicious with pork and gammon, but it goes well with many other dishes.

🔪 25 minutes

Makes about 150 ml /5 fl oz
20 g /¾ oz butter
22.5 ml /1½ tbls flour
15 ml /1 tbls tomato purée
300 ml /10 fl oz chicken stock, home-made or from a cube
1 garlic clove, crushed
2.5 ml /½ tsp dried basil
½ bay leaf
salt and freshly ground black pepper

1 Melt the butter in a small pan and stir in the flour. Cook over a gentle heat for about 2 minutes, stirring. Remove the pan from the heat and stir in the tomato purée, then gradually stir in the chicken stock to make a smooth sauce.
2 Add the crushed garlic, dried basil, bay leaf and salt and pepper to taste.
3 Simmer the sauce, uncovered, for about 15 minutes, stirring occasionally, until it is thick enough to coat the back of the spoon. Remove the bay leaf, taste, adjust the seasoning and serve hot.

Spaghetti with courgette sauce

🔪 35 minutes

Serves 4
30 ml /2 tbls oil
50 g /2 oz butter
2 onions, finely chopped
1 garlic clove, finely chopped
1 green pepper, thinly sliced
450 g /1 lb courgettes, trimmed and cut into
* 5 mm /¼ in slices*
350 g /12 oz tomatoes, blanched, skinned,
* seeded and sliced*
5 ml /1 tsp dried oregano
salt and freshly ground black pepper
350 g /12 oz wholewheat spaghetti
freshly grated Parmesan cheese, to serve

1   To make the sauce, heat the oil and 25 g /1 oz butter in a frying-pan and sauté the onions over a moderate heat for 3 minutes, stirring occasionally. Add the garlic, green pepper and courgettes, stir well and sauté for 2 minutes. Cover, lower the heat and simmer for 10 minutes, stirring occasionally.
2   Add the tomatoes, oregano, salt and pepper and cook, uncovered, over moderate heat for a further 10 minutes. Taste the sauce and add more seasoning if necessary.
3   While the sauce is cooking, cook the spaghetti in a large pan of boiling, salted water for 12–13 minutes, or until tender.
4   Drain the spaghetti and toss it with the remaining butter in a warmed serving dish. Top with the sauce and serve hot, with the cheese handed separately.

Garlic sauce

🔪 20 minutes, plus chilling

Serves 4
100 g /4 oz stale white bread, crusts
* removed*
6 garlic cloves, peeled
salt
250 ml /8 fl oz olive oil
15 ml /1 tbls lemon juice
15 ml /1 tbls white wine vinegar
freshly ground black pepper

1   Cut the bread into pieces and place in a bowl; pour on just enough water to cover and soak for 5 minutes.
2   Turn the soaked bread into a fine sieve and drain off the water. Using a wooden spoon, gently press the bread against the sieve to extract any remaining liquid.
3   Mince or crush the garlic with 2.5 ml /½ tsp salt. Purée the garlic and bread in a blender, or use a pestle and mortar to pound the garlic to a smooth paste and gradually beat in the bread.
4   Add the olive oil, a little at a time, and pound or blend until it is completely absorbed by the bread. When all the olive oil has been incorporated, blend in the lemon juice and wine vinegar. Season and continue

blending the sauce again until it is smooth and creamy. Turn the sauce into a bowl if necessary, cover with cling film, chill for 30 minutes, or until needed.

Creamy mushroom sauce

🔪 15 minutes

Serves 4
225 g /8 oz full fat cream cheese
30 ml /2 tbls freshly snipped chives
50 g /2 oz butter
100 g /4 oz button mushrooms, trimmed,
* wiped and thickly sliced*
salt and freshly ground black pepper

1   In a bowl, beat the cream cheese until smooth and soft. Beat in the chives.
2   Melt the butter in a small sauté pan over medium heat. Add the mushrooms and sauté for 2 minutes. Reduce the heat to low, then add the cream cheese and chive mixture and stir until completely melted. Season well. Continue stirring over low heat for a few minutes more until the sauce is heated through. Use immediately.

Rouille

Rouille is a Provençal sauce for fish – the name means 'rust'. It also goes well with pasta or as a dip with raw vegetables.

🔪 30 minutes

Spaghetti with courgette sauce

Makes 175 ml /6 fl oz sauce
1 large sweet red pepper, grilled, skinned,
* seeded and chopped*
1 small red chilli, seeded and chopped
1 large garlic clove, chopped
25 g /1 oz fresh breadcrumbs
60 ml /4 tbls olive oil
30–45 ml /2–3 tbls warm fish stock,
salt and freshly ground black pepper.

1   Combine the sweet pepper, chilli and garlic in a blender or mortar. Reduce to a purée or pound to a smooth paste.
2   Work in the breadcrumbs, then gradually stir in the olive oil. Slowly beat in the stock and season.

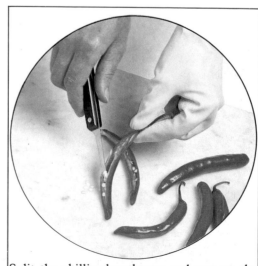

Split the chillies lengthways and remove the seeds. Wash your hands immediately.

Matriciana pasta sauce

 1 hour 20 minutes

Serves 4–6
100 g /4 oz fat salt pork or fat streaky
  bacon, without rind
30 ml /2 tbls olive oil
1 Spanish onion, finely chopped
2 garlic cloves, finely chopped
800 g /1 lb 12 oz canned tomatoes with their
  juice
30 ml /2 tbls tomato purée
1 small red pepper, diced
2.5 ml /½ tsp sugar
salt and freshly ground black pepper
To serve
450 g /1 lb spaghetti or other pasta, boiled

1   Cut the salt pork or bacon into dice.
2   Heat the olive oil in a frying-pan and sauté the diced salt pork or bacon, finely chopped onion and garlic for about 5 minutes, or until it is golden, stirring occasionally.
3   Transfer the sautéed mixture to a small flameproof casserole. Add the juice from the can of tomatoes, then chop the tomatoes and add them too. Add the tomato purée, diced red pepper and sugar. Season to taste.
4   Simmer the sauce gently, uncovered, for about 1 hour. Taste and season again, if necessary, before serving hot, with freshly cooked spaghetti or other pasta.

Soubise sauce

Serve this creamy onion sauce with roast lamb or veal, grilled chops, or ham.

 55 minutes

Serves 4
450 g /1 lb onions, thinly sliced
75 g /3 oz butter
a large pinch of salt
40 g /1½ oz flour
425 ml /15 fl oz milk
150 ml /5 fl oz thin cream
freshly ground black pepper
a pinch of freshly grated nutmeg

1   Melt the butter in a large, heavy-based saucepan over a very low heat. Add the onions and salt and stir well. Cover and sweat very gently, till the onions are soft but not brown.
2   Off the heat, stir in the flour; return the pan to a low heat and stir for 3 minutes. Meanwhile, bring the milk to the boil in a small pan and remove from the heat.
3   Off the heat, gradually pour the boiling hot milk onto the onions, stirring constantly. Simmer the onion sauce gently for 15 minutes, stirring occasionally.
4   Purée the sauce through a fine nylon sieve or an electric blender. Return the purée to the clean pan and reheat gently to simmering point. Stir in the cream and season with salt, pepper and nutmeg.
5   Serve the sauce immediately; or, turn it

Matriciana pasta sauce

into a heatproof bowl, cover with dampened greaseproof paper and stand in a pan of very hot water until ready to serve.

Watercress purée

 25 minutes

Serves 4
4 bunches watercress, about 450 g /1 lb
salt
15–30 ml /1–2 tbls lemon juice
150 ml /5 fl oz thick cream
freshly ground black pepper

1   Trim any coarse stalks and yellow leaves from the watercress and wash it well. Blanch it in boiling salted water for 3 minutes. Drain and refresh under cold running water, then drain again.
2   Put the watercress in an electric blender or food processor with the lemon juice and thick cream and blend until just smooth – take care not to over-blend or it may curdle.
3   Pass the purée through a fine sieve into a small saucepan and season it to taste with salt and freshly ground black pepper. Reheat the purée very gently and serve it at once with fish or veal.

●   It is important to serve the watercress purée as soon as it is ready because keeping this purée waiting before serving will cause it to discolour.

Sorrel sauce

🍴🍴 55 minutes

Serves 4
*300 ml /10 fl oz chicken stock, home-made
    or from a cube*
100 ml /3½ fl oz dry white wine
1 medium-sized onion, thinly sliced
1 medium-sized carrot, thinly sliced
1 celery stalk, chopped
1 bouquet garni
5 ml /1 tsp black peppercorns
50 g /2 oz sorrel leaves, chopped
125 g /4 oz curd cheese

1 Put the chicken stock, wine, vegetables, bouquet garni and peppercorns in a saucepan and boil gently, uncovered, for about 20 minutes or until the liquid is reduced by half.
2 Add the sorrel and cook for 1 minute. Remove the bouquet garni and discard and then blend the liquid with cheese and work until smooth.
3 Gently reheat the sauce and serve.

Pasta with green sauce

Pasta with green sauce

🍴🍴 soaking the mushrooms, then 25–35 minutes

Serves 4
500 g /1lb pasta
salt
15 ml /1 tbls olive oil
freshly grated Parmesan cheese
For the green vegetable sauce
*1 small head broccoli, cut into florets, with
    25 mm /1 in stems*
8 cauliflower florets
salt
*250 g /8 oz French beans, cut into 25 mm /1
    in lengths*
2 medium-sized, unpeeled courgettes, diced
150 g /5 oz butter
15 ml /1 tbls finely chopped fresh parsley
*3 large fresh basil leaves, chopped, or 2.5 ml
    /½ tsp dried basil*
a pinch of freshly grated nutmeg
*4 pieces dried mushroom, soaked for 30
    minutes and chopped*
freshly ground black pepper
150 ml /5 fl oz thick cream

1 Cook the broccoli and cauliflower florets in boiling salted water for 3–4 minutes. Drain and refresh them under cold, running water. Drain again and then reserve.
2 Cook the French beans in boiling salted water for 3 minutes. Drain and refresh them under cold, running water then drain again and reserve.
3 Cook the diced courgettes in boiling water for 2 minutes. Drain and refresh them, then drain again and reserve.
4 Bring a large pan containing at least 3.5 L /6 pt salted water to the boil and add 15 ml /1 tbls olive oil. Add the pasta and bring back to the boil. Give the pasta a good stir and simmer, uncovered, for 8–15 minutes, according to the variety, until *al dente*, that is, cooked but still firm to the bite.
5 Melt the butter in a large saucepan. Add the finely chopped parsley, chopped basil leaves or dried basil, freshly grated nutmeg and chopped dried mushroom. Season to taste with freshly ground black pepper and cook for 5 minutes.
6 Add the prepared vegetables and the thick cream and cook for 2–3 minutes, or until hot and bubbling, stirring well.
7 Pour the green vegetable sauce over the pasta and serve with freshly grated Parmesan cheese.

CHUTNEYS, PICKLES & PRESERVES

Home-made chutneys and pickles are a traditional way of preserving an abundant harvest of fruit and vegetables, to be used later as spicy, tangy relishes or side dishes.

Chutneys are a type of sweet-and-sour, spicy jam, while pickles are vegetables or fruit soaked in brine (salt and water solution) or salt, then bottled, uncooked, in spiced vinegar. Some produce, like beetroot, crab-apples, cooking pears and most fruit and sweet vegetables, are not soaked in brine but are stewed gently in sweetened, spiced vinegar until cooked, but not soft.

Ingredients

The main ingredients in most chutneys and pickles tend to be fairly basic every-day fruit and vegetables, either home grown or those that can be bought cheaply in season, but recipes can be adapted to making smaller quantities with better quality ingredients.

Chutneys: spices and other flavourings are included both to increase the keeping qualities and to add variety. Among the most favoured flavourings are allspice, chillies, cinnamon, cloves, coriander, garlic, ginger, horseradish, mustard and onion.

Any type of sugar may be used – granulated, preserving crystals, Demerara or soft brown. Usually natural, soft brown sugar (such as Barbados sugar) is preferred for the extra richness it gives.

Pickles: use good-quality malt vinegar, which has at least 5% acetic acid content, for most fruit and vegetables. For produce with especially subtle flavours, you can use distilled white cider or white wine vinegars.

Black peppercorns, mustard seed and dried red chillies are three of the standard ingredients of most pickling spice blends.

Equipment

For chutneys and all pickles using vinegar or salt, do not use equipment made of corrosive metals. At the brining and salting stage in pickling always use glass, earthenware or china bowls. Choose a preserving pan or very large saucepan made of stainless steel or enamel, or one with a high-quality non-stick interior finish. Do not use iron, brass or copper pans.

If the ingredients need to be passed through a sieve, use one with nylon mesh. Select storage jars with airtight lids lined with plastic. Transparent paper covers are not suitable.

The method

Chutneys: first core, stone, skin or peel the fruit or vegetables according to type, then chop and put them in the pan. Add the vinegar, spices and sugar – it is best to mix the ground spices first with a little of the vinegar and then stir this paste into the chutney ingredients, this way they blend more readily. Stir all these ingredients over low heat until the sugar has dissolved, then bring to the boil. Simmer until the chutney has thickened and there is no separated liquid; during cooking, the liquid settles into little pools and these must be stirred in.

The cooking time will depend largely on the age and quality of the ingredients. Always taste a little of the chutney to test that all the ingredients are tender.

Once the chutney is cooked, spoon or pour it into jars which have been warmed in the oven at the lowest setting. Cover the filled jars at once with waxed paper circles, waxed side down, then tightly screw on the lids.

Label the jars with the type of chutney and the date and store them in a cool, dark, dry airy place. Use them after 3 months or within 2 or 3 years.

Pickles: to make the spiced vinegar, lightly bruise or crush the spices with a rolling pin, but do not crush them to a powder. If you wish, tie them into a piece of scalded muslin. Steep them in cold vinegar in a covered glass jar for up to two months, then strain. It is then ready for use, but will keep for a year. You can speed up the process by bringing the spices and vinegar to the boil, then cooling. This cooled spiced vinegar can be used immediately. If you want a strong flavour and interesting appearance to your pickles, leave whole spices in the vinegar when pickling large produce such as whole onions or beetroot. Otherwise, remove the bag of spices or strain off loose spices.

As a general rule, allow about 60 ml /4 tbls (25 g /1 oz) of spices to each 1.1 L /2 pt vinegar. Try green or white peppercorns instead of black, or whole cloves to give a strong, penetrating flavour to onions and beetroot pickles. Whole allspice berries and a piece of cinnamon stick pep up the flavour of all kinds of fruit. Dill or fennel seed enhance the flavour of gherkins, cucumber, marrow and courgettes, and coriander seeds add an orangy pepperiness. Also, try adding a piece of dried root ginger or a blade of mace.

To prepare the produce, wash and drain the vegetables or fruit and prepare them according to type. Prick small cucumbers, gherkins or firm vegetables or fruit all over with a sterilized darning needle so the spicy flavour will be taken up more quickly. Preserve small pears and apples whole, but core the apples, or peel, core and quarter them, then drop them in acidulated water to preserve the colour. Gently simmer very tough vegetables or cooking fruit.

To salt and brine, use dry, coarse (cooking) salt for vegetables with a high moisture content – aubergines, marrows, cucumbers and courgettes. Slice the vegetables and layer them in a bowl with 50 g /2 oz salt to each 500 g /1 lb vegetables. Cover the bowl with a plate and leave for 12–24 hours, until the vegetables are crisp in texture and slightly shrunken.

For other vegetables, make up a brine solution using 225 g /8 oz salt to 2 L /3½ pt water. Put the prepared vegetables into a bowl, cover them with brine, then with a large plate. Weight down the plate with a jar filled with water. Then leave the gherkins, cauliflowers and cabbage in brine for 24 hours and onions for 48 hours.

Rinse off the salt or brine under plenty of cold, running water and see that the vegetables are well drained.

To bottle, pack the produce loosely into jars, occasionally giving the jars a firm tap to shake down the level. Do not push the fruit or vegetables down hard or you may spoil their texture and appearance.

Spiced vinegar is usually poured cold over the vegetables to preserve their crispness, but it can be boiled and poured hot over onions, beets and firm fruits. Before you do this, warm the jars. Fill them quickly with the produce and pour on the hot vinegar. Whether using hot or cold vinegar, cover so that it comes to about 5 mm /¼ in above the top of the vegetables, then cover the jars with non-corrosive lids. Label and date the jars, then store them upright in a cool, airy place. Unless stated to the contrary in the recipe, you can use pickles as soon as they are made. However, if you do store them for a while, their flavours will improve.

Piccalilli

⏱🍴 salting the vegetables, then 1 hour

Makes about 6 × 450 g /1 lb jars
1.4 kg /3 lb green tomatoes, quartered and sliced
1 small, firm cauliflower
2 small cucumbers
450 g /1 lb onions
225 g /8 oz firm, white cabbage
400 g /14 oz cooking salt
For the spiced vinegar
1 L /1¾ pt malt vinegar
225 g /8 oz sugar
15 ml /1 tbls ground ginger
30 ml /2 tbls mustard
15 ml /1 tbls turmeric
15 ml /1 tbls mustard seeds
15 ml /1 tbls black peppercorns
1 clove garlic, crushed

1 Prepare the vegetables according to type. Layer them in a large bowl with the salt, cover and leave them for 24 hours. Rinse, then drain the vegetables.
2 To make the spiced vinegar, pour the vinegar into a very large, non-corrosive saucepan. Add the sugar, ground ginger, mustard and turmeric. Put the mustard seed, black peppercorns and crushed garlic into a muslin bag. Add it to the pan. Bring the vinegar to the boil, stirring it to dissolve the sugar.
3 Add the vegetables and simmer gently for 20 minutes until they are tender but still crisp. Remove the spices.
4 Warm the jars in the oven. Spoon the hot pickle into the jars, cover, label and use.

Preserving ingredients

100

Mushroom ketchup

🕐🍴 3–9 days in salt,
then 4 hours

Makes 850 ml /1½ pt
1.5 kg /3 lb mushrooms
150 g /5 oz coarse or sea salt
30 ml /2 tbls allspice
2 blades of mace
*20 peppercorns or 15 ml /1 tbls cayenne
    pepper*
25 mm /1 in piece ginger root, chopped
5 whole cloves
15 ml /1 tbls sugar
125 ml /4 fl oz brandy
125 ml /4 fl oz wine vinegar

1 Trim and clean the mushrooms as necessary, then chop them coarsely. Spread them out in an earthenware or enamel-lined pan and cover them with all but 15 ml /1 tbls of the salt. Mix this into the mushrooms with your hands.
2 Leave them in a cool place or the refrigerator for 3 days, stirring and squashing with a spoon at least once. If you do not have time to cook and finish the pickle immediately, this salting stage may be continued for a maximum of 9 days.
3 When you are ready to make the ketchup, turn the mushrooms and their liquor into a jellybag, or a buttermuslin spread out inside a large colander over a bowl. Thoroughly squash down the mushrooms with the back of a spoon and

then twist and squeeze the bag or cloth to obtain the maximum amount of liquor.
4 Crush the allspice, mace and peppercorns, if using, in a mortar with a pestle and add the ginger root and crush again. Add these flavourings, plus the cloves, to the mushroom liquor with the cayenne pepper, if using, 15 ml /1 tbls salt and the sugar.
5 Pour the liquor into the top pan of a double boiler, bring it almost to the boil, then put the pan onto the boiler containing simmering water. Simmer, uncovered so that the liquid reduces, at the back of the stove, remembering to add more hot water regularly to the bottom pan so that it does not boil dry. Reduce the liquor to 750 ml /26 fl oz – this will take about 2½–3 hours.
6 Sterilize 3 small jars or bottles, for example, 3 × 300 ml /10 fl oz old soy sauce bottles.
7 Strain the liquor to remove the spices and stir in the brandy and vinegar. Pour it into the prepared containers, using a funnel for bottles. Seal tightly; the ketchup should keep indefinitely until opened, then use it up fairly quickly. Add a spoonful or so to taste to sauces, casseroles and soups.

Marrow chutney

For those who like hot spices, this is a good accompaniment to a mild curry. It will also add zing to cold snacks.

🕐🍴 overnight salting,
then about 1¾ hours

Makes about 3.2 kg /7 lb
1 large marrow
about 50 g /2 oz salt
1 kg /2 lb cooking apples
500 g /1 lb onions, chopped
*25 g /1 oz dried root ginger, peeled and
    finely chopped*
500 g /1 lb soft, dark brown sugar
2.5 ml /½ tsp cayenne pepper
850 ml /1½ pt malt vinegar
2.5 ml /½ tsp mustard seeds
5 ml /1 tsp black peppercorns
5 ml /1 tsp dried red chillies
2.5 ml /½ tsp whole cloves

1 Peel the marrow, discard the seeds and cut the flesh into cubes. Layer these in a large china mixing bowl – do not use a metal pan – and sprinkle each layer with salt. Cover the bowl and leave the marrow to stand overnight.
2 The next day, drain the marrow in a colander and rinse it thoroughly in cold water. Drain it well again.
3 Peel, core and chop the apples. Put the marrow and apples into a large vinegar-proof pan with the onions, ginger and sugar. In a small bowl or cup, mix the cayenne pepper with a little vinegar and stir it into the pan with the remaining vinegar and the whole mustard seeds. Tie the peppercorns, chillies and cloves in a piece of muslin or cheesecloth which has been scalded in boiling water, and add them to the pan.
4 Stir over a low heat until the sugar has

Pennsylvanian chow-chow

dissolved, then increase the heat and bring to boiling point. Simmer the chutney for about 1¼ hours, or until the ingredients are tender and there is no excess moisture. Remove the bag of spices from the chutney and discard it.

5 Wash some jars thoroughly and warm them on a board in the oven at the lowest setting. Pour in the chutney to fill the jars. Cover the tops with waxed paper circles, waxed side down, then with vinegar-proof screw or clip-on tops. Label the jars with the name of the chutney and the date and store until you are ready to use it.

Pennsylvanian chow-chow

overnight soaking,
2 hours, plus 6 hours

Makes 3–4 × 450 g /1 lb jars
1 small, firm cauliflower
2 green peppers
2 red peppers
500 g /1 lb French beans
225 g /8 oz sweetcorn kernels
2 medium-sized onions
100 g /4 oz cooking salt
225 g/ 8 oz red kidney beans, soaked
*   overnight and drained*
For the spiced vinegar
1 L /1¾ pt cider vinegar
15 ml /1 tbls mustard seeds
15 ml / tbls prepared mustard
10 ml /2 tsp turmeric
175 g /6 oz soft, light brown sugar

1 Prepare all the fresh vegetables according to type. Make a brine with the salt and 1.1 L /2 pt water. Soak the prepared vegetables for 24 hours. Drain, rinse, then drain them again.
2 Meanwhile, cook the soaked kidney beans in boiling unsalted water for 1½ hours, then drain them. Leave them to cool and then mix them with the fresh vegetables.
3 Pour the vinegar into a non-corrosive pan; add the spices and sugar. Bring to the boil slowly, stirring to dissolve the sugar. Simmer for 3 minutes. Warm the jars.
4 Pack the vegetables into the warmed jars and pour over the hot spiced vinegar. Cover the jars, label and use.

Tomato, celery and red pepper relish

30 minutes

Makes 350 g /12 oz
250 g /9 oz tomatoes
30 ml /2 tbls olive oil
2 celery sticks, finely chopped
1 medium-sized onion, finely chopped
1 garlic clove, finely chopped
5 ml /1 tsp celery seed
1 sweet red pepper, cored, seeded and finely
*   chopped*
45 ml /3 tbls white wine vinegar

1 Scald, skin, seed and finely chop the tomatoes, then reserve.
2 Heat the oil in a saucepan over a low heat. Stir in the celery, onion, garlic and celery seed, reduce the heat to very low and cook until the onion is transparent.
3 Mix in the tomatoes and red pepper. Add the vinegar and bring the mixture to the boil.
4 Remove the pan from the heat and transfer the relish to a bowl. Allow it to become completely cold before serving.

● This relish is not a preserve but will keep for 3–4 days, covered, in the refrigerator.

Pickled onions

2 days soaking, plus 1 hour,
then 3 weeks maturing

Makes 1.5–1.7 kg /3–4 lb
1 kg /2¼ lb pickling onions, trimmed
225 g /8 oz coarse salt
50 g /2 oz sugar
600 ml /1 pt white wine vinegar
5 ml /1 tsp whole cloves
5 ml /1 tsp mustard seed
4 dried red chillies
2.5 ml /½ tsp black peppercorns
1 bay leaf, crumbled

Pickled onions

1 Place the onions in a bowl, cover with boiling water and leave for 5 minutes. Drain the onions and, while they are still warm, rub off the skins. Cut a cross at the root end of each onion to help them stay whole and to help the salt to penetrate.
2 Combine half the salt with 1.2 L /2¼ pt water in a large bowl and stir until the salt has dissolved. Add the onions and cover them with a large plate so they are completely immersed in the brine. Place a weight on the plate and leave the onions to soak for 12 hours.
3 Drain the onions and wash the bowl. Make fresh brine with the remaining salt and 1.2 L /2¼ pt water; add the onions, cover with a weighted plate and leave to soak for 36 hours.
4 Drain the onions and pack them into cleaned, warmed preserving jars.
5 Combine the sugar and vinegar in a stainless steel or enamelled pan. Stir over a low heat until the sugar has dissolved. Add the spices and the crumbled bay leaf. Bring the vinegar syrup to the boil and boil for 5 minutes. Remove the pan from the heat and leave the spiced vinegar to cool.
6 Pour the vinegar over the onions to completely cover. Seal the jars with vinegar-proof covers, label and store.

FREEZING VEGETABLES

With a store of vegetables in the freezer, you always have side dishes and hot appetizers almost ready to hand and, with the minimum of fuss, frozen vegetables can be turned into delicious main-course dishes.

Freezing is the best method of long-term storing for vegetables: few canned vegetables have the quality of quick-frozen ones. If you choose your vegetables carefully for freezing, using young, good-quality produce, your frozen stock may well be of better flavour and tenderness than a hurried, indiscriminate choice of fresh produce.

The freezer comes into its own when you are pressed for time and is particularly good as a store of ready-to-cook vegetables. Freeze vegetables in forms you know will be useful later, or buy types, such as ready-frozen peas, beans and corn, that can be quickly converted into dishes with butter, cream and freshly chopped herbs.

Home freezing is particularly successful for those vegetables which are tedious to prepare; it allows you to arrange the preparation time to suit yourself, rather than doing it before a meal, when you are often pressed for time. Podding fresh peas and beans comes into this category, of course, but there are even more time-consuming vegetables which many cooks dislike for this reason — knobbly Jerusalem artichokes, salsify and pickling onions among them. Happily, the blanching process necessary for freezing vegetables means they can be kept ready-prepared in the freezer.

Blanching vegetables before freezing them means that they are slightly cooked, usually in boiling water, and take less time to finish cooking than fresh vegetables. Therefore, frozen vegetables can be transformed into an interesting side dish by simply braising them with a little butter and cream and the addition of a few tablespoons of stock, wine or vermouth. If you are using a frozen vegetable for a recipe that quotes

fresh, the frozen vegetable needs about half the cooking time. Liquid in the recipe can also be reduced by about half.

Tips for home freezing
● Look for young vegetables in peak condition; vegetables past their prime are tough and stringy and they will not improve in the freezer.
● Economy in purchasing is necessary to pay for the electricity storage costs for some months. Either grow and freeze your own vegetables, buy direct from the producer or look out for bulk-buy bargains.
● Peas and beans, which need a large amount of podding time, may well be better bought in quantity ready-frozen from a bulk supplier if you do not have access to cheap, high-quality, fresh produce.
● Leafy vegetables, such as lettuce, cannot be stored in anything resembling their raw form, and watery vegetables such as cucumbers, whole tomatoes and marrows are not a great success after thawing.
● Vegetables that have been frozen are not pleasant eaten raw, even if frozen uncooked.
● Most blanched vegetables can be stored for 1 year; cooked vegetables and purées will keep for 6 months.

Blanching and freezing
Blanching: the great majority of vegetables should be blanched before freezing. This destroys the enzymes which cause discoloration and loss of flavour and vitamins during storage. Prepare vegetables for blanching as you would for cooking. Roots, such as carrots, should either be small or else sliced into manageable sections.

To blanch vegetables, plunge them into

Vegetables for freezing

salted, boiling water. For this job you need a large saucepan and a wire mesh basket. It is important that the water returns to boiling within 1 minute of the vegetables being

Blanching, cooling and freezing

Plunge the vegetables in a wire basket into a pan of boiling water. Blanching starts from the moment the water returns to the boil.

To cool, plunge the blanched vegetables into iced water. Chilling time should not be more than the blanching time.

Drain and thoroughly dry the cooled vegetables. Open freeze or pack immediately into appropriate containers.

submerged, so do not blanch more than 500 g /1 lb vegetables at a time and reduce this amount if necessary. The wire basket should be in the pan while the water is being brought to the boil, so it is also heated. Only when the water is at a fast boil should the basket be lifted out and the vegetables put in. Immerse them in the water and time the blanching from the moment the water comes back to the boil. Do not cover the pan but keep it over a fairly high heat throughout the blanching. Each vegetable has its own optimum blanching time (see chart).

Chilling: to stop cooking and speed up chilling, which is the secret of trapping in freshness, cool the vegetables under cold, running water, then chill swiftly by submerging in iced water. Make several batches of ice cubes for icing the water, ahead of time. Change the water as it becomes tepid. The golden rule is that the cooling time should never exceed the blanching time.

Drain the blanched vegetables thoroughly, then allow to dry on absorbent paper and chill in the regrigerator before freezing.

Open freezing: this is the method to use if you wish to bag vegetables like peas in bulk but keep them free-running so you can easily pour out individual portions. Spread the vegetables out on baking trays in a single layer and freeze uncovered. When firm, bag and label, then return them to the freezer.

Packaging: most vegetables have a fairly solid texture so rigid packaging is not essential in most cases. Gussetted polythene bags are a sensible and cheap choice, with the added advantage that the contents are easily visible, though this does not mean that labelling should be forgotten. However, cauliflower florets and delicate vegetable shapes are best open frozen, then packed in rigid containers.

Use a special freezer vacuum pump or straw to suck out as much air as possible before sealing firmly with freezer tape. The polythene bags can be used several times as long as they are carefully washed and dried between uses.

Other ways to freeze vegetables

Freezing raw: although this is the quickest way to freeze, there are disadvantages to freezing raw vegetables. Storage time is much reduced – 6 weeks maximum is a good rule – or discoloration will follow.

Try freezing raw, small button mushroom caps, pepper strips and rings, celery trimmings and onion slices. Add these to slowly cooked dishes such as casseroles.

Fat scalding: ready-prepared chips are useful if you have a family that loves them. Fat scalding is the best method. Deep-fry them for 2 minutes only, then drain and cool on absorbent paper. Open freeze, then bag

and label. They can be deep fried from frozen but do not overload the deep frier as the fat should return to its original temperature as quickly as possible.

Purées: as we have seen, many vegetables make successful purées and this is a good way to freeze vegetables with a high water content. Purées of celery, cucumber, lettuce and watercress retain the subtle flavour of the fresh vegetables. Tomatoes, potatoes, Jerusalem artichokes (which have knobbly shapes, awkward for freezing whole) and spinach all make successful purées.

Since purées freeze so well, it is worth extending your range to carrots, turnips, and other vegetables you might normally ignore. They can be served as a side dish or as an unusual topping to a shepherd's pie. Diluted with stock, cream or milk, these also make quick soups.

To freeze purées and soups, pack them into rigid containers, leaving a 10 mm /$\frac{1}{2}$ in headspace for expansion during freezing. Or, as a space saver, freeze as ice cubes.

Fully cooked dishes: sautéed mushrooms freeze well – and this is a convenient way to have them ready in the freezer. Beetroot has to be fully boiled before freezing. Casseroles with root vegetables in them will freeze and ratatouille is well known for surviving in the freezer without changing. Stuffed vegetables also freeze well.

FREEZING VEGETABLES

VEGETABLE STORAGE TIME	PREPARATION	BLANCHING COOLING TIMES	TIPS
Artichokes **Globe** 6 months	Cut off stalks at the base and remove damaged and coarse outer leaves. Wash thoroughly.	7–10 minutes according to size. Add 15 ml /1 tbls lemon juice to each 1.1 L /2 pt blanching water. Drain thoroughly upside down.	
Jerusalem 3 months	Scrub thoroughly and then peel. Cook in a little stock or tomato juice with finely chopped onion, until tender. Blend or liquidize.		Pack in rigid containers or in pre-formed polythene bags. Serve as a vegetable purée or add stock and/or cream to make a soup.
Asparagus 9 months	Separate into thick, medium and thin stems. Wash and trim but do not tie into bundles yet.	2–4 minutes according to stem thickness.	Tie into bundles of 6–10 stems, packing tips to stalks. Separate bundles with non-stick freezer paper and pack into rigid containers.
Avocados 1 month	Peel and mash, or blend to a pulp. Add 15 ml /1 tbls lemon juice to each avocado.		Pack in rigid containers or pre-formed polythene bags. Use as a base for cream soup or as a savoury party dip.
Beans **Broad** 12 months	Shell	3 minutes	Use only very young, small beans.
French 12 months	Rinse and dry, snip off ends, leave whole.	2 minutes	
Runner 12 months	Wash, trim and slice into 25mm /1 in lengths.	1 minute	
Beetroot 6 months	Only small, baby beetroots are worth freezing. Cook whole until tender. Allow to cool.		To serve, slice and cover with vinegar or reheat in a parsley or cheese sauce.
Broccoli 12 months	Remove coarse stalks, cut into small sprigs and wash.	3–5 minutes according to thickness of stems.	Pack in 1–2 layers in rigid containers, tips to stalks.
Brussels sprouts 12 months	Remove outer leaves, wash.	3 minutes	Only freeze young, small sprouts which are very firm.
Carrots 12 months	Trim, scrape, dice or leave whole.	4 minutes	Use only small, young carrots.
Cauliflower 6 months	Cut off base and break into florets of even size.	3 minutes	15 ml /1 tbls lemon juice added to the blanching water helps retain colour. Use rigid containers to store.
Celeriac 6 months	Wash and trim. Cook until nearly tender. Peel and slice.		Pack in layers separated by non-stick paper in containers.
Celery 6 months	Trim, pull off strings, wash thoroughly and cut into 25 mm /1 in lengths.	2–3 minutes	Not suitable for eating raw after freezing. Add to casseroles or to sauces.
Corn on the cob 12 months	Choose small or medium cobs. Remove leaves and any threads. Trim ends.	4–5 minutes, depending on size.	Pack individually in foil. Thaw before cooking, or strip off kernels and pack in polythene.

VEGETABLE STORAGE TIME	PREPARATION	BLANCHING COOLING TIMES	TIPS
Courgettes 12 months	Wash small, young ones. Cut into 10mm /½ in lengths.	Sauté in butter or blanch for 1 minute.	Can also be frozen cooked in ratatouille.
Mushrooms **Button** 3 months	Wipe clean; do not peel.	Sauté in butter for 2 minutes. Drain on absorbent kitchen paper.	
Flat 3 months	Chop finely, add seasoning and sauté in 25 g /1 oz butter to each 200 g /7 oz mushrooms until dry.		Store in small quantities in rigid containers.
Onions **Large** 6 months	Peel and slice into rings.	1 minute	Good for using in casseroles. Onion should always be double-wrapped to prevent the smell filtering out.
Small 6 months	Wash and peel but leave whole.	4 minutes	
Parsnips 12 months	Trim, peel and cut young parsnips into fingers.	2–3 minutes	
Peas, green 12 months	Shell, grading carefully according to size.	1 minute	Only freeze young ones as the starch in peas turns to sugar as they age.
Mange tout 12 months	Wash and trim ends.	2–3 minutes	
Peppers, green and red 12 months	Wash, cut open and remove the stems and seeds. Leave in halves or cut into thin slices.	3 minutes	Freeze green and red separately to prevent cross-flavouring.
Potatoes **New** 3 months	Scrape; boil for a few minutes less than usual.		Cook new potatoes from frozen in boiling water for 3–5 minutes. Drain and toss in butter. Open freeze mashed potatoes and pack in rigid containers. Re-heat Duchesse potatoes in a hot oven and deep fry croquettes. Open freeze chips.
Mashed 3 months	Freezes well as croquettes or Duchesse potatoes.		
Chipped 3 months	Peel and cut into chips.	Part-fry in deep fat for 2 minutes.	
Spinach 12 months	Use young leaves; wash and trim stems.	2 minutes. Press out water on absorbent kitchen paper or in a clean tea-towel.	Best to blanch 225–350 g /½–¾ lb at a time so the leaves do not stick together.
Swedes 12 months	Trim, peel and cut into cubes.	3 minutes	Alternatively freeze as a cooked purée.
Tomatoes 12 months	Plunge first into boiling water, then cold, to loosen skin. Peel, core and seed. Simmer with no extra liquid until soft. Blend to a purée or sieve.		Pack in rigid containers.
Turnips 12 months	Trim, peel and dice small, young ones.	2½–3 minutes	Alternatively freeze as a cooked purée.

VEGETABLE GARNISHES

A well-chosen garnish adds texture, colour and flavour to both hot and cold dishes. Here we show you how to make simple vegetable garnishes with a very sophisticated look.

A garnish should be simple and fresh. It should also be compatible in flavour with the main ingredient of the dish and, if the dish is hidden by a sauce, as a guide the garnish should relate to what is under the sauce. Arrange all garnishes decoratively, either around the edge of the dish or in the centre of the food.

The garnishes described in this chapter look sophisticated, yet are very simple to make. The only equipment you need is a small, sharp knife. Vegetable garnishes are perfect for decorating salads, cold meats, platters and sandwiches. The 'chrysanthemums' and spring onion 'flowers' are excellent with Chinese food and open sandwiches, while the gherkin 'fans' are particularly good for decorating pâté and smoked fish hors d'oeuvres. Celery curls look most effective floating on the surface of soups. Use lemon twists for garnishing fish and white meat dishes, or any dish made with lemon mayonnaise.

Carrots: grated raw carrot looks attractive floating on the surface of a pale, creamy soup; add a herb sprig for a touch of extra colour.

To make carrot flowers to garnish a salad, thinly pare strips of carrot lengthways, roll them up and secure with cocktail sticks. Put them into iced water for an hour, then remove the sticks, uncurl the strips and arrange them on top of each other at different angles to form petals (see picture).

Cut slices from a large carrot, remove the centres with an apple corer, and use as holders for thin, julienne strips of celery; if these are immersed in iced water for a time, the celery will curl attractively. Use to garnish canapés or hors d'oeuvres or large platters of cold meat.

Use aspic cutters or tiny biscuit cutters to stamp out a variety of carrot shapes for use in salads and soups.

Tomatoes: use tomato slices, quarters or wedges for quick and easy garnishes; halve them by cutting around their middles in a zig-zag pattern with a small, sharp knife, or make roses with thinly pared tomato peel (see picture).

Mushrooms: to make an attractive garnish from button mushrooms, leave them whole and slice through the stems and caps to make T-shapes. Minaret mushrooms (see picture), are a classic, but extremely simple-to-make garnish for the top of a fish fillet or any bland white meat, such as veal or poultry.

Onions: small, peeled pearl onions make

A variety of carrot shapes can be made from thick rings of carrot using a sharp knife, aspic or tiny biscuit cutters.

Make carrot holders from hollowed-out carrot rings filled with julienne strips of celery and leaves of flat-leaved parsley.

Thinly pared strips of carrot make the petals of this flower. Use a stuffed olive for the centre, anchored with a cocktail stick.

attractive 'chrysanthemums' (see picture). The easiest way to peel fresh onions is to drop them into boiling water and then turn off the heat. Take the onions out, one by one, and slice off the top and bottom – the skin will then slip off and the juices will not irritate the eyes.

Spring onions, on the other hand, can be formed into tassels or spring onion flowers (see pictures).

Use any of these onion decorations to garnish salads or a cheese board.

Celery: make crisp celery curls (see picture), to decorate and enhance cold platters, sandwiches and cheese boards. Another idea for celery is to make delicate julienne strips.

Radishes: because of their pretty, striking colour, radishes make excellent garnishes simply sliced. Otherwise, make 'waterlilies' (see picture).

Gherkins: use cocktail gherkins to make fans, or chop finely and use to garnish

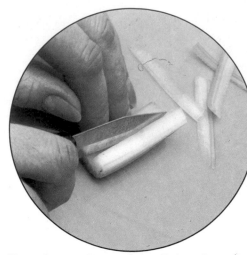

For tomato waterlilies, cut round the middle of the fruit in a zig-zag with a small, sharp knife. For roses, thinly pare away the peel in a spiral, and coil it around your finger.

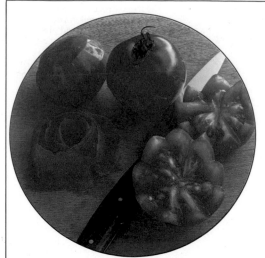

For celery curls, cut the stalk into 5 cm /2 in lengths. Slice lengthways into narrow strips. Leave in iced water for 1 hour for the celery strips to curl. Drain and pat dry.

To make spring onion tassels, cut off most of the green tops, then make several slits close together down from the top. Put the onions in iced water until the tops curl back.

For chrysanthemum onions, cut a small peeled onion into 4, stopping just short of the base. Cut again into 8, then 16. Open out and immerse in iced water for 1 hour.

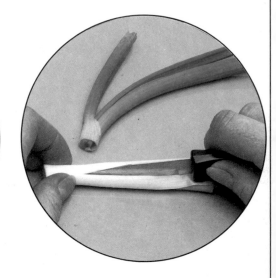

For spring onion flowers, remove the bulbs and greens leaving 7.5 cm /3 in of stalk. Shred, leaving 25 mm /1 in of the white stalk whole. Leave in iced water for 1 hour.

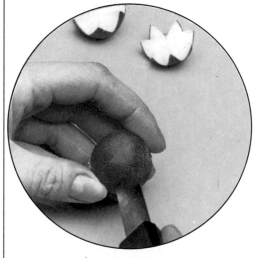

For radish waterlilies, use a sharp knife to make small V-shaped cuts around the middle. Pull the 2 halves apart, then immerse in cold water for about 1 hour.

For Minaret mushrooms, make skin-deep, curving cuts through the caps, not meeting on top. Reverse the knife and make fresh cuts a fraction away; remove the strips.

To make gherkin fans, use a sharp knife to slice a drained cocktail gherkin 3 or 4 times lengthways, almost to the stalk end. Ease the slices apart to open like a fan.

Index

à la grecque 92-5
adzuki (aduki) 89
aligot 32
ALMONDS: Brussels sprouts with 14
celery and Gruyère bake with 57
ANCHOVY: broccoli alla siciliana 69
mixed bean salad with tomatoes 80
appetizers, à la grecque 92-5
ARTICHOKE, GLOBE:
blanching 36
freezing 106
preparation 8
artichoke hearts à la grecque 94
deep-fried artichoke hearts 24
ARTICHOKE, JERUSALEM:
freezing 106
preparation 8
fritters 27
purée 33
ASPARAGUS: to cook 10
freezing 106
preparation 8
green bean and lettuce salad with 78
Italian baked 66
spring vegetable medley 11
aspic 70
assiette verte 79
au gratin 57
AUBERGINE: curried 64
French mould 75
fried, in miso sauce 52
fried slices 29
fritters with piquant sauce 25
gratin 59
Imam bayeldi 40
Provençal-style vegetables 36
ratatouille 66
Sicilian vegetable hors d'oeuvre 78
soufflés 62
stuffed 78
tomato omelette with 18
AVOCADO: freezing 106
baked in tomato shells 41
chilled cucumber soup with 86
hot purée 31
mousse with watercress 74
BACON: Belgian warm salad 77
braised cabbage with tomatoes 45
braised peas with 43
country red cabbage with 78
quick corn casserole with 68
red cabbage campagnard 69
shallot casserole 67
baking 56-63
BAMBOO SHOOTS: general 49
spinach with 52
barley: baked mushroom casserole with 68
basil: Provençal vegetable soup 85
BATTER: for deep-frying 22
beer 29
tempura 26
BEAN SPROUTS: general 49
gado gado 53
spring rolls 24
stir-fried 51
BEANS, DRIED see also individual types of bean
general 88-91
BEANS, FRENCH OR GREEN see also Runner beans
freezing 106
Belgian warm salad 77
with button onions 13
Creole 18
gado gado 53
Italian bean mould 72
lettuce and asparagus salad with 78
mixed bean salad with tomatoes 80
purée 33
bechamel sauce 87
beef: stuffed baked potatoes 40
beer batter 29
BEETROOT: blanching 36
freezing 106
Belgian warm salad 77
black beans 89
black-eyed beans 89
blanching 36, 104-5

blenders 30
boiling 8-15
BOUILLON:
onion and garlic 93
tomato with raisins 92
braising 42-7
breadcrumb coatings for deep-fried vegetables 22
BROAD BEANS: freezing 106
preparation 8
with herb butter 12
soup with parsley 84
BROCCOLI: freezing 106
preparation 8
alla siciliana 69
au mirepoix 47
braised 44
broccoli and raisin platter 76
Chinese mushrooms and 55
purée 31
with quick hollandaise sauce 13
BRUSSELS SPROUTS:
blanching 36
freezing 106
preparation 8
with almonds 14
au gratin 63
purée 32
soup 85
bubble and squeak 18
BUTTER, SAVOURY: herb 12
melted butter sauce 10
BUTTER BEANS: general 89
in hot yoghurt sauce 90
CABBAGE: blanching 36
preparation 8
appetizer with olives 77
braised with tomatoes 45
bubble and squeak 18
gado gado 53
herby cabbage and celery 46
juniper 19
sauerkraut 77
stuffed 36, 38
cabbage, red see Red cabbage
caramelized turnips 13
CARROTS: freezing 106
garnishes 34,108
preparation 8
braised with black olives 47
celery hearts à la grecque with 94
creamy vegetable terrine 73
Crécy potatoes 67
herbed mustard carrots 16
italienne 20
julienne of potatoes, celery and 12
leeks vinaigrette with 81
Moroccan appetizer 79
purée 34
shallot casserole 67
spring vegetable medley 11
CASHEW NUTS: savoury marrow with peanuts and, 38
stir-fried mushrooms with mange tout 51
casseroles 64-9
CAULIFLOWER: freezing 106
preparation 8
chakchouka 64
deep-fried 28
florets à la grecque 93
gado gado 53
little vegetable towers 75
loaf 74
tarts with cream 58
CELERIAC: freezing 106
hot mousse 72
purée 32
CELERY: freezing 106
garnishes 110
preparation 8
celery, almond and Gruyère bake 57
celery hearts and carrots à la grecque 94
Chinese braised vegetables 52
deep-fried 29
herby cabbage and 46
julienne of potatoes, carrots and 12
potato cake with 21
tomato and red pepper relish with 103
chakchouka 64
CHEESE, HARD: aligot 32
braised chicory with cheese sauce 46

broccoli alla siciliana 69
Brussels sprouts au gratin 63
cabbage and olive appetizer 77
celery, almond and Gruyère bake 57
Crécy potatoes 67
gratin of baby turnips 63
stuffed baked potatoes 40
stuffed peppers 36
chestnut, water see Water chestnut
CHICK-PEAS: general 89
falafel 89
hummus 91
CHICORY: braised 44
braised with cheese sauce 46
CHILLI: general 48
rouille 97
Chinese braised vegetables 52
CHINESE CABBAGE: general 49
in cream 51
stir-fried sweet and sour 51
vegetables in coconut milk 49
Chinese courgettes 55
Chinese fried rice with mushrooms 54
Chinese mushrooms and broccoli 55
Chinese steamers 9
Chinese-style mushrooms 51
chips 26, 105
CHUTNEY, PICKLES AND RELISHES:
general 100
marrow chutney 102
mushroom ketchup 102
Pennsylvanian chow-chow 103
piccalilli pickle 100
tomato, celery and red pepper relish 103
coconut: vegetables in coconut milk 49
cold dishes 76-81
coriander 48
CORN (Maize; Sweetcorn):
freezing 106
croquettes 25
Mexican courgette casserole with 67
quick bacon casserole with 68
country red cabbage with bacon 78
COURGETTE:
blanching 36
freezing 107
preparation 8
à la grecque 94
buttered 28
Chinese 55
creamy vegetable terrine 73
deep-fried 28
little omelettes 19
Mexican corn casserole with 67
Provençal-style vegetables 36
ratatouille 66
soufflé 60
spaghetti with courgette sauce 97
spring rolls 24
spring vegetable medley 11
stuffed appetizer 81
cream, soured: baked potatoes with 58
CREAM AND SOFT CHEESE:
creamy mushroom sauce 97
sorrel sauce 99
cream sauces 10
creamed button onions 59
creamed chopped spinach 11
creamed peas with lettuce 15
creamy mushroom sauce 97
creamy tomato sauce 96
creamy vegetable terrine 73
Crécy potatoes 67
Creole green beans 18
CROQUETTES: baked potato 62
sweetcorn 25
croûtons 86
CUCUMBER: chilled avocado soup with 86
with fresh dill 80
soup 83
tomato mould with 72
curried aubergines 64
curried new potatoes 9
deep frying 22-9
DILL: cucumber with 80
lemon potatoes 15
pumpkin purée with 32
double boilers 9
EGG see also Omelette; Soufflé
coatings for deep-fried vegetables 22

pipérade 17
spinach with pimento and hard-boiled eggs 20
falafel 89
FAT: for deep frying 22
fat scalding 105
for sautéeing 16
FENNEL: à la grecque 95
soup 84
with tomatoes 16
FLAGEOLET BEANS: general 89
parslied 91
flower steamers 8-9
food mills 30
food processors 30
freezing 104-7
French aubergine mould 75
French mushroom soup 83
FRITTERS: Japanese mushroom 26
Jerusalem artichoke 27
parsnip 26
gado gado 53
garam masala 48
GARLIC: general 48
hummus 91
onion bouillon with 93
Provençal vegetable soup 85
purée 33
sauce 97
garnishes 108-10
ghee 49
gherkins: garnishes 110
ginger 49
gnocchi, potato 12
gratin of aubergines 59
gratin of baby turnips 63
gratin of mixed vegetables 57
Greek vegetable soup 83
green sauce 99
ham: vegetable terrine 70
HARICOT BEANS: general 89
minestrone 82
mixed bean salad with tomatoes 80
in tomato sauce 90
herb butter 12
herbed mustard carrots 16
herby cabbage and celery 46
herby mushrooms 39
hollandaise sauce 13, 74
hummus 91
Indian spice blend 53
Italian baked asparagus 66
Italian bean mould 72
Japanese mushroom fritters 26
Jerusalem artichoke see Artichoke, Jerusalem
julienne of potatoes, celery and carrots 12
juniper cabbage 19
ketchup, mushroom 102
kidney: Len Evans' stuffed mushrooms 41
kitchri 66
lamb: stuffed vine leaves 38
LEEKS: preparation 8
carrots vinaigrette with 81
purée with scallops 30
in red wine 43
rich leek and onion double-crust pie 61
watercress vichyssoise 87
lemon: dill potatoes 15
lemon grass (sereh powder) 48
Len Evans' stuffed mushrooms 41
LENTILS: general 89
marrow rings stuffed with 91
red lentil soup 83
spiced 90
LETTUCE: creamed peas with 15
fresh lettuce soup 87
green bean and asparagus salad with 78
lima beans 89
little courgette omelettes 19
little potato loaves 60
little vegetable towers 75
MANGE TOUT: freezing 107
preparation 8
stir-fried mushrooms with 51
vegetables in coconut milk 49
MARROW: au gratin 58
chutney 102
marrow rings with lentil stuffing 91

111

savoury marrow with peanuts and
   cashews 38
Matriciana pasta sauce 98
mayonnaise chantilly 10
Mexican corn and courgette
   casserole 67
minestrone 82
mirin 48
miso sauce, fried aubergines in 52
mixed bean salad with tomatoes 80
monosodium glutamate 49
Moroccan carrot appetizer 79
MOULD, HOT SAVOURY:
   general 70
   French aubergine 75
   Italian bean 72
   little vegetable towers 75
mouli legumes 30
MOUSSE AND MOULD, COLD
SAVOURY: *general* 70
   avocado and watercress 74
   tomato and cucumber 72
MUNG BEANS: *general* 89
   kitchri 66
MUSHROOMS: *freezing* 107
   garnishes 108-10
   general 49
   à la grecque 93
   baked avocado in tomato shells 41
   baked barley casserole with 68
   Chinese braised vegetables 52
   Chinese broccoli and 55
   Chinese fried rice with 54
   Chinese-style 51
   creamy sauce 97
   deep-fried stuffed 24
   French soup 83
   in green packets 45
   herbed carrots 16
   herby 39
   Japanese fritters 26
   ketchup 102
   Len Evans' stuffed 41
   little vegetable towers 75
   oven-braised 44
   shallot casserole 67
   spinach with bamboo shoots 52
   stir-fried with mange tout 51
   nutmeg, whipped swedes with 34
oils: *Oriental-style vegetables* 49
OLIVES: braised carrots with 47
   cabbage appetizer with 77
   mixed bean salad with tomatoes 80
OMELETTES: *general* 16
   aubergine and tomato 18
   little courgette omelettes 19
ONION: *blanching* 36
   freezing 107
   garnishes 110
   bouillon with garlic 93
   button onions à la grecque 93
   creamed button onions 59
   fried rings 27
   green beans with button onions 13
   pickled 103
   Provençal-style vegetables 36
   rich leek and onion double-crust
      pie 61
   roast stuffed 39
   soubise sauce 98
   soufflé soup 86
   soup with watercress 84
onion, spring: *garnishes* 110
orange, sautéed sweet potatoes with 19
Oriental-style vegetables 48-55
oven-braised mushrooms 44
PARSLEY:
   broad bean soup with 84
   parslied flageolets 91
PARSNIP: *blanching* 36
   freezing 107
   preparation 8, 56
   roasting 56
   fritters 26
   pasta with green sauce 99
PEANUTS: gado gado 53
   savoury marrow with cashews and 38
   pea-pod soup 84
PEAS *see also* Mange tout
   freezing 107
   preparation 8
   braised with bacon 43
   creamed, with lettuce 15

purée Saint-Germain 35
tarts 60
   with water chestnuts 10
peas, split: purée 90
Pennsylvanian chow-chow 103
PEPPERS:
   blanching 36
   freezing 107
   chakchouka 64
   cheese-stuffed 36
   pipérade 17
   quick corn and bacon casserole 68
   ratatouille 66
   rouille 97
   stuffed courgette appetizer 81
   tomato, celery and red pepper
      relish 103
piccalilli pickle 100
pickled onions 103
Pickles *see* Chutney
PIES AND TARTS: cauliflower and
   cream tarts 58
   pea tarts 60
   rich leek and onion double-crust
      pie 61
pimento: spinach with hard-boiled
   eggs and 20
pinto beans 89
pipérade 17
piquant sauce 25
pistou sauce 85
pommes Anna in darioles 73
pommes parisiennes 17
porringers 9
POTATOES: *blanching* 36
   deep frying 22
   fat scalding chips 105
   freezing 107
   preparation 8, 56
   aligot (purée) 32
   baked croquettes 62
   baked with soured cream 58
   baskets 25
   Belgian warm salad 77
   bubble and squeak 18
   chips 26, 105
   Crécy 67
   curried aubergines 64
   curried new potatoes 9
   garlic purée 33
   gnocchi 12
   julienne of celery, carrots and 12
   lemon diced 15
   little potato loaves 60
   pommes Anna in darioles 73
   pommes parisiennes 17
   potato cake with celery 21
   puréed 35
   roast 56, 57
   sautéed new potatoes with herbs 18
   shallot casserole 67
   skirlie mirlie 11
   spiced potato cakes 53
   spring vegetable medley 11
   stuffed baked 40
   watercress vichyssoise 87
potato, sweet: sautéed with orange 19
preserves 100-3
Provençal-style vegetables 36
Provençal vegetable soup 85
pulses *see also individual types*
   general 88-91
pumpkin purée with dill 32
purée Saint-Germain 35
purées 30-5, 105
quick corn and bacon casserole 68
quick hollandaise sauce 13
radish: *garnishes* 110
RAISINS: broccoli and raisin
   platter 76
   tomato bouillon with 92
   ratatouille 66
RED CABBAGE *see also* Cabbage
   with bacon 78
   campagnard 69
red kidney beans 89
red lentil soup 83
RICE: cheese-stuffed peppers 36
   Chinese fried rice with mushrooms 54
   kitchri 66
   Provençal-style vegetables 36
   stuffed vine leaves 38
rice wine 48-9

rich leek and onion double-crust
   pie 61
roasting 56-7
rouille 97
RUNNER BEANS *see also* Beans,
   French
   freezing 106
   à la grecque 95
   with yoghurt sauce 14
saké 48-9
SALADS:
   Belgian warm (potato) 77
   green bean, lettuce and asparagus 78
   mixed beans with tomatoes 80
salting and brining vegetables 100
SAUCES, SAVOURY: *general* 96
   bechamel 87
   cheese 46, 63
   courgette 97
   cream 10
   creamy mushroom 97
   creamy tomato 96
   garlic 97
   green 99
   hollandaise 74
   hot yoghurt 90
   Matriciana pasta 98
   mayonnaise chantilly 10
   melted butter 10
   miso 52
   piquant 25
   pistou 85
   quick hollandaise 13
   rouille 97
   sorrel 99
   soubise 98
   standby tomato 96
   tempura 27
   tomato 72, 90
   vinaigrette 10
   watercress purée 98
   yoghurt 14
saucepans 8
sauerkraut 77
SAUSAGE-MEAT:
   herby mushrooms 39
   oven-braised mushrooms 44
   roast stuffed onions 39
   stuffed cabbage 38
sautéing 16-21
scallops, leek purée with 30
shallot casserole 67
Sicilian vegetable hors d'oeuvre 78
skirlie mirlie 11
sorrel sauce 99
soubise sauce 98
SOUFFLÉ AND HOT SAVOURY
   MOUSSE *see also* Mould
   aubergine soufflés 62
   courgette soufflé 60
   hot celeriac mousse 72
soufflé onion soup 86
SOUP: broad bean and parsley 84
   Brussels sprout 85
   chilled avocado and cucumber 86
   cucumber 83
   fennel 84
   French mushroom 83
   fresh lettuce 87
   Greek vegetable 83
   minestrone 82
   pea-pod 84
   Provençal vegetable 85
   red lentil 83
   soufflé onion 86
   watercress and onion 84
   watercress vichyssoise 87
SOY SAUCE: *general* 48
   spinach with 54
soya beans 89
SPAGHETTI: with courgette sauce 97
   with Matriciana pasta sauce 98
spiced lentils 90
spiced potato cakes 53
spiced vinegar 100
SPICES: *general* 48
   Indian blend 53
SPINACH: *freezing* 107
   preparation 8
   with bamboo shoots 52
   creamed chopped spinach 11
   little vegetable towers 75
   mushrooms in green packets 45

with pimento and hard-boiled eggs 20
   with soy 54
split pea purée 90
spring onion *see* Onion, spring
spring rolls 24
spring vegetable medley 11
standby tomato sauce 96
star anise 48
steamers 8-9
steaming 8-9
stir-fried bean sprouts 51
stir-fried mushrooms with mange
   tout 51
stir-fried sweet and sour Chinese
   leaves 51
stuffed vegetables 36-41
SWEDE: *freezing* 107
   preparation 8, 56
   roasting 56
   whipped, with nutmeg 34
sweet potato *see* Potato, sweet
tahini: hummus 91
tempura batter 26
tempura sauce 27
TERRINES:
   general 70
   cauliflower loaf 74
   creamy vegetable 73
   vegetable 70
Thai stir-fried vegetables 52
TOMATOES: *freezing* 107
   garnishes 54, 108, 110
   aubergine omelette with 18
   baked avocado in tomato shells 41
   bouillon with raisins 92
   braised cabbage with 45
   celery and red pepper relish with 103
   chakchouka 64
   creamy sauce 96
   cucumber mould with 72
   fennel with 16
   gratin of aubergines 59
   haricot beans in tomato sauce 90
   Italian bean asparagus 66
   marrow au gratin 58
   Matriciana pasta sauce 98
   mixed bean salad with 80
   pipérade 17
   piquant sauce 25
   Provençal-style vegetables 36
   quick corn and bacon casserole 68
   ratatouille 66
   sauce 72, 90
   Sicilian vegetable hors d'oeuvre 78
   standby sauce 96
   stewed fresh tomatoes 21
   stuffed aubergines 78
   stuffed courgette appetizer 81
tuna: Sicilian vegetable hors
   d'oeuvre 78
turmeric 48
TURNIP: *blanching* 36
   freezing 107
   preparation 8, 56
   roasting 56
   caramelized 13
   gratin of baby turnips 63
   skirlie mirlie 11
veal: Provençal-style vegetables 36
vegetable hotpot 64
vegetable terrine 70
vegetables in coconut milk 49
vichyssoise, watercress 87
vinaigrette 10
vine leaves, stuffed 36, 38
vinegar, spiced 100
WALNUTS:
   cheese-stuffed peppers 36
   country red cabbage with bacon 78
   stuffed cabbage 38
water chestnut, peas with 10
WATERCRESS:
   avocado mousse with 74
   purée 98
   soup with onion 84
   vichyssoise 87
WINE:
   braised broccoli 44
   leeks in red wine 43
woks 49
YOGHURT: butter beans in hot
   yoghurt sauce 90
   sauce 14